Manifest Perdition

Ville de Lisbone et Flote des Indes

Manifest Perdition

SHIPWRECK NARRATIVE AND

THE DISRUPTION OF EMPIRE

Josiah Blackmore

University of Minnesota Press

Minneapolis / London

Published with support of the Camões Institute, Portugal.

Frontispiece: *Ville de Lisbone et Flote des Indes* [City of Lisbon and (East) Indies Fleet], from Joseph François Lafitau, *Histoire des découvertes et conquestes des portugais dans le nouveau monde*, 1733.

See pages 177 and 178 for copyright and permission information.

Published by the University of Minnesota Press
111 Third Avenue South, Suite 290
Minneapolis, MN 55401-2520
http://www.upress.umn.edu

Library of Congress Cataloging-in-Publication Data

Blackmore, Josiah.
    Manifest perdition: shipwreck narrative and the disruption of empire / Josiah Blackmore.
      p.   cm.
    Includes bibliographical references (p.).
    ISBN 0-8166-3849-7 (hc : alk. paper) — ISBN 0-8166-3850-0 (pbk.: alk. paper)
    1. Shipwrecks—Early works to 1800.   2. *História trágico-marítima.*
   3. Portugal—History—Period of discoveries, 1385–1500.   I. Title.
    G525 .B57 2002
    910.4'52—dc21

                          2001006996

Printed in the United States of America on acid-free paper

The University of Minnesota is an equal-opportunity educator and employer.

12 11 10 09 08 07 06 05 04 03 02   10 9 8 7 6 5 4 3 2 1

Pedro, lashed to the mast,
believes he has glimpsed
through the storm's
pearly membrane
God's dark face swooping
down to kiss—as the main
sail, incandescent under
pressure, bursts
like a star. The ship
splinters
on the rocks . . .

At least one man happy
to have lost everything.
His crew will make it home
with tales of strange lands
and their captain's untimely
demise.

Rita Dove, "The Sailor in Africa"

Contents

ACKNOWLEDGMENTS

ROM THE FIRST, CREAKY EXPRESSIONS of this project as a paper at the Learned Societies of Canada conference in Ottawa in the spring of 1993 to its final form here, I have had the advice and counsel of many people for which I am grateful. At the University of Toronto, a number of colleagues and students heard the ideas in this book in various forms, and always responded helpfully and with interest. For scholarly and personal generosity, I want to thank Aida Baptista, James Burke, David Higgs, Manuela Marujo, Andreas Motsch, Stephen Rupp, Ricardo Sternberg, and Jill Webster. Wendy Rolph, when she was administering the Department of Spanish and Portuguese, helped seek out sources of research support. Consequently, I wish to thank the Connaught Foundation Research Council for research funds. The personnel of the Robarts Library and the Thomas

Fisher Rare Book Library provided exceptional scholarly resources and help in acquiring bibliographic items. Among the treasures of the Fisher's remarkable Stanton Collection is an *editio princeps* of the *História Trágico-Marítima*; I often thrilled in the breath of contact with that rarity, running my fingers over the covers and across the impressions of type on its pages as Gomes de Brito and his first readers must have done.

Many colleagues and friends outside of Toronto provided encouragement and shared ideas along the way. Gregory Hutcheson offered detailed and immensely useful criticism of this book at an early stage, and Leora Lev has been a constant source of searching and demanding questions. In the past, now, and always, Nancy Ratey stands apart. Also swirling in this minuet of acknowledgments are Andrew Damian Pratt, Carla Mazzio, and Anna Klobucka. To Joaquim-Francisco Coelho I owe the discipline of letters and literature. Mary Gaylord and Tom Conley added to the book's completion in important ways, as did my students at Harvard in the spring of 1997. As long as I live I will not forget the intellectual camaraderie I shared with Gad Gross (tragically killed in Kirkuk, Iraq, in 1991) when we were both residents of Adams House, much as I will not let the memory of my friend and classmate, Estela Berger, fade away, or that of the years spent discussing Portuguese literature and future projects with her on A-level of Widener Library. For more recent exchanges of ideas at conferences or in cafés, thanks to Fernando Arenas, Vincent Barletta, Paul Dixon, and Rafael Mérida-Jiménez. Rita Dove graciously allowed me to reproduce words from one of her poems as the epigraph. This book, in any way, would not have seen the light of day without the support of my parents, Josiah H. and Joyce Blackmore. At a crucial point, my father helped sort out the complexities of nautical terminology.

I would like to thank the reviewers for the University of Minnesota Press, K. David Jackson and David Haberly, for helpful comments, queries, and challenges; they are rigorous and generous readers both. To the efficient and cheerful editorial staff at the Press (I must mention Pieter Martin and Laura Westlund) I am also grateful. In particular, I want to say what a fun privilege it has been working with Richard Morrison again. His belief in this and other projects, together with his humor and scholarly professionalism, has been the *primum mobile* keeping this study in constant motion.

I remain indebted to all named here, and offer these pages as a bookish coda to bookish favors rendered.

ON THE TEXTS AND TRANSLATIONS

*T*HE PORTUGUESE SHIPWRECK NARRATIVES studied in this book were, almost invariably, first printed as individual pamphlets and sold as such in bookshops. The characteristic manner of displaying the pamphlets for sale (and others like them, on a multiplicity of topics) by hanging them over cords or strings gives us the generic designation "string literature," or *literatura de cordel*. In many instances, the shipwreck stories were reprinted (sometimes in counterfeit editions) and modified, so there is frequently more than a single extant version of any one narrative. The differences between versions—including matters such as woodcuts or title pages, in addition to the modification of content—as well as the number of versions mean that the bibliographic and textual histories of the shipwreck narratives are often as messy as the shipwrecks they describe. Readers interested in the bibliographic complexities of Portuguese shipwreck literature should consult the studies by Boxer ("An Introduction" and "Some Corrections"; Duffy [21–43] also summarizes details, but his comments should be read in conjunction with Boxer's studies).

In the early eighteenth century, Bernardo Gomes de Brito collected a dozen narratives and published them as a two-volume anthology, the *História Trágico-Marítima* (HTM) or *Tragic History of the Sea.* Hence, several of Gomes de Brito's texts are but one moment in the life of the shipwreck narratives. But because his anthology constitutes the standard corpus of Portuguese shipwreck literature, the HTM versions are used as the basis of study in this book. For those narratives that do exist in multiple variants, generally the differences between versions reside in the level of detail or the extent of elaboration of certain episodes. These differences, however, do not affect the underlying nature of the shipwreck account as I argue for it in the following pages.

It has been something of a critical commonplace to assume that the expanded versions of some of the narratives as they appear in the HTM are the result of Gomes de Brito's own pen. Yet, there is no evidence to support the hypothesis that it was Gomes de Brito alone who revised the narratives—all that we have is the fact of the variants themselves. A correlate of this speculation is that the earlier versions of the narratives are "true" while the later variants are inferior or "error-ridden." Rather than imputing a dynamic of corruption to the textual history of shipwreck narrative (characteristic of some branches of textual criticism), it is better, I think, to take the existence of variants as evidence of the vitality of the genre, of its ability to capture the interests of readers and printers over the years who desire, in their own way, to participate in the telling of shipwreck. For this reason, the narratives of the "apocryphal" third volumes of the HTM (that is, the volumes that bear no explicit signs of Gomes de Brito's editorial supervision or that boast no overall Inquisitional imprimatur) fall fully within the purview of shipwreck narrative proposed in the present study (for bibliographic information on the third volume, see Martocq and *O livro História Trágico-Marítima*).

I cite individual narratives throughout in short-title form according to the name of the ship(s) in each. I use italics to indicate the narrative itself and roman characters to indicate the name of the ship. For example: "the *S. João* narrates the wreck of the S. João." I use the two volumes of Neves Águas (Europa-América) and Lanciani, *Sucessos* for quotations of narratives of the first and second volumes of the HTM (I cite the *S. João, S. Bento, Conceição, Águia/Garça,* and *Santiago/Chagas* from Lanciani's edition); I use Pereira for third-volume narratives, and the *editio princeps* of the HTM housed in the University of Toronto library for Gomes de Brito's dedication and the Inquisitional *licenças.* I respect the orthography of all printed sources, so I do not modernize spelling or accentuation of earlier materials. I use Blackmore, Boxer, Ley, and Theal for published English translations of some of the narratives, sometimes silently modifying the words of the latter three translators. All unattributed translations of primary and secondary sources are mine.

For the reader's reference, I provide here the full titles of the principal shipwreck narratives included in this study as they appear in the HTM:

S. João: Relaçaõ da muy notavel perda do Galeaõ Grande S. Joaõ em que se contaõ os grandes trabalhos, e lastimosas cousas que acontecèraõ ao Capitaõ Manoel de Sousa Sepulveda, e o lamentavel fim, que elle, e sua mulher, e filhos, e toda a mais gente houveraõ na Terra do Natal, onde se perdèraõ a 24. de Junho de 1552.

S. Bento: Relaçaõ Summaria Da Viagem que fez Fernaõ D'Alvares Cabral, Desde que partio deste Reyno por Capitaõ mór da Armada que foy no anno de 1553. às partes da India athè que se perdeo no Cabo de Boa Esperança no anno de 1554. Escrita por Manoel de Mesquita Perestrello Que se achou no ditto Naufragio.

Conceição: Relaçaõ do naufragio da nao Conceyçaõ, de que era capitaõ Francisco Nobre, a qual se perdeo nos baixos de Pero dos Banhos aos 22. dias do mez de Agosto de 1555. Por Manoel Rangel, o qual se achou no dito Naufragio: e foy depois ter a Còchim em Janeiro de 1557.

Águia/Garça: Relaçaõ da Viagem, e Successo que tiveraõ as naos Aguia, e Garça Vindo da India para este Reyno no Anno de 1559. Com Huma Discrição da Cidade de Columbo, pelo Padre Manoel Barradas da Companhia de JESUS, Enviada a outro Padre da mesma Companhia morador em Lisboa.

S. Paulo: Relaçaõ da Viagem, e Naufragio da Nao S. Paulo Que foy para a India no anno de 1560. De que era Capitaõ Ruy de Mello da

Camera, Mestre Joaõ Luis, e Piloto Antonio Dias. Escrita por Henrique Dias, Criado do S. D. Antonio Prior do Crato.

S. António: Naufragio Que passou Jorge de Albuquerque Coelho Vindo do Brazil para este Reyno no anno de 1565. Escrito por Bento Teixeira Pinto Que se achou no ditto Naufragio. (See the edition of Fernando de Oliveira Mota for the 1601 version of this narrative.)

Santiago: Relaçaõ do Naufragio da Nao Santiago No anno de 1585. E Itinerario da gente que delle se salvou. Escrita por Manoel Godinho Cardozo. E agora novamente acrescentada com mais algumas noticias.

S. Tomé: Relaçaõ do Naufragio da Nao S. Thomé Na Terra dos Fumos, no anno de 1589. E dos grandes trabalhos que passou D. Paulo de Lima Nas terras da Cafraria athè sua morte. Escrita por Diogo do Couto Guarda mòr da Torre do Tombo. A rogo da Senhora D. Anna de Lima irmãa do dito D. Paulo de Lima no Anno de 1611.

The distribution of all the HTM narratives, volume by volume, is as follows: Volume 1: *S. João, S. Bento, Conceição, Águia e Garça, S. Maria da Barca, S. Paulo.* Volume 2: *S. António, Santiago, S. Tomé, S. Alberto, S. Francisco, Santiago/Chagas.* Volume 3: *Conceição, S. João Baptista, N. S. do Bom Despacho, N. S. de Belém, Sacramento/Atalaya, S. Lourenço.*

PROLOGUE

QUI NAVIGANT MARE

*A*s DUSK FELL ON A STORMY DAY off the east coast of
Africa in the spring of 1552, Captain Manuel de Sousa
Sepúlveda called out to master and pilot and asked what
was to be done to help his distressed ship. Head for shore!—*arribar*!—
came the reply, and, with winds buffeting the prow and lightning bolts
flashing through the sky, the great galleon S. João made for land. But
then the tempest became more violent. The sea breaking over the side of
the ship threatened to send it to the depths with each swell; the raging
storm denied the ship approach to the shore. For three days crew and
passengers feared for their lives in the treacherous latitudes near the
Cape of Good Hope as the unleashed forces of nature pummeled the
Portuguese vessel overburdened with cargo from India.

Respite seemed then to arrive with a calming of the winds. But soon another storm of such intensity beset the galleon that the already-tattered sails were ripped from their yards, rigging was torn from the deadeyes, and the swollen sea battered the hull so relentlessly that crew members could not keep a footing. The intricate architecture of masts and yardarms exploded into pieces as water pounded the ship. "Then it seemed," the anonymous author of the *Account of the very remarkable loss of the Great Galleon São João* would later write, "to please God to make an end of them, as later happened" (Blackmore 6). Yet, even in the heart of the unforgiving tempest, feverish work remained. Clinging to hope, hands on deck hacked away at the standing mainmast with axes in a desperate attempt to rid themselves of this potential hazard in a rough sea, but their work was not long as the winds seized hold of the mast and effortlessly—almost mockingly—hurled it into the ocean. Makeshift sails were scrambled together, but they were of little use: the rudder was rotten, the ship could not be steered, and the S. João veered uncontrollably toward the craggy shore.

The captain and his crew hurriedly decided that "[t]he only way to save their lives . . . was to allow themselves to be carried along until they sounded a depth of ten fathoms, and then drop the long boats" (8). And so it happened: several trips were made in the lifeboats to bring the first of nearly five hundred people on board the S. João to the dubious safety of the alien and rocky shore. Some drowned on the ship-to-shore run, and those who survived eventually would witness the lifeboats smash to pieces against the beach. Others watched as the S. João

> broke in two, one half from the mast forward and the other from the mast to the stern. In about one hour these two pieces became four. The decks were broken open, so the merchandise and crates came to the surface. Many of those on board struggled to cling to the boxes and pieces of wood in order to get to land. More than forty Portuguese and seventy slaves died this way. The rest came to land as God pleased: some on top of the waves, and some under, and many were wounded by the nails and wood. In about four hours the galleon was completely destroyed. Not a single piece of it any longer than a couple of feet could be found. The sea delivered all the pieces onto the beach in a great fury. (10)

Shipwrecked. Manuel de Sousa Sepúlveda, his wife Leonor de Sá and their children, and the remaining crew and passengers would afterwards make an arduous march through uncharted Sofala as they negotiated the brutal business of staying alive. Food and water would be scarce. Sepúlveda would gradually lose his mind and his command. His wife and infant children would die. He would bury them with his bare hands in the sand, and, speechless with grief, would wander off into the jungle never to be heard from again. As he made his way into the savage recess of nature, where "[w]andering through that wilderness, he certainly must have been devoured by tigers and lions" (24), Sepúlveda walked off the pages of history and into those of national legend. He and Leonor would soon emerge as Portugal's—and Europe's—most famous shipwreck victims, symbol and icon of personal tragedy in dangerous and volatile times. They are shipwreck experience personified. The story of their suffering (published c. 1555–64) inscribed them into the heart and mind of a historical era and catapulted them to literary fame: the tale of the S. João famously captured the attention of Luís de Camões in his *Os Lusíadas* (1572), as it did that of Spanish "Golden Age" dramatists together with numerous other writers, playwrights, and translators in Portugal and abroad for almost the next five hundred years.[1]

The tragic tale of Captain Manuel de Sousa Sepúlveda's untimely demise stands today as the earliest surviving example of a remarkable storytelling project cultivated in Portugal from the sixteenth through the seventeenth centuries: that is, the writing and printing of shipwreck narratives occasioned by the many wrecks of Portuguese ships on the perilous *carreira da Índia* (India route), the trading route between Portugal and ports of the subcontinent (usually Goa or Cochin) opened up by Vasco da Gama's historic 1497 voyage and maintained during the heyday of empire.[2] This itinerary took ships (the *naus da Índia,* or East Indiamen) laden with eastern riches through hazardous waters that spelled the end to a vast amount of material goods and to a dizzying number of lives; "on account of this staggering wealth," José Saramago observes in a 1972 essay, "people died in all possible ways" (cvii). The *carreira da Índia* was the "lifeline" (McAlister 251) of the *Estado da Índia* (State of India), which was "the name given . . . to the whole of maritime East Africa and Asia from the Cape of Good Hope to Japan" (Boxer, *Race Relations* 41).[3]

But there were survivors of these wrecks, and many of them subsequently returned to Portugal to tell their stories in print, either in their own voices or through those of intermediaries. These shipwreck narratives (*relações* [or *relatos*] *de naufrágios*) enticed and captivated readers with the dramatic, extraordinary, and gory details of shipwreck and survival in faraway lands. They are prose litanies of deplorable hardships away from home, of the constant threat of piracy, treachery, starvation, mutiny, and murder, of the inevitable presence of fear, death, and disease in the violent struggle to remain alive. Shipwreck parades disaster before us with its "stress upon minutiae, [the] sovereignty of the accidental" (Blanchot 3) in incidents that are truly tragicomic: a rotten, stinking tiger's head infested with maggots is found on the beach in one account and is the basis of a soup, guarded at gunpoint; in another, starving castaways attempt to eat live crabs and are clawed mercilessly in the lip; and one castaway dinner consists of roasted sandals. Then there are the poignant, devastating moments, such as the story of Sepúlveda and Leonor, or of the woman lowered into a lifeboat as the S. Tomé sinks in the middle of the ocean who pleads to a nurse still on board the doomed ship to release her infant child to her, a request the nurse refuses. It is no wonder these narratives gripped the imagination of a landbound populace, and it is no wonder we can read them at a distance of centuries and still feel their pull, siren-texts echoing the insidious currents of sea and wind that delivered sailor, captain, aristocrat, merchant, priest, slave, woman, and child equally and indifferently onto the rocks.

Affectively, the appeal of the shipwreck stories is obvious, accessible to readers across the generations. They provide a collective instantiation of a more universal, metaphoric imaginary that Hans Blumenberg in his *Shipwreck with Spectator* calls a "nautical metaphorics of existence."[4] But affective appeal aside, the Portuguese shipwreck narratives at the center of this study (the *História Trágico-Marítima* [Tragic history of the sea]) occupy a privileged position in the textual history of maritime Europe because they inaugurate the genre of prose text known as the shipwreck narrative (or "shipwreck literature," as I will alternately call it), a genre that will flourish in Portugal and will eventually expand northward, reaching the pens of Dutch, English, and French writers.[5] Born during the epoch of the colonial empires that in Portugal encompassed Asia, Africa, and the New World, the Portuguese stories introduce the individual shipwreck narrative onto the Western literary map. Although, of course, the theme of shipwreck and tales about wrecks date back to antiquity, it is during the expansionist campaigns in Portugal that the shipwreck account emerges as a distinct mode of narrative in which shipwreck functions as the sign and break in the ideological fastness of reigning forms of historiographic discourse.[6]

Manifest Perdition proposes that shipwreck narrative is a practice of prose writing, defined not solely by the thematic presence of shipwreck in a text but by a relationship between calamity and writing, where a certain kind of experience generates a certain kind of text. The shipwreck text, one of breakage, rupture, and disjunction, precludes the possibility of a redemptive reading, and in this messy openness presents the greatest blow to the predetermined success of national expansion and its textual analogue.

It is precisely within the pervasive and prolific historiographic culture attendant on southern European expansionist activity of the fifteenth to seventeenth centuries that we must both situate the shipwreck narrative and argue for its unsettling or disruptive agenda. Shipwreck literature exposes and promotes breaches in the expansionist mentality and in the textual culture associated with that mentality. The Portuguese narratives appear when discursive productivity is at the service of maritime campaigns, when the Portuguese and Spanish states are expanding their borders and transplanting their politico-cultural grids overseas. These disaster authors emerge from a historical consciousness in which overseas expansion figures prominently (we should not forget that Portuguese expansion begins with the capture of the North African city of Ceuta in 1415, almost eighty years before Christopher Columbus set sail); the official reports of expansion, such as those produced by Columbus, Hernán Cortés, or Pero Vaz de Caminha, find a fierce resistance in the pens of the shipwreck writers. *Manifest Perdition,* then, argues for a reassessment of the shipwreck text in relation to the imperialistic, textual agenda of early modern Iberia by positing that shipwreck narrative, though born of conquest/expansionist historiography, is, in reality, a type of counter-historiography that troubles the hegemonic vision of empire evident in the accounts of the canonical actors of colonialism. Collectively, the shipwreck narratives undermine the master historiographic narrative of imperialism in all its cultural, political, and economic valences, upsetting the imperative of order and the unifying paradigms of "discovery" or "conquest" textuality. In such a context, the *História Trágico-Marítima* creates its own field of critical relevance that ripples outward from Portugal to encompass the entirety of the ideological climate of expansionist

Iberia, a peninsula in the throes of maintaining its strongholds in Asia and the New World.

The shipwreck narratives originally appeared in print as pamphlets *(fol-hetos)*. These pamphlets, a form of ephemera known as "string litera-ture" *(literatura de cordel)* owing to the practice of hanging them over cords or strings to display them for sale, made the shipwreck stories ac-cessible to an eager reading public as soon as they came off the press.[7] Doubtless there were many more shipwreck pamphlets printed than have survived, because the fascination with the dramatic and the unusu-al coursing through the shipwreck stories was fueled by the fact that in them, the names of brothers, husbands, cousins, neighbors, or parents of many of their readers figured as participants. Some two hundred years after the earliest extant shipwreck pamphlet (the story of the S. João) was printed, a Lisbon editor by the name of Bernardo Gomes de Brito (1688–1760?) collected and reprinted twelve of them as a two-volume anthology in 1735–36 with the title *História Trágico-Marítima*.[8] A third, undated volume (sometimes called the *Colecção de naufrágios* [Collec-tion of shipwrecks]) containing another six narratives soon appeared, al-though scholars traditionally doubt its "authenticity" in that it is unlike-ly this volume was produced by Gomes de Brito's editorial hand.[9]

Had it not been for Gomes de Brito's interest, most or all of these shipwreck narratives might not have survived. The HTM was published at a time when interest in the exotic, the strange, the monstrous, and the marvelous ran high, as the proliferation of pamphlets ("popular" litera-ture, according to some) in the eighteenth century proves.[10] Hence our shipwreck anthology is really a product of two different historical peri-ods, for there is a distance of almost two hundred years between the pub-lication of the HTM's first narrative (the S. João) and Gomes de Brito's compilation. We might think of the HTM as a case study in how texts travel through time or through historical and cultural ideologies, as will be considered in the last chapter.

The eighteen narratives of shipwreck are an extremely heterogeneous collection—the variety of writers sponsors a wide and kaleidoscopic dif-ference in tone, style, level of detail, and general narrative shape, not to mention the often pronounced differences in the survival experience or the self-consciousness of the shipwreck story as a narrative. On the one hand, this variety heightens their readerly appeal, and, on the other, presents no small challenge to the critic; for if there are overarching ideas that travel through the three volumes, even the most cursory reading of the HTM reveals that shipwreck literature is a mutable and often highly idiosyncratic form of narrative. Despite certain formal similarities between the narratives, these stories are as variegated in tone, vision, language, erudition, and field of reference as the multifarious company of clerics, soldiers, cosmographers, shipwrights, cartographers, noblemen, and pharmacists who wrote them. The narrative reports of pervasive despair and unexpected deliverance, shipwreck literature as a whole traces a vertiginous psychological journey. It is by nature unruly, and, like the shipwreck victims themselves, we must be prepared for anything as we make our way through the HTM. We must navigate a discernible path through texts often so distinct from one another that they seem to be products of entirely different writerly agendas altogether.

A discernible path, though, is something that even the critical history of these narratives cannot present, the plurality of readings of these texts being as resistant to clean categorization as the intricacies of the tales themselves. At the outset, there could be no stronger testament to the narratives' problematic nature, and a quick overview of the HTM's critical history can help us understand this.

It was Boxer ("An Introduction" 89–99) who first sketched a glimpse of the rocky critical road traveled by the *História Trágico-Marítima* and I would like to revisit a few moments in its history. We begin with Luís de Camões (1524?–80), perhaps the most famous reader of the story of Manuel de Sousa Sepúlveda and the loss of the S. João. Camões included the story in his *Os Lusíadas* (The Lusiads, 1572), the ten-canto poem about expansionist Portugal's past and prophetic future that resides at the center of the Portuguese canon. For Camões, this shipwreck tale stands as an emblem of the dire cost of empire, and represents not so much a tragic heroism as the conviction that empire contains disaster at its core, that it is built on the seeds of its own undoing. Years later, in the dedication of his anthology to D. João V, Gomes de Brito underscores the narratives as singular and constituent moments of Portuguese history. He declares that, by his act of editorial dedication, the stories are inducted into the monarchic and institutional consolidation of the past. This, Gomes de Brito claims, mitigates—even overturns—the horror of shipwreck by subsuming it within the otherwise glorious march of national history. In like spirit, Manuel de Sá, in his inquisitorial license printed in the first volume of the HTM, enjoins readers to "glory [in] the heroism of those magnanimous spirits."[11]

Camões's and Gomes de Brito's understanding of shipwreck as first and foremost a historical circumstance was lasting and influential. Shipwreck can admit one to the historical archive. This historical inflection of the shipwreck stories lasts to our day—and for obvious reasons. Generally, shipwreck is contextualized within the history of empire, and is related negatively to it. In the first monographic study of the *História Trágico-Marítima* and its circumstances, James Duffy reads the narratives as evidence of the decline of empire in the East, observing that "the eighteen narratives of shipwreck are simultaneously the negation of a heroic concept and the affirmation of a national decline. It is this candid picture, not the dramatic or epic mural, which is the significance of the *História trágico-marítima*" (47). Boxer reiterates the antiheroic or antiepic nature of the tales, remarking that "they give us the seamy side of the Portuguese 'conquest, navigation, and commerce'" (*Tragic History* vii), but he also recognizes their value as literary and ethnographic documents.

The literary treatment of the shipwreck narratives presents a similar history of varied assessment. Ramalho Ortigão, one of the founders of Portuguese realism, enthuses in 1876: "the most extraordinary work in Portugal written in prose is the *Historia tragico-maritima*" (19), complemented on the poetic side by nothing other than *Os Lusíadas*. Not only is shipwreck narrative on a canonical par with Camões, it is the highest expression of realist writing, a model of exteriority in which sentiment finds no place, as Ortigão overstatedly claims about the narrative of Sepúlveda and the wreck of the S. João. Albino Forjaz de Sampaio follows Ortigão's thinking somewhat when he notes the "literary brilliance, historical interest, and purity of language" he sees in the narratives, "model moments of good and legitimate Portuguese prose" that, because of their uniqueness to Portugal, boast a "patriotic value" (3:352–53).

If Sampaio's exuberance is heir to Ortigão's, so is João Gaspar Simões's reading of shipwreck literature through the lens of realism. In his book on the Portuguese novel, Gaspar Simões counts shipwreck narrative as one of the possible realist sources of modern Portuguese fiction while at the same time noting the problems it presents to generic classification; the narratives are a "confusion between a commemorative document, descriptive memory, travel account, a draft or direct annotation of facts, [and a] literary creation in the strict sense" (1:189). This generic uncertainty is reiterated by other critics, who alternately see shipwreck narrative as belonging properly to novels of chivalry, epic and antiepic texts, travel literature, or chronistic writing.

Duffy, for his part, eschews the "literary merits" of the narratives, noting that they "do not seem to warrant a more evolved literary treatment than they have already received" (v), which was relatively little at the time he was writing. This sentiment is implicitly echoed in many of the standard histories of Portuguese literature that either mention the narratives in passing or omit them altogether. Only recently has the *História Trágico-Marítima* begun to enjoy a critical renaissance in literary studies, thus overcoming Duffy's pronouncement of 1955.

I begin the study in chapter 1 by exploring two competing understandings of *naufrágio* (shipwreck) in the Iberian literary tradition, and

Figure 1. Woodcut from the 1601 edition of the *S. António, Naufragio, que passou Iorge Dalbuquerque Coelho, Capitão e Governador de Pernambuco.*

how these understandings are emblematic of the way shipwreck has been read over time and how they prepare for the conflicting meanings shipwreck takes on in the narratives themselves. I consider first medieval lyric, most notably Alfonso X's *Cantigas de Santa Maria* (Songs of Holy Mary), as the most significant literary ancestors of the HTM in the symbolic complexities ascribed to the literary representation of shipwreck. How shipwreck has traditionally been related to the heroism of empire occupies the second part of the chapter, with a focus on *Os Lusíadas* and the figure of the giant Adamastor, by far Camões's most provocative and controversial poetic figure.

Chapter 2 studies the shipwreck text in more theoretical terms, arguing that the shipwreck narratives collectively manifest a counterhistoriographic impulse to the official textual culture of imperialism. The status of the shipwreck text as one of breakage and rupture derives in part from the idea of discourse *(discurso)*, a notion encompassing both ships and texts; thus the forced abdication of a discourse by a ship (that is, a ship's inability to respond to the coordinates of a predetermined course meant to seal off a voyage under the aegis of "success" or "accomplishment") creates a rupture in a symbolic imaginary where the controlled, forward-moving ship manifests a hegemony of empire or official culture. The narrative account of that rupture—the shipwreck text—consequently has implications for the culture of textuality as one of supposedly unbreachable knowledge or power.

Chapters 3 and 4, in contrast to the more general considerations of chapter 2, present close readings of selected narratives and explore the symbolic, metaphoric, and thematic agendas common to HTM texts. Chapter 3 studies a series of maroonings or shifts away from paradigms of order and the strictures of historiographic writing. Chapter 4 explores the significations of the body—of humans, of ships, of texts—as the presiding presences in shipwreck narrative. These chapters seek to reveal a poetics of the shipwreck text—that is, how shipwreck writers imagistically structure the shipwreck narrative—in its particularities and complexities.

Chapter 5 returns to critical readings of the HTM, but this time from the perspective offered by the eighteenth-century Inquisition in the *licenças,* or licenses for publication printed in Gomes de Brito's volumes that were authored by Inquisitional censors. These *licenças* constitute the first essays of literary criticism on the shipwreck narratives, and reveal how the texts of two centuries past were received institutionally in Gomes de Brito's time. In the shipwreck licenses, we find an attempt to steer the turbulent body of shipwreck narrative, to commandeer the disruptive potential of shipwreck narrative by admitting it into the canon of national heroism. In a sense, the licenses attempt to rescue the shipwreck narratives from themselves.

"Qui navigant mare enarrent pericula ejus"—"Let those who sail the sea narrate its dangers," intones Ecclesiasticus 43:26. The biblical injunction places the responsibility for telling stories of the dangerous sea on the shoulders of those who have experienced it firsthand. It marries maritime peril and text. The collective story that unfolds throughout the pages of the HTM acts as a concrete, historicized response to this mandate because many of the writers express the conviction that they suffer and write about shipwreck because it is mandated by the *Verbum Dei*. In this there is an odd sense of comfort to be found by those who experience and write about shipwreck—the Portuguese experience and narrative of wreck, recognized by Ecclesiasticus, emerge as a kind of long, maritime gloss on the book of Job, on the realities and terrors of forced exile and wandering. Fernando Pessoa echoes the pervasiveness of pain and sorrow in Portuguese maritime history, and the need to conquer it, somehow, in his "Mar Português" (Portuguese sea): "O salty sea, so much of whose salt / Is Portugal's tears! / . . . / Whoever would go beyond the Cape / Must go beyond sorrow."[12]

What are the vagaries, the inscrutabilities of the *pericula maris*? Enter the sea-danger authors, the shipwreck writers.

1

A SHIPWRECKFUL SHIP

*T*O SET SAIL: This simple act is rife with historical specificity for a maritime nation, an inevitable presence in its literary and cultural identities. At the same time, it is universal, an archetype, a metaphor encompassing life, fortune, and existence. To set sail means, at once, to move from certainty to uncertainty, from safety to danger, from the known to the unknown, from the banal to the new, from boundaries and limits to the untraceable. It unleashes a range of potentialities, both calamitous and auspicious. One can sail into new knowledge and possibility, into new worlds and paradises, or disappear under the waves into death and oblivion. There is something philosophically sobering about going to sea; there are dangers at every turn, but also, for expansionist Iberia, pots of gold waiting just over the horizon. To confront the sea by launching oneself into it is to confront primordial chaos, to take a precarious perch on the edge of the abyss. "Among the elementary realities we confront as human beings," writes Blumenberg, "the one with which we are least at ease is the sea" (7). The sea is both *terminus a quo* and *terminus ad quem*. Despite the lands skirting its edges, the sea cannot be contained or delimited—it is the very principle of resistance, of limitlessness. The sea, ultimately, is unknowable, a cypher, "an occult frontier facing silence, absence, nothingness" (Jackson, *Builders* 13).

The shipwreck stories in one way express the fulfillment of the deepest fears about the sea and the attempts to domesticate it. The ship—a unit of form over formlessness, an artifice or construct over that which cannot be contained or structured—fails to render an abridgment between its occupants and chaos. It is, ironically, chaos's very agent. The failed negotiation between humans and the sea via ships suffuses the shipwreck narratives as the dyad *naufrágio e perdição* (shipwreck and perdition) rings ominously throughout the HTM, the paired ideas informing the preoccupations of all shipwreck writers, the weighty presences under which the writers characteristically labor to tell their world.

Shipwreck and perdition represent more than just two sides of a disastrous coin, two realities hovering menacingly over the heads of the India route passengers. As notions relating humans to catastrophe, they are at once synonymous and discrete: shipwreck itself can be considered a form of perdition and of loss, or it can lead to a greater perdition, a trigger-event to a more general experience of loss. In subsequent chapters, I will look closely at shipwreck and perdition as operative concepts within the shipwreck texts themselves. In this chapter, though, as a necessary preliminary to that discussion, I explore two competing meanings of *naufrágio* in the Iberian literary tradition that are emblematic of the way shipwreck has been read over time and how they prepare for the conflicting meanings ascribed to shipwreck in the narratives themselves. First we consider shipwreck as a means to spiritual salvation in the medieval lyric, specifically the *Cantigas de Santa Maria* (Songs of Holy Mary) of Alfonso X, el Sabio (1221–84). Alfonso X stands out in Iberian history as a monarch of exceptional literary and scholarly abilities who oversaw and participated in a massive textual/cultural productivity encompassing poetry, history, law, and science.[1] These poems of divine intervention and miraculous deliverance are key precedents to shipwreck literature in that they, more than any other corpus of medieval (Iberian) texts, present shipwreck as a complexly symbolic and allegorical motif. Next we move forward several centuries to scrutinize the shipwreck passages in Luís de Camões's *Os Lusíadas* (1572). Camões's poem, itself contemporary with the earliest accounts of shipwreck, proposes a lasting, influential reading in that it locates shipwreck oppositionally to empire, yet still within the fabric of empire, a reading to which Gomes de Brito himself and his Inquisitional censors in the eighteenth century would subscribe. The medieval poetry and Camões's canonical mastertext demonstrate how shipwreck and its partner notion perdition evolve over time. The conflictual meanings manifested in both poetic traditions help explain why critical response in modern times to the shipwreck narratives has often been divided.

NAUFRÁGIO E SALVAÇÃO (SHIPWRECK AND SALVATION)

Alfonso X's *Cantigas de Santa Maria,* poems in praise of the Virgin or that recount her miraculous intervention in human affairs, are important precursors to the shipwreck narratives in that a subset of these *cantigas* narrate Mary's intervention occasioned by shipwreck or storms at sea. These *cantigas* work ship distress into a highly wrought, symbolic plenitude in which catastrophe finds explanation as the product of a Christian, salvational fatalism—ideas that often reappear in the shipwreck narratives of later centuries. The dynamic of perdition and salvation plays itself out dramatically and therefore didactically as Alfonso inscribes shipwreck within the allegorical narrative of Christian devotion.[2]

The Learned Monarch's poems participate in the broader literary production of the Galician-Portuguese lyric "school," that is, the poetry composed in the Galician-Portuguese language between the twelfth and fourteenth centuries. This school includes a large corpus of secular love poetry in which the tumultuous and plaintive inner world of emotion frequently finds expression through images of sea-swept landscapes and the banalities of maritime life. One example suffices to suggest how intricately maritime and human nature are intertwined in this poetic, love-bound universe. Here is a poem by the Galician poet Meendinho:

> I was at the chapel of Saint Simon
> and enormous waves surrounded me,

while awaiting my friend,
while awaiting my friend!

I was in the chapel, before the altar.
There surrounded me enormous waves of the sea,
while awaiting my friend,
while awaiting my friend!

And enormous waves surrounded me.
I have neither oarsman nor boatman,
while awaiting my friend,
while awaiting my friend!

There surrounded me enormous waves of the sea.
I have no oarsman, nor can I row,
while awaiting my friend,
while awaiting my friend!

I have neither oarsman nor boatman.
Lovely, I'll die in the depths of the sea,
while awaiting my friend,
while awaiting my friend!

I have no oarsman, nor can I row.
Lovely, I'll die in the grasp of the sea,
while awaiting my friend,
while awaiting my friend![3]

This *cantiga* stands for a wide and complex array of texts in which the Galician-Portuguese poets depict a world where love, suffering, and the sea symbolically coalesce, where emotion and sentiment, like ships, suffer wreck.[4] In particular, the poems in the voice of a woman (*cantigas de amigo* or "lover's songs") typically enunciate a suffering *(coita)* caused by a yearning for a lover who is absent, frequently because he has traveled far from home overseas. Absence as a poetic premise anticipates the aprioristic absence in the accounts of shipwreck (i.e., the absence of a completed, round-trip voyage, or even of the integral body of the ship). The world dominated by amorous torment and the difficulty or impossibility of release from it in the lyric maps perdition as leitmotific in the flow of existence. In contrast to Alfonso's religious texts, the secular poems, like the shipwreck narratives, present no assured mechanism of salvation, only the dim hope of a distant and postponed relief.

We begin our study of Alfonso's sacred lyric obviously but necessarily with the acknowledgment that such lyric explicitly or implicitly glosses biblical instances of shipwreck. The story of Jonah or Paul's shipwreck at Malta are two well-known examples, in addition to other passages such as the line from Ecclesiasticus noted earlier or verses 23–29 of Psalm 107, where seagoing merchants experience the terror of storm-tossed ships:

> Some went down to the sea in ships,
>> doing business on the great
>>> waters;
> they saw the deeds of the Lord,
>> his wondrous works in the deep.
> For he commanded, and raised the
>> stormy wind,
>> which lifted up the waves of the
>> sea.
> They mounted up to heaven, they
>> went down to the depths;
>> their courage melted away in
>> their evil plight;
> they reeled and staggered like
>> drunken men,
>> and were at their wits' end.
> Then they cried to the Lord in their
>> trouble,
>> and he delivered them from their
>> distress;
> he made the storm be still,
>> and the waves of the sea were
>> hushed.

The relationship sketched by the psalmist here between terrifying storms at sea and the hand of God is a premise for Alfonso's devotional lyric in which tempestuous seas and shipwreck at once manifest divine fury and serve as the basis for Mary's interested intercession.[5] Furthermore, there is an obvious parallel between the merchants "doing business on the great waters" and the worldview of the later Portuguese shipwreck writers, who often appeal to the biblical legitimation of shipwreck as the only available explanation to the sense-defying experience of wreck. It is in these appeals that we may locate an attempt to ascribe a latent redemptive quality to the shipwreck experience, even if it means suffering a fierce, divine retribution for the rampant sin of *cobiça* or avarice as that which drives the relentless and life-endangering pursuit of *carreira da Índia* wealth.

"A ship was in peril . . . in a great storm at sea" ("Hūa nave periguada andava . . . pelo mar en gran tormenta), writes Alfonso in *cantiga* 313. Alfonso's adjective *periguada* boasts a neat semantic efficiency. Generally, it means "in peril" or "endangered," but here it acquires a further shade of precision—when used to describe a ship at sea, the word means "in peril *of shipwreck*." A shipwreckful ship: the danger in potentia threatens to become a danger realized. The capacity for wreck latent in every seaborne ship builds the tension in Alfonso's poetic narrative, gearing the listener or reader to celebrate when Mary intervenes in the final stanzas. But if the *nave* of poem 313 is saved from wreck and oblivion, its ghost sails on, forever *periguada,* a mainstay of the Iberian cultural and poetic imagination. In the image of the shipwreckful ship pulses a collective anxiety about the inescapable proximity to, and negotiation of, the sea.

Ships, storms, and wrecks are commonalities of daily life that gain transcendence by playing roles in the drama of divine intervention and salvation. In the *cantigas,* they prompt despair and mortal terror, and in so doing, allow for Mary's intercessional grace. In the Marian texts, the troubled experiences of seafaring are implicated in Alfonso's narrative act of homage, where storytelling itself manifests Alfonso's devotion (Snow, "Alfonso" 129). Hence there is an overall, divine narrative at work, one independent of the individual miracle stories recounted as Alfonso inscribes the troubles of ships and their occupants within the story of spiritual exemplarity. Alfonso's narrativizing of shipwreck rejuvenates this poetic and biblical topos as one that favors the quotidian life of a maritime nation. Similarly, Gonzalo de Berceo (c. 1190–1264?), in his *Milagros de Nuestra Señora* (Miracles of Our Lady), presents the image of Mary's guiding grace as a ship in the Prologue to his series of miracle poems.

> The Blessed Virgin is called Star,
> Star of the Seas, Longed-For Guide
> She is watched by mariners in peril
> for when they see Her, their ship is guided.[6] (Mount and Cash 25)

Toward the Prologue's end, Berceo folds the image of the inhabited, endangered ship into his own poetic itinerary:

> May the Glorious One guide me so that I may complete the task
> for I would not dare to undertake it otherwise.[7] (27)

Berceo, like a mariner on a ship in distress, appeals to Mary to be his pilot, to guide his pen and therefore his narrative journey. *La nave guiada* performs a clear exegetical function in that the narrative, and narration of, the miracles is the path to salvation. Berceo thus writes his *milagros* as an act of helmsmanship under Mary's command. Navigation is a metaphor for the correct negotiation of the Word of God, and these few prefatory verses cast the *Miracles* under the metaphoric sign of the ship and maritime voyage.

Let us return to Alfonso's *cantiga* 313, the full text of which follows:

> This is about the ship which was in peril at sea, and those who were on board called on Holy Mary of Villa-Sirga, and the storm calmed at once.

> *There where all the saints have no power to lend assistance, the Virgin of whom God chose to be born can do so.*
> For it is right and fitting that She be quicker to offer Her grace than any other saint, since God chose to take on Her flesh and become a man to save us through Her, and He made Her Fount of Virtues and gave Her His power.
> *There where all the saints have no power to lend assistance. . . .*

> Therefore, I wish to tell you a miracle of Hers, and I know you will praise Her name. And I shall tell you even more; you will recognize for certain that She manifestly has wisdom from the Great King in order to perform such a miracle.
> *There where all the saints have no power to lend assistance. . . .*

The Holy Virgin Mary of Villa-Sirga performed this miracle with
Her power, as I learned. Pay heed to it and may it not displease you,
for I take delight and pleasure in praising Her deeds.
There where all the saints have no power to lend assistance. . . .

A ship was in peril, as I learned, in a great storm at sea, and all the
people on it were in great affliction. As I heard it, the ship was already broken. Then the sea began to rise
There where all the saints have no power to lend assistance. . . .

rapidly and swell more and more, churning up the sand, and the
night became very dark because of the storm, black as pitch. Furthermore, they saw many people on the ship dying all around them.
There where all the saints have no power to lend assistance. . . .

Therefore, they shouted and called on the Lord God and Saint Peter
and Saint James, Saint Nicholas and Saint Matthew and many other
male and female saints, promising that they would gladly be their
pilgrims if anyone would come to their aid.
There where all the saints have no power to lend assistance. . . .

All were in danger and mortal fear and thought for certain they were
as good as dead. However, a priest who was there had heard tell of
the miracles of the Holy Virgin
There where all the saints have no power to lend assistance. . . .

which She performed and performs in Villa-Sirga for all who go
there to ask mercy and help for the troubles they have and are immediately and completely cured. When he saw the desperate situation,
he offered his body and those of his fellows on board to Her
There where all the saints have no power to lend assistance. . . .

and said: "Good men, let us now with all our hearts call on the Holy
Virgin Mary of Villa-Sirga, and let no one abstain. Let us ask Her for
pardon, for Her holy power will not fail us."
There where all the saints have no power to lend assistance. . . .

They knelt down as best they could while the priest said: "Mother of
Our Lord, since you win pardon for the sinner from your Son, look
not to our errors, by your grace, but have pity
There where all the saints have no power to lend assistance. . . .

"for us who are in trouble, and may your goodness and your virginity, through which the world is preserved, avail us now. Come to our aid, Good Lady, for you have the power and wisdom to do so, and without you we cannot defend ourselves from this affliction.
There where all the saints have no power to lend assistance. . . .

"Since you in Villa-Sirga restore sight to the blind and revive the dead by the power you have, come to our aid, Holy Virgin, for we do not believe we shall live until dawn, but you can free us from this plight."
There where all the saints have no power to lend assistance. . . .

When the priest had said this, he raised his eyes to Heaven and then with all his heart sang "Salve Regina" in honor of the Virgin Mother. A dove white as newfallen snow came onto the ship,
There where all the saints have no power to lend assistance. . . .

and at that very moment the ship was illuminated with a brilliant light. Each one set himself to saying his prayers to the Gracious Lady, and then all began to bless Her name.
There where all the saints have no power to lend assistance. . . .

The sea became very calm, and the night cleared. The next day the ship came safely to port, and each one on the ship, as he had promised an offering at Villa-Sirga, did not fail to comply.
There where all the saints have no power to lend assistance. . . .

As offering they made a very large chalice that the priest took to Villa-Sirga where the Virgin performs many miracles, as She takes pleasure in doing. Therefore, let us beseech Her to cause us to live well.
There where all the saints have no power to lend assistance. . . . (Kulp-Hill 379–80)[8]

Ship, sea, and danger merge in this *cantiga* as symbols and embodiment of extreme tribulation. This poem is characteristic of others in the corpus in its alignment of sea distress with the salvific frame and movement of the text, where shipwreck plays a part in a larger, allegorical narrative.

The rubric of this *cantiga* tells us only that here is the story of an endangered ship, a crying out to Saint Mary of Vila-Sirga (i.e., Palencia), and the subsequent abating of the storm. Alfonso steers our understanding of this premise in a certain direction by presenting the Encarnation in the first stanza, inviting us to hold in our minds the fleshly body of Christ as the image we will carry through the narrative along with the more dramatic and explicit presence of the distressed ship, and of Mary. Alfonso's own response to these divine bodily presences is characteristically an authorial pleasure.

The first three stanzas serve as a kind of prologue to the kernel event, that is, the story of the shipwreck-endangered ship. These introductory stanzas rehearse the lesson to be derived from the subsequent events, a lesson appearing with only minor variations in other *cantigas*. This prologular teaching, common to many of the poems, serves two purposes: first, it allows each *cantiga* an autonomy in that the lesson will not be lost if the text is read or recited in isolation, and second, it creates a salvific redundancy that travels from *cantiga* to *cantiga,* an intertext placing each individual poem in a metonymic relation to the masterstory represented by the Marian songs in their collective entirety. This is perhaps why the illuminator of the lavish *Códice rico* chooses the distressed ship as his first miniature in the pictorial account of *cantigas* 33 and 112 (see Figures 2 and 3), because it is this image that initiates the miracle story proper after the prologular verses, the image in which we may locate the individuality (the localized "gloss" on the common narrative) of each *cantiga*.

The ship in 313 labors through the sea "in a great storm" ("en gran tormenta") and because of this its occupants, in like manner, suffer "great affliction" ("mui gran coita"). The storm and the sea have already broken the ship's back, and this augments the terror the travelers feel, their *coita* increasing and swelling like the sea growing in its fury. As the ship is beset by a fierce physical storm, the passengers are beset by a fierce spiritual one. Before any one person can be saved, many must die, the tempest thus making the ship a place of exemplary sacrifice and a public spectacle of the forced recognition of the body's mortality. Such affliction prompts all to cry out and invoke the maritime saints with promises of pilgrimages in exchange for survival.

The miraculous intervention in the final stanzas works on the metaphoric triangle equating the body of Christ to the body of the ship and to the body of those on board. The Encarnation authorizes physical, bodily suffering to occur as part of a salvational plan. The ship experiences

Figure 2. Miniatures of *cantiga* 33 from Alfonso X, el Sabio, *Cantigas de Santa Maria,* from *El "Códice rico" de las cantigas de Alfonso x el Sabio: ms. T.I.1 de la Biblioteca de El Escorial* (Madrid: Edilán, 1979). Reprinted by permission of the publisher, Edilán.

torment like the human body and transmits this torment to those on board. *Nave* (ship) and *tormenta* (storm) are one side of the symbolic coin; *gente* (people) and *coita* (affliction) are the other. This *coita,* as we learn in line 36, is mortal—it presages death, it ultimately is linked to the survival of the soul.[9] Ships relate to storms as humans relate to affliction. In medieval devotional logic, and in Alfonso's poetic imagery, the torment of the body serves a redemptive end.

The distressed ship's body as the site of danger and death becomes transformed into the space of supplication in the second half of *cantiga* 313: whereas in the sixth stanza the chaotic invocation of saints is heard, in the ninth the single voice of the *crerigo* (cleric) rises above the din and begins a prayer. So it is that the extremities of distress and terror allow the ship, a focus of worldly danger, to function as a place of prayer, a church. As Kolve demonstrates, the physical spaces of church and ship in medieval literature and imagery are frequently superimposed, even at the lexical level: "the very word 'nave' . . . comes from the Latin *navis,* meaning 'ship,' and the 'ship's keel' roof that characterizes certain church naves . . . may represent a translation of that symbolism into architectural fact" (315–16).[10] In keeping with the bodily nature of the images that structure this *cantiga,* the cleric's supplication entails an offering up of his body and of the bodies of those on board (l. 44). The christological body imagery thus comes full circle as the events of the *cantiga* reenact the Passion. The shipwreckful ship, we might say, is a kind of floating pageant-wagon, the trials and terrors of seaborne danger inciting an impromptu passion play, but one in which lives are at real risk. This dramatization reaches a climax as the ship is illuminated from above and is released from the dangers of the storm with the appearance of the white dove. In the image of the dove, Alfonso makes a double reference to the story of Noah and to the Holy Spirit as the agent of Mary's impregnation, the motific act of embodiment announced in the opening stanza. The dove, which never returns to the ark after being released by Noah for the third time in Genesis 8, would seem to return now to the terrified passengers in an assurance that the narrative of divine grace may be repeated. This is the same assurance the few remaining survivors of the shipwreck in Gonzalo de Berceo's "The Shipwrecked Pilgrim" (El náufrago salvado) experience as they witness a flock of white doves emerge from the sea, the transformed souls of those who had drowned in the wreck.

The body/ship metaphor, one that is fundamental to the shipwreck narratives (as we will see in subsequent chapters) appears in *cantiga* 267 in what amounts to a coincidental anticipation of the HTM circumstances where a Portuguese merchant, traveling in a heavily populated ship, encounters a storm at sea on his way to Flanders:

> . . . near the coast of the Great Sea of Spain, while that ship was traveling with many people on board, the sea rose that day with a great storm and became very rough.
>
> It struck the ship so fiercely with its powerful waves that those people thought they would surely die there. . . .
>
> The merchant was then at the side of the ship on top of a boom, and a heavy, powerful wave came and struck him in the chest, and he was thrown into the sea.
>
> The ship moved away from him through the sea a good distance, as God is my aid. However, the devil, who always works against us, tried to drown him there.
>
> While struggling thus in that storm, he remembered the Virgin. . . .
>
> "Remember, My Lady, that I have promised you to go to your house, this is well known. But you, strength and shield of the unfortunate, save me, My Lady, for I suffer great torment." (Kulp-Hill 324–25)[11]

Just as the stormy sea inundates the body of the ship, so also does it overtake the body of the merchant, who must in like fashion negotiate the rough waters of the sea. Alfonso emphasizes the identical disposition of ship and human as vessels on the waves in the throes of tribulation with *"atormentado"*: both *tormenta* (storm) and *tormento* (suffering) are present in this adjective, so the merchant's anguish here is etymologically linked to the duress caused by a storm—in fact, it is inseparable from it. Alfonso qualifies the human body by an adjective he otherwise reserves for ships alone. Now metaphors of one another, both ship and merchant eventually reach the safety of dry land in the salvific movement characteristic of these *cantigas*.

The troping of the human body as a ship (and vice versa) allows for a further metaphoric reading in which single bodies are juxtaposed to communities through the conceit of the body overboard. To be cast out of the ship is to be cast from the community of belief, to be temporarily excommunicated. The separation of the individual from the community symbolized by a conflictual relation with ships and the sea realizes the potential of *periguar* (to be in danger) in the broken body of the ship. The stranded body is often highlighted in the Marian songs because the fact of being separated from the collective is itself a terror, a falling outside of grace or a descent into sin. This is the fear the merchant in 267 feels, or the unnamed pilgrim who falls into the sea in 33 as he attempts to jump from the foundering ship into a lifeboat. Here, after the pilgrim undergoes the salvational experience of mortal terror (i.e., his terror acts as a necessary requisite to his rescue), he is guided across the waves by Mary and reaches port safely even before the ship itself does (see Figure 2 for the narration of this *cantiga* in miniatures). *Cantiga* 33 emphasizes the allegorical nature of the individual, since Alfonso tells us in line 21 that the pilgrim ship contains "more than eight hundred pilgrims" ("romeus mais d'oitocentos"), and the salvation of one is the salvation of all.

The lone body committed to water within the frame of devotion may be a female body as well. In 383, during a pilgrimage to the Holy Land, a woman loses her footing and falls into the sea in the presence of her child as she attempts to board a ship:

> They [mother and daughter] . . . begged the man who owned the ship to take them and tried to board the ship quickly. They were in great haste
>
> to enter and were climbing a ladder from the boat into that ship. The daughter went up first. Then the mother, trying to be nimble and climb quickly, fell into the water fully clothed. (Kulp-Hill 467)[12]

The woman cries to the Virgin for help, who rescues her by pulling her safely from the sea at a place other than the point where she fell in; the miraculous rescue presupposes an equally miraculous passage through water.[13] Similarly, in 86, a pregnant woman, on her way to the sea-enclosed Mont-Saint-Michel, gets swept away by the waves. Mary's arrival calms the water and aids with the birth of her child (see Figure 3).

These two poems mobilize a plurivalent symbolism eddying outward from the archetypal sanctity of the mother and child pair, as maritime accidents appeal to Mary's maternal grace. Water unmistakably emerges as an important component of Alfonsine Marianism. If the endangered maternal body alone might suffice to explain Mary's intervention, the association of that body with water multiplies its symbolic appeal. The bearer of life, the maternal body is itself given new life by a submersion in water, a baptism that, given the perilous context here, reiterates water's dual nature as life-giver and death-deliverer. Kolve remarks on the "symbolic submission to water," on "its power to destroy and its power to give and sustain life" (321). The sacramental function of water in the *cantigas* derives from the sea as an analogue of the water of the womb (hence the woman with her daughter and the pregnant woman), the naturally transubstantiating water that renders the seed of life into flesh. We might consider the *cantigas* in this regard as medieval evidence of Gaston Bachelard's poetico-philosophical propositions about water. Although we do not find in Alfonso's poems the milky water of the sea (representative of mother's milk) as Bachelard argues for maternal and feminine water, we do find the message that "[w]ater gives us back our mother" (131), that the sea is "one of the greatest and most constant maternal symbols" (Maria Bonaparte, qtd. in Bachelard 115). It is possible to consider the woman's fall of 383 as a leap into the sea and therefore into the unknown (because of doubt or despair?): "the *leap into the sea,* more than any other physical event, awakens echoes of a dangerous and hostile initiation. It is the only, exact, reasonable image, the only image that can be experienced of a *leap into the unknown*" (Bachelard 165).

The conflictual relation between ships and the sea resulting in the broken body of the ship may explain why this form of being in danger elicits Mary's special interest and sympathy. In several *cantigas* the body of the ship is either split or broken.[14] In particular, the breaking of the mast marks the moment when a ship may be decisively considered as lost (this notion appears everywhere in the HTM), so dismasting is both a real danger and a symbolic turning point in both the poetic and prose shipwreck narratives. Consider this stanza from *cantiga* 172:

for there was such a great storm that the mast was broken and the sail torn to shreds. He saw himself in such trouble that one night he

Figure 3. Miniatures of *cantiga* 86 from Alfonso X, el Sabio, *Cantigas de Santa Maria,* from *El "Códice rico" de las cantigas de Alfonso x el Sabio: ms. T.I.1 de la Biblioteca de El Escorial* (Madrid: Edilán, 1979). Reprinted by permission of the publisher, Edilán.

promised that if he landed safely in port, he would go as a pilgrim to the holy altar of Salas. (Kulp-Hill 207)[15]

A ship's configuration as (or similarity to) a church suggests that the dismasting of a ship represents the splintering or endangering of a community of faith. In this reading, the broken, shipwreckful ship appeals to Mary because, as a church, there is an equivalence between it and the broken body of Christ. The breaking of the mast parallels the breaking of Christ's body on the cross.[16] Part of the mast's structure is the crossbeam *(trave)*, so together, *masto* and *trave* form a crucifix, and the affliction of the ship mirrors Christ's affliction.[17] In the *N. S. do Bom Despacho,* we find a direct allusion to this motif as the crew affixes a crucifix to the mizzenmast at a particularly terrible moment of storm at sea (114).

How appropriate, then, that at this breakage Mary comes to the rescue, her presence comforting the broken, tormented God and the potential break with God (if we read the distressed ship as a community losing, or having lost, its faith) emblematized by the split mast. We might think of the ship's mast as an arm reaching heavenward in a gesture of dramatic verticality—it is a "tormented" limb uplifted in supplication, a prayerful, desperate message from the afflicted passengers on board.[18]

As a close to these thoughts on Alfonso's poems and as a way of anticipating the shipwreck narratives with their own, ship-informed symbolism, consider the following moments from two of the narratives. In the *S. João Baptista,* Francisco Vaz de Almada writes of the disabled ship and its separation from a ship of Dutch corsairs:

> And in all these miseries we thought that it was a punishment from God that the enemy ships had separated from us, since it was an unprecedented thing that a dismasted and rudderless ship in such remote and stormy latitudes should be able to make any port at all. In which a miracle of the Virgin was manifestly displayed, as I have said above. (*Tragic History* 194)[19]

Almada's manifest miracle, in contradistinction to Alfonso's miracles, is an incidental occurrence, and does not locate his story within the redemptive world of the lyric—that is, here is no miracle story in which the trials of shipwreck are unexpectedly relieved by an act of interceptive grace. Closer to the style of the *cantigas* or Berceo's *Miracles* is the following passage from João Baptista Lavanha's *S. Alberto,* occurring near the end as the castaway experience in Africa is brought to a close:

> Nuno Velho, seeing the veneration which they [Kaffirs] showed to the most holy cross, bade a carpenter make a cross from a tree which stood close by (happily and fortunately grown in that Kaffraria, since from one of its branches was made the symbol of our salvation), which was soon made. . . . This was a triumph of the Holy Cross, worthy of being celebrated like those of Constantine and Heraclius, for if those most Christian and pious emperors liberated the True Cross from their enemies . . . so this one (the image of that) was raised and hoisted . . . in the midst of Kaffraria, the centre of heathendom, over which it is triumphing today. And since by clinging to this sweet wood the world was saved from its shipwreck, may it please God Our Lord to enlighten the understanding of these heathen, so that clinging to this faithful cross which was left to them, they may be saved from the perdition and blindness in which they live. (*Tragic History* 171–72)[20]

The "sweet wood" is the wood of grace that saves the world from the shipwreck of original sin, except that it is really the natives' salvation that is at stake rather than the Europeans'. This wood, unlike medieval wood, now exemplifies a worldly, conquistatorial ideology or preoccupation on the part of the Europeans rather than standing as a purely otherworldly symbol of divinity. Equally noteworthy is the reference to trees, one fraught with cultural significance in the (Galician-)Portuguese world. When we see the tree here, Lavanha tells us we simultaneously see the cross-raw material and artifice overlap, and in so doing obliterate time, as if to say that trees, from the first sapling, are already crosses. There is a folding together of the timelessness of divinity and the time-boundedness of earthly existence. The crossing of time, from the earthly into the divine, is accomplished arboreally. Crosses and ships blend imperceptibly through the image of the tree; shipwreck and salvation live in the roots of the cruciformed ships-to-be. Such is the hope when the survivors of the N. S. de Belém head into the African jungle to gather wood to build a rescue boat: "we went into the jungle, and in the name of Our Lady of the Nativity we blessed the trees, everyone making a vow that if she brought us to salvation to any port on the other side of the Cape of Good Hope we would sell the ship and donate the proceeds in this kingdom [Portugal] to the nuns of Saint Martha."[21] Gonzalo Fernández de Oviedo y Valdés, official chronicler of Carlos V and author of the encyclopedic history of the New World titled *Historia general y natural de las Indias* (General and natural history of the Indies) (1535), lists the natural materials out of which sails are made, and then remarks: "but let us leave aside the sails, no more to blame than the wood of trees . . . since out of them the ships and masts and antennas are made."[22] Oviedo makes this comment in the last book of his history, the *Libro de los naufragios* (Book of shipwrecks).[23] These episodes in fact are miracle stories in the style of Alfonso X or Berceo. Ships and sails for Oviedo are natural objects put to unnatural use (in this he reiterates the ancient idea of sailing or seafaring as unnatural), but this sentiment is safely ensconced in the shipwrecks book as opposed to the history "proper" and serves to heighten the temerity of Oviedo's historical actors. He sounds a note of heroism tragically attained, one that eventually should lead to safety: "we live in tempest," Oviedo writes, citing Seneca, "let us die in port."[24]

Figure 4. Mary and child appear above the dismasted ship in a woodcut from the 1601 edition of the *S. António, Naufragio, que passou Iorge Dalbuquerque Coelho, Capitão e Governador de Pernambuco.*

NAUFRÁGIO E PERDIÇÃO (SHIPWRECK AND PERDITION)

In the medieval devotional lyric, shipwreck ultimately leads to salvation in an overall narrative of spiritual redemption that frames the shipwreck miracles and preempts any understanding of perdition as a permanent state. Shipwreck is a trial on the altar of faith. For Alfonso X and Berceo, it presents no lasting danger that cannot be healed by heaven's intervention; it exists wholly outside the issue of national self-identity, and preexists the evangelical, political, and cultural imperatives of expansion. We now move forward in time some three centuries to consider the presence of shipwreck in the machinery of the expansionist state as it appears in *Os Lusíadas,* the central expression of imperial ideology in Portugal and a text so heavily nationalistic that it has been located at the epicenter of the Portuguese literary canon ever since its publication in 1572. This poem, which takes as its historical basis the opening of the sea route to India by Vasco da Gama's fleet in 1497–99, has done more to shape the understanding of the relationship between shipwreck and empire—especially empire as a heroic enterprise—than any other work. It is beyond the scope of these comments to offer even a partial account of the staggering body of criticism on Camões's poem; rather, what I want to do is isolate a few instances of this ten-canto text and consider them as emblematic of an exegetical tradition, of how shipwreck has been typically conceptualized as part of the voracious sweep of imperial desire.

As Vasco da Gama and his company sail down the west coast of Africa and are about to round the Cape of Good Hope, a terrifying apparition addresses the Portuguese travelers. This specter is Adamastor, an anthropomorphic manifestation of the Cape who materializes precisely at the midpoint of both Vasco da Gama's voyage and Camões's text (canto V). Adamastor upbraids the Portuguese for their daring in violating again a natural boundary (the cape) that had only been breached a few years earlier by another Portuguese (Bartolomeu Dias, in 1488) and then delivers a series of prophetic pronouncements outlining the death and loss to be experienced by Portugal in her campaign to reach the corners of the globe. At one point, the giant predicts, "If what I think be true, each year your fleet / Shall look on many a shipwreck, and immense / Variety of ruin shall befall, / Till death itself shall be least ill of all" (V, 44, v–viii),[25] and then declares:

Here will another come, of fairest fame,
A knight, a lover, and of liberal mind,
Bringing with him that most delicious dame,
Love, of his mercy, for his love designed,
Whom their sad fortune and dark fate shall claim
Here in my country, angry and unkind,
Which, though it let them through rough shipwreck live,
'Tis but the sight of greater ills to give.

Starving to death, they shall see children dear,
Begot and born in love beyond compare,
And the fierce Caffirs, envious of her gear,
From the sweet lady all her vesture tear,
And limbs, so beautiful and crystal clear,
Naked in the sun and frost and windy air,
After the long march when her delicate feet
Have suffered the beach sands' ferocious heat.

Their eyes shall see, such as escape again
From so much misadventure and distress,
The lovers in their misery remain
Deep in the hot implacable wilderness.
There, when for bitter tears of grief and pain
The very stones seem not so merciless,
Those two, in close embrace, their souls shall free
From the fair prison of their agony. (V, 46–48)[26]

Adamastor, by telling the story of Manuel de Sousa Sepúlveda and Leonor de Sá, casts this shipwreck narrative squarely into the center of the cultural mythology created by Camões's pen and given dark expression in this episode. It is at this point that Adamastor narrates his own story to the terrified onlookers. A Titan, he became enamored of Thetis one day after seeing her naked. The goddess Doris deceives Adamastor by claiming that she can arrange a meeting between the giant and the goddess of the waves, but when Adamastor appears at the designated place and runs to embrace his beloved, he finds that he has been tricked, and holds in his arms not a nymph but a mountain: "When I thought that face angelical to press, / I was unmanned and, dumb, still as a stock, /

Became a rock joined to another rock" (V, 56, vi–viii).[27] So begins a metamorphosis:

> This flesh of mine was changed into hard clay.
> My bones, of crags and rocks, took on the cast.
> These limbs you see, this form and body, lay
> Stretched out in the great waters. And at last
> Into this promontory faraway
> The gods transmuted all my stature vast.
> And, that I might endure redoubled ill,
> The sea of Thetis circle round me still. (V, 59)[28]

The figure of Adamastor and the images associated with him resonate strongly with shipwreck and its presence in the project of empire.[29] For, as an anthropomorphic figure of the Cape of Good Hope (also known as the Cape of Storms), Adamastor is also shipwreck awesomely incarnate because the Cape and its vicinity were the site of numerous wrecks on the India route. But it is important to note that Adamastor, once he finishes speaking, never really disappears—he just returns his form back to the land from which he was temporarily released by the passage of the Portuguese fleet,[30] and it is understandable that Camões should have Adamastor narrate the story of Sepúlveda and Leonor because it strikes such a sympathetic chord with his own. In the final moments of the *S. João,* both husband and wife are committed to the African countryside in defeat much as Adamastor returns to the earth in a reenactment of his defeat by Thetis. Here is a new, symbolic defeat at the hands of the Portuguese who disregard his ferocity and proceed through the tumultuous waters to their destination. Adamastor surely feels special empathy for Leonor, because she physically merges with the African land by burying herself in the sand after being beaten and disrobed by the natives.[31] Like Adamastor, Leonor's story is also one of love punished by the forces of nature. Although Adamastor may well be thought of as existing "on the border between the animate and the inanimate" (Lipking 215), he is also a living body and the land itself, a commitment of body to earth, a "telluric symbol of death and transfiguration . . . the conversion of flesh into earth" (Jackson, *Builders* 23). Adamastor and Leonor are each figures of death caused by desire: Adamastor dies (or is literally petrified) by his desire for Thetis, a mythological scenario through which we might also read him as representative of the sacrifice of African (and Portuguese) bodies for the sake of land and resources, the objects of imperial desire;[32] Leonor dies after a gesture in which she allows her body to be consumed by the African sand while still holding her children, a moment of maternal despair caused by *carreira da Índia* greed.[33] Finally, it is possible to link the tale of Sepúlveda and his wife to the struggle of the gods played out through Camões's poem. As Venus protects the Portuguese, Bacchus hinders and obstructs them. Adamastor, as a figure of frustrated desire, manifests Bacchus's presence as the troubling conflation of fate, symbol, and presentiment, part of a Baroque code permitting classical gods and fates to represent archetypal conflicts in Camões's poem, conflicts that we could just as easily consider as acted out in the shipwreck narratives also, albeit without the explicit references to the mythological figures.[34]

Adamastor's speech in canto V is anticipated in the preceding canto as Vasco da Gama's fleet prepares to depart from the Lisbon (more properly, Belém) shore. An old man from the district of Restelo appears suddenly and delivers a harangue to the sailors, excoriating the vanity of fame that drives expansion and the communal ills it causes. The Old Man of Restelo (Velho do Restelo) voices an explicit anti-imperialist argument:

> Glory of empire! Most unfruitful lust
> After the vanity that men call fame!
> . . . .
> What thy vast vengeance and thy sentence just
> On the vain heart that greatly loves thy name!
> What death, what peril, tempest, cruel woe,
> Dost though decree that he must undergo!
> . . . .
> Spring of adultery and abandonment,
> Empires and realms and wealth consuming whole,
> And, as we know, only too provident!
> Thy powers for high and noble men extol,
> More worthy of their curse malevolent,
> And call thee fame and glory's plenitude,
> Names whereby witless men their souls delude.
> What new disasters dost thou now prepare

Figure 5. The encounter with Adamastor in canto V of *Os Lusíadas*, from *La Lusiade de Louis Camoëns* (Nyon, 1776).

Against these kingdoms and against their seed?
What peril and what death for them to bear,
Under some mighty name, hast thou decreed?
What mines of gold now dost thou promise fair?
What kingdoms?—promise lightly made indeed!
What fame dost thou propose? What legend glorious?
What palm? What triumph? And what war victorious? (IV, 95–97)[35]

It is telling that the Old Man delivers his imprecation at the moment of the ship's departure, the significant moment in shipwreck narratives that marks a ship's first failure because, in almost all cases, the ship will not return. The Old Man's monologue enacts a negative narrative moment, a type of undertow in the ineluctable and otherwise forward-moving realization of empire. In fact, we could consider the Old Man of Restelo's speech as an enactment of shipwreck narrative, that is, as a discursive moment that counters or disrupts the official discourse of imperialism.[36] The harangue stands in opposition to the stanzas immediately preceding it—clearly a strategy to emphasize this brief eruption of shipwreck discourse—in which Camões invokes the glory and pomp attendant on Vasco da Gama's departure. Shipwreck functions as a symbolic tool by which failure can be related to empire, and in this sense both Adamastor's speech and the Velho do Restelo's act as conjoint shipwreck narratives. Camões's recognition of disaster or failure in his poetic vision is, like the HTM narratives, ambiguous and problematic. There exists the possibility of allowing shipwreck (and the shipwreck prophecies) to be part of the cost extracted by empire, a discordant note in the otherwise "epic" discourse of the poem. Yet, as Lipking observes, grievance itself can exert a unifying or binding force: "For one way a poet can speak for a nation . . . is by expressing the grievances that hold it together" (205). The fate of Sepúlveda might stand in contrapuntal relation to imperial achievement or embody a collective lament about empire.[37] So the prophecies about, and presence of, disaster, function doubly in Camões as both inimical to imperial achievement and inherent to it. Banks reminds us that "in *Os Lusíadas* one finds a tautological voice which predicts the consequences of the Portuguese voyages while assuming their success" (4). Subrahmanyam similarly remarks that "the *Lusíadas* simply cannot be read as a critique of Portuguese expansion from an insider. . . . To do so would be to set aside the thrusting weight of the text in its dominant (and most understood) mode" (158–59).

To consider shipwreck as cleanly and binarily opposed to empire is to enter shaky critical territory because it simplifies both Camões's poem (and, by extension, the shipwreck narratives) and the fact of shipwreck as a common occurrence in the course of empire. Although it is not possible to read *Os Lusíadas* as an "epic" text in the univocal mold, neither is it possible to read the text as a wholesale condemnation of it. Indeed, it would seem that Camões intentionally construes the relationship between national glory and failure in equivocal terms, weaving shipwreck and disaster into the very fabric of imperial design rather than conceiving of it simply as a regrettable cost. In the Camonian understanding of epic, disaster exists coterminously with an espousal of imperialist ideologies, so there is no cause and effect between the two: empire exists alongside shipwreck, alongside its own undoing.

The simultaneous existence of shipwreck and empire appears in another moment near the end of the poem as we witness the success of Vasco da Gama's voyage as he and his crew enjoy the company of the nymphs on the Isle of Love (Ilha dos Amores). As Tethys displays a model of the universe, indicating the parts of the globe the Portuguese will reach in the future, she pauses to consider the Mekong River, and remarks:

> In his bosom, gentle and compassionate,
> He shall receive the sea-drenched Epic Song
> That fled the wreck, in sad and piteous state,
> Upon the shoaling reefs where the gusts throng.
> Hunger shall be, and danger grim and great,
> Till they at length shall do that shameful wrong
> To him whose lyre, with its sonorous sound,
> Shall make him far less happy than renowned. (X, 128)[38]

An echo of Adamastor's voice can be heard here, unrecognizable now because it issues from the mouth of the alluring sea goddess but present nonetheless because it proclaims a final shipwreck prophecy. Adamastor haunts these verses, a spectral presence lurking behind the Mekong wreck. Most readers of *Os Lusíadas* find in this stanza a biographical reference to Camões's own experience of shipwreck on the S. Bento in

China in 1554, a reading that begins with the comments Manuel de Faria e Sousa makes in his erudite, annotated edition of the poem (1639).[39] Yet whatever biographical facts might lie behind these lines, the image consolidates crucial symbolic motifs elaborated throughout the entire text. Moser, for one, hypothesizes that it may be "fraught with symbolic meaning" ("Camões' Shipwreck" 215), reading, through Almeida Garrett, an equation between the "sinking ship from which the *Lusiads* were saved with the Portuguese ship of state" (215). This is certainly plausible, but what about the explicit link forged between shipwreck and text? We imagine Camões swimming to shore with a waterlogged text *(o Canto molhado)*: the text, like Camões, is a shipwreck swimmer, a survivor of the wreck. Shipwreck, for all its destructive power, is the mechanism by which *Os Lusíadas* survives; in a gesture of high irony, the obliterating force of shipwreck has saved the poem for posterity.

Camões proposes a problematic dependence between shipwreck and empire through textuality. Iberian empire was largely, even predominantly, textual in nature, so the writing of texts served to perpetuate empire and assure or manifest its survival; textuality, in this capacity, is a sign of power and the maintenance of hegemony. Yet, as Tethys's vision demonstrates, shipwreck or disaster also allows for a textual productivity. The correlation between shipwreck and text dismantles a binarism that would otherwise allow us to equate texts with the success of empire and the absence of texts with its failure or demise: disaster is a gap in the narrative of empire that nonetheless is represented by a moment of textual survival. Symbolically, this erasure of boundaries, this impossibility of a facile schema of success and failure, cohesion and disaster, resides in Camões's decision to represent text and water as coterminous. The elemental affinity created by shipwreck (the liquidating of the text, we might say) means that the text now shares characteristics with water—it has gained a fluidity, a currency, a transitivity. Because it travels over the water, the text is a ship and shipwreck swimmer simultaneously. Camões incorporates written discourse into the triumvirate ship/water/travel that constitutes the epistemological frame of empire, and of its representation in his poem. Out of shipwreck, the poet tells us, come texts. Disaster sends them, waterlogged but intact, to the readers waiting on shore.

2

THE DISCOURSE OF THE SHIPWRECK

"SHIPWRECK," WRITES FERNAND BRAUDEL, "is always the most significant moment" (32).[1] I take Braudel's observation with its flatly superlative assessment of shipwreck in his essay on historiographic models and apply it freely to the context at hand, that is, to the significance of narratives of shipwreck within the historiographic productivity of maritime Iberia (especially Portugal). The tradition of shipwreck writing is a disruptive chapter in expansionist historiography, a narrative practice of representing disaster that (partially) establishes itself outside the official parameters of textual production and authority by which the workings and benefits of empire enter narrative representation. The shipwreck narrative breaks apart, or breaks away from, the monolithic practice of state writing, and shipwreck emerges not so much as an isolated event as it does an idea, a force, a resistance to order and cohesion. In this chapter, I want to advance ideas about possible meanings of shipwreck and what it means to write about it from within a legislated culture of textuality.

IN THIS SHIPWRECK

When the anonymous author of the *S. João,* the earliest surviving shipwreck account, begins the prologue with the words "The matter narrated *in this shipwreck*" (3) ("Cousa é esta que se conta *neste naufrágio*" [185]; my emphasis), the writer establishes an equation that will underlie all subsequent shipwreck narratives: shipwreck is both event and text, an experience of disaster and the narrative account of that disaster. *Naufrágio,* a moment of rupture in which loss becomes realized concretely and symbolically, encompasses also the narrative representation of loss. The shipwreck narrative is a second, or reenacted loss, and there exists an attempt on the part of the shipwreck authors to recuperate or repair loss through the agency of narrative. Although on the whole such a recuperation fails at a symbolic level—there is no complete restoration of the damage done to the ship and its passengers, either as icons of state, culture, or narrative, as will become clearer in the ensuing pages— the fact that the shipwreck story can be told at all is a sign of a certain kind of salvation; for even if the shipwreck authors are disaster personified, they are also all survivors, like Camões's waterlogged manuscript. So it is that salvation lies in the reality of the printed page, a deed of survival clinging to its authors like seaweed to drenched clothes. This survivalist lens allows us to invoke Blumenberg again because survival creates an authorial positioning that makes the shipwreck narrative loosely akin to the "safety of the spectator position."

The imbrication of shipwreck with text, a folding together of historical and narrative loss, happens through the medium of the concept of discourse *(discurso),* a keystone of both nautical and narrative practice. A *discurso* is the route of a ship, its itinerary, and it is also the route a writer creates and the reader follows. *Discurso* is the path of the ship and the path of the narrative, and is even a synonym for narrative itself. When Manuel de Mesquita Perestrelo refers to the "discourse of the voyage" ("discurso da viagem"), he is referring to the path traveled by him and his fellow passengers of the S. Bento, on water and on land; when he mentions the moment when the S. Bento is no longer able to "navegar direita" or "sail correctly," or remarks that the ship "goes off course" *(de-sandar)*, he ascribes a waywardness and an implicit, unavoidable un-doing to the idea of prescribed itinerary, course, or voyage. At one point in the *S. Tomé*, Diogo do Couto, speaking of the lifeboats put into use after the wreck, narrates the events of one boat, then switches to the other: "so finally they remained where they were for the time being; and there we will also leave them, to return to the other boat in which was Captain Estevão da Veiga" [*Tragic History* 91].[2] Couto's narrative trajec-tory here and elsewhere follows the trajectory of lifeboats, the course of unpredictable wandering after the wreck. Royal cosmographer João Baptista Lavanha speaks of the "discourse of this account" ("discurso desta Relação") in the *S. Alberto*, while Joseph de Cabreira, author of the *N. S. de Belém* (who served as the doomed ship's captain) juxtaposes dis-course as an idea of order with the confusing multiplicity of opinions on how to help the troubled ship: "given everything in this labyrinth of opinions, and guided by the best discourse (i.e., rationale), I gave orders to launch the lifeboat."[3] Later, Cabreira remarks on "this entire dis-course of afflictions" (68) ("todo este discurso de aflições"), and here discourse means the shipwreck narrative itself, a narrative manifesting the irrational path of affliction, hunger, loss.

The equation between text and wreck, between *discurso* and *nau-frágio*, negatively refigures the more general alliance between writing and the voyage that lies at the center of expansionist textuality where the redaction of documents serves as tools and guarantors of empire. If, for instance, we consider the writings of Columbus as one of the founding moments of the text-voyage, then his introductory remark in the *Diario del primer viaje* (Diary of the first voyage) is significant: "and to do this I decided to write this entire voyage in great detail, day to day noting everything I did and saw and experienced, as will be seen in what fol-lows."[4] This is Columbus's first and perhaps most striking instance of what Kadir terms an "interested usage of words" (62) in which rhetoric and ideology overlap; Kadir further remarks that "we are dealing with rhetoric and rhetorical constructs and, inasmuch as these protagonists take their words to be identical with their acts or as their actions' faith-ful echoes, we are dealing with ideologies" (ibid.). The ideologies at work in Columbus and other writers of the Spanish or Portuguese states are grounded in a range of justifications of dominance and control—

cultural, economic, or evangelical—under the sign of "conquest." As Columbus makes clear, this (self-)authorizing dynamic happens through writing and the text: thus, the "ideology of the text" is an expression we may posit to mean both the ideology(-ies) expressed in a text and the willed use of the text as an instrument of ideology. Columbus's postponement within the text of the narration of events that have already transpired, signaled by "as will be seen in what follows," creates the illusion of a forward-moving series of historical actions and revelations that the diary records in increments as they happen. If, in Columbus's case, the New World, in its staggering newness, effects a break with previous ways of knowing or conceiving of the world, then this newness emerges safely under a backward-looking writerly perspective that guarantees knowledge and authority through the conceit of the forward-moving voyage and the textual rendering of that voyage. Through Columbus's pen, we read the enterprise of the Indies authoritatively by moving backwards and forwards at once; the account of a rocky epistemological voyage already partially tamed is presented as one in the making.

Columbus's authoritative back-writing happens from an already consolidated position of power in relation to conquered lands and people; this dynamic loses potency in the shipwreck authors. True, they draft their accounts after the fact like Columbus and his successors, but the coalescence of text and voyage begins to disintegrate as an exercise of powerful and authoritative hermeneutics (one that ideally wields, promotes, and consolidates ideologies) because the shipwreck voyage, a priori, is a failed enterprise. I will return to this later, but for now suffice it to say that the shipwreck author looks back on a voyage textually within a discursive culture that demands that such historiographic reckoning inexorably lead to a position of knowledge and power. The shipwreck narrative undoes, or begins to fall outside of, the hermeneutic iron bonds successfully linking writer, voyage, and text, where these notions coalesce seamlessly as a manifestation of European politico-cultural power and its textual correlates.

Let us return to the shipwreck accounts and to *discurso*. In the *S. Paulo*, Henrique Dias troubles the smooth synchronicity of writing and voyage when he speaks of "our terrible voyage and our perdition" ("nossa ruim viagem e nossa perdição") by reconceptualizing the relationship between voyage and outcome as one of loss or absence, where a discourse or trajectory acts as a form of dispersal or ruin. Consider Dias's move from writerly concerns to an ignorance of the course of the ship in the following passage:

> If I were to write of our daily misfortunes and misadventures (for not a single day passed without them) this would be a lengthy process and would cause more weariness than pleasure to the reader (since long things, as the Poet affirms, are habitually disdained and held in little esteem, while short things are pleasing). I will therefore limit myself to recording as briefly as possible the notable things that happened to us, both in our voyage as in our shipwreck, noting the dates on which they occurred. I will stick as closely to the truth as I can, for where my skill and my words fail, the truth is enough to ornament and embellish my narrative. The route that the ship made every day, and the directions that determined it with the various sightings taken, I leave to those charged with these matters, namely, men of the sea who have their rutters with departures and degrees marked, as this is not my profession and since I was such a novice on the sea. This trip was the first time I left the country and I didn't even know the standard compass-points. (*Further Selections* 61)[5]

Dias proposes to write both voyage and shipwreck, two forms of itinerary or *discurso* that stand in a dissociative relationship to one another, and this tension between a forward-moving, plottable, and coherent route ("voyage") and its opposite ("shipwreck") surfaces in the author's admission of ignorance about the technicalities of nautical science. It is no mistake that Dias sketches a portrait of the shipwreck writer at the time of this wreck as someone inhabiting a space of unknowing that is characterized by an explicit reference to disorientation: "I . . . didn't even know the standard compass-points." From the outset, Dias casts his narrative outside the directionality and control emblematized so cogently in maritime trajectories by the compass; the "discourse" of this account is founded on a conflictual relation between a nautical route that was followed and one that Dias does not know yet paradoxically chooses to record. Dias's shipwreck route soon emerges as one of aimlessness, a discourse entirely distinct from the ship's (allegedly) calculated and regulated route. His experience of wandering or marching haphazardly—"at daybreak, we began to walk, in no order and without accord" ("rompendo a alva, começámos a caminhar, sem ordem nem concerto") (225), he remarks at one point—is characteristic of this and virtually all shipwreck narratives in that the survival march is distinguished by disorientation and by unknowingly walking in circles. One of the effects of shipwreck is to reduce the idea of itinerary to an impassable redundancy, where a supposed movement forward is in reality a movement backward, where one can walk for leagues (as do the survivors of the S. João) only to find one has unwittingly doubled back to the march's place of origin. The shipwreck route is the road to nowhere.

In writing the wreck and its aftermath, the shipwreck writer could not be further from empire, writing, and the metaphor of nautical directionality invoked by Bernal Díaz del Castillo in an early chapter of his *Historia verdadera de la conquista de la Nueva España* (1632) (True history of the conquest of New Spain): "you [the readers] will find the conquests of New Spain clearly, as they must be seen. I want to take again my pen in hand, as a good pilot takes soundings, discovering shoals in the sea ahead, when he senses they're there."[6] As a *discurso* (a route and a representation), then, shipwreck effects a forced abdication of knowledge on the part of the writer who would otherwise construct an authority of the European subject moving through (and dominating) extra-European spaces. This authority, we have seen, rests on the seamless imposition of successful voyage and text. So it is, in a similar attitude, that González Fernández de Oviedo speaks of the order of empire in the introductory pages of his *Historia general y natural de las Indias* (General and natural history of the Indies), where the successful return to Europe of ships loaded with goods (1:28) demonstrates the controlled and victorious manifestation of empire. Oviedo goes on to assert that one of his historiographic objectives in compiling the "glorious *Chronicle of Spain*" ("gloriosa *Chrónica de España*") (1:28) is to relate "the order of the route and navigation from Spain to these parts, the rise and fall of the sea and its tides, the turns to northeast and northwest of the compass needles, and other matters convenient to the discourse of history."[7]

If the shipwreck narrative can be regarded as a platform on which the dissolution of the power relations obtaining between expansionist activity and its textual analogue may begin to be glimpsed, it also embraces more generally a number of thematic topoi typical of the Baroque aesthetic, and a brief consideration of these topoi helps situate shipwreck within this aspect of a cultural and aesthetic imagination. We might, for instance, consider the terror of shipwreck or storm, sickness, hunger, and exposure to the elements as an anguished disillusion (Portuguese *desengano,* Spanish *desengaño*), a Baroque conceit that, in the shipwreck tales, appears in graphic detail.[8] But the negative, pessimistic tenor of the Baroque aesthetic and its conceits generally harbor an injunction to locate the positive and the useful: Baroque art may be filled with tragedy, but we can laugh at it; the confused order of the universe may be exalted as sublime, as an aesthetic ideal. It is precisely these other sides of themes, such as misery, mutability, disillusion, and confused order, that the shipwreck narratives generally lack; they are powerfully negative because they systematically or characteristically suggest no redemption.[9]

One conceit that is especially prevalent in shipwreck texts is disordered order, an ancillary aspect of the broader idea of the "desconcerto do mundo" (disorder of the world) that is in itself a "sorrowful reflection on cosmic confusion and disorder, on the senselessness of the world and of life" (Silva, *Maneirismo e barroco* 236). Through the conceit of disordered order—the *conjunctio oppositorum, discordia concors,* or *dissimilium concordia*—the world emerges as a struggle of oppositions. Through these oppositions a harmony becomes apparent. Yet when the shipwreck authors invoke the notion of disordered order, the harmonic aspect is attenuated, if not eradicated altogether. Disordered order becomes a device by which a lack of meaning receives emphasis. Consider the following examples. At the beginning of the *S. Bento,* Perestrelo remarks on the loading of the ships in India that are about to depart for Portugal, among which the S. Bento stands out because of its "greatness, fortitude, and goodness" ("grandeza, fortaleza, e bondade") (218). He then observes that the ship was doomed because of the burdensome amount of cargo the officials haphazardly wanted to place in its holds. "Nonetheless," Perestrelo continues, "once the best order was bestowed on this disorder, and the said ships were prepared with cargo and necessary items, they sailed for this country."[10] Order is granted to the body of the ship in a slapdash and certainly tenuous manner, and it is precisely this fragile arrangement of order over disorder that will cause the ship's destruction. Later, Perestrelo tells how, after surviving a rainstorm at night, the company awakes and returns to the beach that was the site of the wreck. There,

[we] found it strewn with dead bodies disfigured by hideous wounds and deformities, which gave evidence of the painful death they had suffered. Some lay above and some underneath the rocks, and of many nothing was visible but heads, arms, or legs, and their faces were covered with sand, boxes, and other things. . . .And truly there was a confused order to all that misadventure had ordered. (Theal 1:222)[11]

Perestrelo is taken aback at the "confused order" caused by misadventure and shipwreck, and his almost awestruck recognition of this happens as he realizes the extent of the chaos, one that will only become amplified in the subsequent pages of his narrative. The arrangement of order over disorder at the commencement of the narrative has reappeared after the shipwreck (confused order begets confused order, Perestrelo seems to be saying), but it is one that affords no understanding of a harmonic principle of the cosmos or of Perestrelo's own place in it—quite the contrary. This moment of realization punctuates the sense of chaos and disorder and negates the possibility of an edifying or sublime understanding of the structure of the world.

We find a similar instance in the *S. Paulo,* but here the juxtaposition of disordered order with the chaos caused by shipwreck occurs within the context of a homiletic attempt to negate the chaotic experience of wreck. Father Pedro Manuel Álvares delivers an impromptu sermon in an attempt to restore harmony after shipwreck in Sumatra, as mutual suspicion among the survivors increases:

In these suspicions . . . we spent the day in vigilance, both of the enemy and of each other, an ambivalent vigilance in that we didn't know if anything was certain or not, since there was no one who would believe or trust in anyone other than himself; at daybreak the next morning the Father Manuel Álvares convoked and assembled everyone together. And standing in front of an altar which he had made, with a retable of Our Lady, he began to make an admonitory speech, using very prudent words, worthy of such a pure man and so necessary at this time to bring everyone into agreement *[concórdia]* and unanimity, saying: "Most beloved brothers in Christ, let us recall that holy saying of the Gospel that a kingdom divided against itself cannot stand; and with concord *[concórdia]* small things grow into

great, whereas with discord *[discórdia]* great things decline and di-
minish. I must remind you, brothers, that with all the other great
ships which were wrecked in the region of the Cape of Good Hope,
like the galleon *[São João Baptista]* and the *São Bento* and many others, one of the things which led to the total death and destruction
of the survivors was the discord which prevailed among them. . . ."
(*Further Selections* 74)[12]

Discord and concord are not purely aesthetic notions but the in-
structive theme of a homily. Even more significant is the fact that in this
sermon Álvares acts as a reader of shipwreck, and his exhortation to fellow survivors is to create a harmony from a pall of discord, to learn the
lesson of the Baroque precept. It is also an attempt to inscribe the chaotic experience of the S. Paulo and of all shipwrecks into a divine plan,
and in this respect Álvares's brief speech recalls the function of shipwreck in Alfonso X's and Berceo's poetry.[13]

Of all the shipwreck motifs commensurate with the Baroque aesthetic, the theatricality of experience, or the world as a stage, finds privileged
expression in the shipwreck authors, as the image of the broken or
doomed ship repeatedly populates the pages of the narratives. The extremity of the shipwreck experience pushes not only at the bounds of
credibility and knowability, but at the limits of (verbal) representation,
and so compels many authors to imbue their writings periodically with
an ekphrastic rhetoric.[14] The doomed or wrecked ship is a spectacle, as
so many of the writers remark, that is "horrendous" or "pitiful." But the
ship is also a space in which theatrical representation occurs, as Cardoso's
narrative of the *Santiago* makes clear: the ship is a floating stage where
numerous religious processions and performances take place "among the
waves of the sea" ("entre as ondas do mar").[15] The double function
of the ship as theatrical space and theatrical spectacle is in line with
Maravall's observation that "[i]f reality is theatrical, if the spectators find
themselves submerged in the great theater of the world, what they contemplate on the stage is a theater to the second degree" (200). What
Maravall calls "theater to the second degree" might also be termed
"metatheater," and it is just this aspect of shipwreck that Afonso Luís
writes about at the end of the S. António. The battered ship is put on display in Lisbon:

Dom Henrique, cardinal in this kingdom of Portugal, who was then in charge of the government, sent a galley to tow the said ship up-river, which it did, and the ship was laid up in front of the Church of St. Paul, which is now a parish. And during the time of a month or more that she lay there, an amazing number of people came to see her, and they were all utterly astounded at seeing what a wreck she was, and they gave great thanks and praise to Our Lord for saving those who came in her from the deadly perils they had undergone. (*Further Selections* 153–54)[16]

The display of the S. António in the Lisbon harbor recalls the final scene of Gil Vicente's *Auto da Índia* (1509), the expansionist-era farce in which a married woman commits adultery in the absence of her husband seeking wealth on the India route. Much to her disappointment, her husband returns safely to Portugal, thereby putting an end to her sexual escapades. The play closes as the wife takes an interest in the wealth her husband has brought back:

WIFE: Is the ship well laden?

HUSBAND: She's decked out so sweetly.

WIFE: Let's go there, I implore you, to see it.

HUSBAND: Would you be pleased by this?

WIFE: Yes, because I'm much out of sorts.

They go to see the ship and so ends this first farce. (Vicente, *Three Discovery Plays* 159)[17]

To those who might find in Vicente's play a criticism of expansionist policy, a lampooning of the agenda of the state, Ana Paula Ferreira observes: "As the playlet that is performed between the two major public scenes of maritime expansionism (departures and returns), Gil Vicente's *Auto da Índia* can properly be regarded as a sort of *entremés* that alleviates the dramatic tension of the official play of history thereby ensuring its successful accomplishment" (108). Ferreira correctly emphasizes the public nature of the ship display in her interpretation, an idea that recalls the notion (rehearsed by the shipwreck authors) of the shipwreck narrative as benefiting the common good (*bem comum* or *bem público*) via the printing press. The difference between Vicente's play and Luís's narrative[18] is that Luís's narrative is no *entremés*; it does not function to produce a farcical laugh that ultimately allows for the reassertion or successful accomplishment of the official play of history, but serves instead as a public reminder that such an "official play" may in fact fail, and definitively at that. There is no ludic contract between Luís and his readers as there is between Vicente and his audience, which allows, ironically, for a laughing sideways glance to be cast on expansionist activity as a way of reaffirming its validity. It might conceivably be argued that the very fact of the S. António's return acts as such an affirmation because in virtually all shipwreck narratives, of course, there is no ship left to return. But against such a reading we must consider a scene immediately following the one just cited in which the ship's captain, Jorge de Albuquerque Coelho, arrives home:

> I only wish to relate one more incident, to show the terrible hardships which we had endured and the condition of those who survived in this shipwreck. Jorge d'Albuquerque, having started on his pilgrimage from Belém to Nossa Senhora da Luz, accompanied by some of us, took the road via Nossa Senhora da Ajuda. Meanwhile, his friends and relations in the city being informed of his arrival, his cousin Dom Jerónimo de Moura, son of Dom Manuel de Moura, and many other persons at once went out to meet him. On being told that he had already landed and where he was going and what route he was taking, they went after him. And on catching up with us as we were walking along in procession, Dom Jerónimo greeted us and asked us if we were those people who had been saved with Jorge d'Albuquerque. When we replied 'Yes,' he asked us: 'Is Jorge d'Albuquerque going in front, or behind, or is he taking another route?' And Jorge d'Albuquerque, who was standing right in front of him, answered: 'Senhor, Jorge d'Albuquerque is not in front, nor behind, nor is he taking another route.' Dom Jerónimo, thinking he was joking, was rather annoyed, and told him not to make jokes but to answer the question he had been asked. Jorge d'Albuquerque thereupon retorted: 'Senhor Dom Jerónimo, if you saw Jorge d'Albuquerque, would you recognize him?' He answered that he would. 'Well then, I am Jorge d'Albuquerque, and you are my cousin Dom Jerónimo . . . And you can see from the state I am in, what I have been through.' And although they had both been brought up together, and it was

not a full year since they had last seen each other, and although they had been familiar and intimate friends for a long time, Dom Jerónimo thought he looked so utterly different that he still did not recognize him. It was then necessary for Jorge d'Albuquerque to show him certain marks on his body, which finally convinced him, whereupon he embraced him with many tears, astounded at how greatly his appearance had altered; and so it was with all the rest of us. (*Further Selections* 156–57)[19]

This scene is reminiscent of chapter 29 of Bernal Díaz del Castillo's later *Historia,* in which Jerónimo de Aguilar, after having lived among the Mexicans for some time, has become so altered in bodily appearance that he is unrecognizable to his compatriot Hernán Cortés. When Cortés asks, "What has become of the Spaniard" ("¿Qué es del español?"), Aguilar responds, "It is I" ("Soy yo"). But whereas the European-gone-native in Castillo's history foreshadows the new subject to emerge from the encounter between the old world and the new, between the European and the native, in Luís's narrative the nonrecognition happens at home at the moment of return. What Luís flags in this scene with its comic undertones is the impossibility of return after the experience of shipwreck, at least as it functions within the template of expansionist activity where the return home happens as a recognizable—and victorious— correlate of the departure.[20] Once departed, an icon of an outward-bound *pátria,* here personified by Coelho, goes into exile and is radically transformed. Distressed sea voyages produce a gap, an alienation that can never be entirely reassimilated back at home. If empire is on one level the enactment of a national self-identity abroad, then Coelho's experience suggests that this identity has suffered shipwreck and has been left in pieces. The return home is more akin to being washed ashore; as culture and identity travel in the shipwreck tale, they are broken into pieces and rendered unfamiliar and unrecognizable.

WRITING PERDITION

Through the double referentiality of *discurso,* as we have just seen, the shipwreck writers posit an equation between wreck and text. The *discurso* as an itinerary that is diverted or undone and represented as such narratively—the discourse of shipwreck—underlies the axiomatic notion to the writing and reading of shipwreck literature that it is a narrative of rupture, breakage, and disjunction in which the context of maritime expansion plays a critical role. Shipwreck writing emerges as a practice of prose when textuality flexes its muscle as a primary tool and engine of empire and colonization, as systems of representation negotiate between the Old World and other worlds to wrestle cultural, political, religious, and social difference into familiar patterns of sociopolitical order. Shipwreck narrative is bound up, negatively, in the project of a nation's self-constitution and identity as it attempts to move beyond the limits of the *pátria* or home country. The world no longer exists as it did in the Middle Ages: new projects of knowing are at stake when the shipwreck writers work as received epistemological traditions creak and groan under the weight of expansion and empirical newness. Shipwreck is the sign of this epistemological break, of a previous world crashing against the shoals of its own demise. The centrality of controlled (maritime) itinerary as an agent of culture, political power, and expanding nationhood is unhinged. If shipwreck happens mostly on the India route as recounted in the HTM, Afonso Luís's narrative of the *S. António* also locates the shipwreck experience and its dynamic of breakage in the New World. Portuguese shipwreck writing, because of this straddling of empires, functions somewhat differently than shipwreck in the writings of Columbus or Cabeza de Vaca, who are immersed exclusively in the New World.

Critical studies on the HTM in recent years seek to define the thematic or structural formalities of the shipwreck account (e.g., Lanciani, *Sucessos* 69–150) or consider, through literary theory, the status of issues such as the narrator or the representation of the real (e.g., Seixo and Carvalho).[21] In general the tendency has been to posit shipwreck literature as a category of travel narrative, but this is far too broad a characterization to be of extensive critical use because so many texts of early modern Iberia were, to some degree or other, travel accounts.[22] More important is the recognition that shipwreck narrative is a form (or "minor genre") of historiographic or chronistic writing, but shipwreck narrative must be understood as more deeply and problematically related to the discursive productivity of expansionist Iberia, for such a productivity gives birth to shipwreck writing at the same time that shipwreck texts break away from the aims of historical texts produced under the Crown by countering their hegemonic agendas. Scholars acknowledge that the shipwreck texts disturb the imperialist agenda,[23] but the fact of their place in the weave of expansionist textuality needs to be made essential, rather than incidental, as the birth moment of shipwreck narrative.

In this sense, Giulia Lanciani's proposition that the shipwreck narrative is related to the ideology of conquest is useful, although while Lanciani finds an affirmation of such ideology I find its resistance or undoing. Lanciani argues:

> The ideology underlying these accounts is . . . the well-known ideology of the civilizing and evangelizing mission entrusted by Providence to the Portuguese . . . [it is] an ideology that . . . cannot be absent from the shipwreck accounts: even if in many of them vestiges of an explicit theoretical formulation may not be found, the ideological motivation, in all of them, is inextricably combined with the other components and certainly had its part in bestowing success on this literary genre. (*Sucessos* 67)[24]

There can be no doubt that conquistatorial ideologies do appear in the narratives, but we need to consider the degree to which these ideologies dominate the texts and determine the weltanschauung of their authors. Just as we may find gestures toward the ideological affirmation of expansion, or redemptive overtones through the consolation of a Christian fatalism (ibid., 59), so do we also find the opposite, and it is this negative, disruptive element that shapes the vision of the writers and emerges from the collective as the counterideological impulse of the tales. In this the shipwreck accounts fiercely resist unilateral interpretation, and there is a problematic relationship between the claims shipwreck authors sometimes make (such as the affirmation of European superiority over the inferiority of indigenous populations, a mainstay of expansionist thought) and the evidence of the narratives. The presence or fact of ideological moments in the disastrous context of shipwreck troubles a reading that would make the shipwreck text a platform for expansionist thinking, and speaks to an emptying out of such claims, to a hollow discursive practice that has lost validity. There is little peremptory affirmation of expansionist thinking here for the simple reason that these are not conquest texts: they narrate no successful campaign of conquest or the implantation of a Portuguese politico-cultural order, nor do they testify to a victorious exercise of the *império*. If shipwreck narratives seem to espouse an official mentality, such an espousal functions as a

remnant or echo of such ideologies. Although we find passages that explicitly reiterate the expansionist mentality, such as chapter 4 of Amaral's
narrative of the Santiago/Chagas,[25] we also find moments like the following, when Francisco Barreto, captain of the Águia, delivers a speech
to his men during troubles at sea:

> Gentlemen and knights, friends and companions, you must not be
> downcast nor saddened at the thought of our making the land which
> lies ahead, because it could be that God is bringing us to a land where
> we will be able to conquer another new world and to discover a
> greater India than that which is already found. For I have here gentle-
> men and knights for comrades, with whom I would dare to under-
> take any conquest or enterprise whatsoever, however arduous and dif-
> ficult it might be. (*Further Selections* 33)[26]

This speech claims our attention because of its provisional character, of
its inscription of the prospect of empire under the uncertain syntagm "it
could be." We know that the end of this narrative brings no new world
and no greater India, so Barreto's speech only confirms the failure of its
premises.[27] This speech presages a moment focusing on textuality that
occurs when the occupants of the doomed companion ship of the Águia
(the Garça) seek Barreto's help:

> As soon as it was daylight, the *Garça* launched a *manchua* with four
> sailors and the scrivener of the ship, called João Rodrigues Pais, who
> came to the flagship of Francisco Barreto with a note from the cap-
> tain of the *Garça* for him, which read as follows:
> "Sir, it is very necessary for the service of God and of our lord the
> King that your worship should come here; and by the brevity of this
> note, you may guess what is happening here. I kiss your worship's
> hands." (*Further Selections* 39)[28]

It is not difficult to sense the irony here, as the *escrivão da nau* (scrivener
or ship's secretary), the onboard official of textual culture, brings a desperate cry for help in the stiff formalities of notarial rhetoric. Pais's writing, unlike Camões's waterlogged poem, announces the absurdity of official textual culture and the eventual failure of the expedition.

The imposition of readings on the shipwreck tale that somehow attempt
to find a redemption in these texts smooths over the shipwreck text as

one that refuses to find easy closure from an ideological perspective. Even in formal characteristics we find a resistance and mutability, because the shipwreck account participates in the genre instability characteristic of prose writing during the sixteenth and seventeenth centuries and that defined earlier, critical attempts at classifying these texts (are they chronicles? sailing diaries? journalism?).[29]

In this sense alone the shipwreck narrative breaks apart the idea of generic or historiographic determinancy, and contains what Maria Alzira Seixo terms a "tragic sense of representation." This tragic sense, according to Seixo, happens as a model of the physical world, static in nature and manifested in classical texts, is broken as travel literature brings newly discovered worlds to bear on the text, recording an "impossible" voyage that nonetheless takes place (i.e., the shipwreck narrative). She states:

> [I]f all classical writing revolves around a model of a possible representation of the physical world that is, at the same time, sustained by literary models of antiquity, and if travel literature puts into question the constitution of these models (themselves anterior to the discoveries, and static) via the changing, complementary, and diverse nature of the newly discovered and recognized world, then the shipwreck narratives seem to be at the heart of this problematic by the very way they articulate this problematic in that this representation is fractured at the core of its constitution. Yet it is the fracture of that representation or, as was already mentioned, the impossibility of a voyage that nevertheless takes place which constitutes the essential aspect, in my opinion, of the tragic dimension of these writings. ("Les récits" III)

Seixo posits the crucial idea of breakage *(brisure)* as a theoretical notion present in the texts, but where Seixo sees the breakage of the shipwreck text occurring against classical representations of the world through the lens of travel literature, I argue that this breakage happens against the authorizing, hermeneutically sealed culture of historiography. The break of shipwreck literature happens not just as an "impossible voyage" takes place but as a text, structured as a historiographic account, fails to achieve, or manifest, the claims to hegemonic authority and power implicit in historiographic tradition.

At the outset, the shipwreck narratives are stories of lived failure given that any voyage undertaken for the purposes of material acquisition or conquest that does not achieve these goals is one of defeat. In this, shipwreck represents on a first symbolic level the breaking apart of the ship of state as an economic entity and as the agent of imperialism and colonization. But, more disturbingly and significantly, the shipwreck narratives are evidence of the disruption of what might be termed an order of empire, both as a praxis and as a flow of hegemonic and authoritative texts produced by the official historians and writers of the realm.[30]

It is productive to conceive of the shipwreck texts as a type of counter-historiography, to use José Rabasa's term, a conglomeration of writings that collectively work against or resist the claims of the official chronicles.[31] Part of the messiness of shipwreck narrative, part of its dialectic of rupture and disjunction, as we remarked apropos of Lanciani's statement earlier, is that it often allies itself with the ideologies underlying expansionist textuality rather than overtly repudiating them, but we should never forget that when the shipwreck authors do make expansionist gestures (present in thematic moments such as the placing of a *padrão* [pillar surmounted by a cross] in the sands of Africa amid native "barbarians" or the redaction of often extensive ethnographic accounts of indigenous populations), these always occur in drastically transformed circumstances that impugn the evidence of the official texts. One of these transformations is aprioristic: in the shipwreck story, the Portuguese presence in other lands is always accidental, not purposeful, and the satellite culture of the metropole represented by the inhabitants of the ship is at a disadvantage in its relations with indigenous peoples and its exercise of supposed cultural superiority. The power dynamic has been reversed. The redaction of texts, rather than being generated by a determined exercise of power, is now a product of failure.

Shipwreck narrative relates itself both partially and disjunctively to the tenets of historiographic imperialism. On the one hand, it acknowledges and narrates disaster, yet on the other, it still maintains a stronghold on historiographic mainstays such as the idea of a providential scheme for European action and experience. As opposed to the univocality of the *cronista-mor* (official chronicler of the realm) before his material and his text, that is, the single voice unifying a diversity of sources and materials into a lone and state-authorized historiographic speaker, the collective evidence of the shipwreck tales is of a multiplicity of voices (some official, some not, some named, some anonymous) working from a multiplicity of vocational backgrounds and a shifting range of interest in the success of the India route as a national or state enterprise.

In these shifting positionalities we may locate an important aspect of the counterimpulse of shipwreck narrative. They are neither conquest texts nor unilateral condemnations of the expansionist mentality.[32] In this, the counterhistoriographic vein of these narratives derives from their interstitial quality, located problematically between an exercise of empire and its attendant textual culture and the reality of the cracks and breakages the shipwreck writers record. Moreover, the presence of unofficial voices in the *História Trágico-Marítima* instantiates an alternate, historiographic subject position, a position from which the history of the state is being told accidentally by those who have no official connection to it but who witness it nonetheless, and write about it, from a perspective informed by self-interest and the simple demands of survival. The counterhistoriographic nature of shipwreck narrative may be thought of as an allowance for alternate (or unofficial) narrating positions in addition to the stories of failure and loss happening under the supervision of the state.

Let us consider a moment in the *Santiago* that speaks to a confounded relationship between experience and writing, between empirical maritime reality and the later redaction of a story that falls outside the certainty of the reading of signs typical of mainstream conquest or imperial texts. As the ship rounds the Cape of Good Hope, there ensues a heated discussion about whether it has entered the Baixo da Judia (Jew's shoal) appearing on the ship's map. This contentious discussion precedes the wreck of the ship, and the reading of signs punctuates the dispute:

> There was great doubt as to whether this was the Jew's shoal, or another one. There was no lack of those who maintained this was the Jew's shoal. The reasons for this opinion are: they say that the shoal on which this ship wrecked is at the same latitude as the Jew's shoal . . . and that there is not another such shoal showing on the old sea charts, which now, on account of a new shoal, must be written anew. . . . Those that say that this wasn't the Jew's shoal are motivated by more convincing reasons, which are . . . three days before the

wreck many birds were sighted; on Sunday they saw many more birds and on Monday, the day the ship wrecked, when afternoon fell there were considerably fewer birds. The opposite should have been the case if this had been the Jew's shoal because there are so many birds on it. . . . Finally, given the information that existed about the Jew's shoal, compared with what was seen on this shoal on which the ship wrecked, there could be no greater folly than to try to make the two shoals into one. . . . The response to this is that the maps are wrong . . .[33]

How far this passage is, after another century of expansionist navigation, from Columbus's first diary in which he authoritatively reads all new signs that come across his path unfettered by the maps or *cartas* of previous navigators. The dispute about the shoal in the *Santiago* foregrounds a rupture that the imminent experience of shipwreck causes between the world and representations of it in the empirically based knowledge of sea charts. The correspondence between maps and the world in shipwreck narrative is one of error: either the maps are wrong, or the crew's sightings are wrong and the maps are correct. The sighting of birds, the cypher virtually all mariners assume to read authoritatively, is here rendered obscure and unknowable. Were the birds indicative of a certain geographical region, or were they a shipwreck prophecy, a foreboding omen as they appear in the pages of the earlier chroniclers such as Zurara? Definitive exegesis of the natural world suffers a severe blow in the *Santiago,* and the result of the contention its author Cardoso describes is that the maps must be rewritten. We might find nothing more than a moment of cartographic clarification here, but what occurs is not really a modification of maps, but rather the recording of a series of events testifying to hermeneutic uncertainty. Ironically, the stabilizing element of his description is the certain location of the shipwreck in time and not the more scientific knowledge of a geographical point already mapped. The regulated and measured mechanisms of organizing experience meaningfully (including knowledge of geographical space, hours of the day, or latitude) disappear or dissolve almost to the point of uselessness in the shipwreck experience. The prescriptive tools of travel and navigation (charts, rutters, astrolabes) lose power to such a degree that they serve, in an absurd inversion of their original intention, as trading truck to be exchanged for food.[34]

THIS, OUR EDIFICE OF WRITING

"In the first *Decade,* because it was the basis of this, our edifice of writing, in some way we wanted to imitate the manner of architects in material edifices."[35] So writes João de Barros (1497–1562) in the prologue to his second *Década da Ásia* (Decade of Asia), the second installment in his expansively conceived history of Portugal in Africa, Asia, Europe, and Brazil, so ambitious a project that neither he nor his successor Diogo do Couto was able to finish it.[36]

João de Barros stands out in Iberian Renaissance historiography as an unflinching apologist of the ideology of expansion. In his historiographic corpus he takes the Roman historians as models (especially Livy); in the project of producing a historical record worthy—both in breadth and scope—of Portuguese imperial campaigns abroad, Barros is joined principally by two other history writers: Fernão Lopes de Castanheda (d. 1559) and the *História do descobrimento e conquista da Índia pelos portugueses* (History of the discovery and conquest of India by the Portuguese [1551–61]), and his successor in the *Decades* project, Diogo do Couto (1542–1616). In this section, I will suggest how we can posture shipwreck narrative against the official historiographic record.

The official voice of Portuguese historiography (that is, the voice representing the interests of the Crown) was instituted formally in 1434 by D. Duarte when he created the post of *cronista-mor* (royal chronicler) and appointed Fernão Lopes (fl. 1434–54) as its first incumbent. From that point on, historiography was, by definition, official. Lopes came to exercise this post in mid-career, and he completed the first two parts of his final project, the *Crónica de D. João I* (Chronicle of King John I) before stepping down and allowing the duty of chronicler to pass to Gomes Eanes de Zurara (c. 1420–73/74). With Zurara's appointment, the historiographic gaze of the *cronista-mor* turns to overseas expansion, as Zurara's initial task was to complete the *Crónica de D. João I,* which he did with a third part known as the *Crónica da tomada de Ceuta* (Chronicle of the seizure of Ceuta), the account of the Portuguese capture of Ceuta in 1415. With his next work, though, the *Crónica dos feitos . . . da Guiné* (Chronicle of the Deeds . . . of Guinea), Zurara immerses himself more fully into recounting the rapidly growing fervor of Christian imperialism, for this chronicle narrates the series of naval expeditions down the west coast of Africa under the supervision of the Infante D. Henrique, known to the English-speaking world as Prince Henry, "the Navigator."[37] *Guiné* depicts an increasing exercise of maritime might fueled by all of the ideological valences we find in later imperial texts.

Zurara regards the office of the chronicler in ways distinct from his predecessor because his writing task is considerably different from the landbound histories penned by the more medievally informed Lopes. As the debut chronicler of Iberian expansion, Zurara acts under a historiographic imperative that requires narrative and *res gestae* to coalesce in a structured act of exegesis—that is, the acting and writing of history must be conceived and executed as a harmonious whole where the text does not so much "record" action as it does complete it; the text manifests, in a finalizing manner, the ineluctability of an interpretation of the past in accordance with Christian imperialist doctrine.[38] Central to Zurara's conception and practice of historiography is the notion of "to order" *(ordenar)*, a polysemous verb that encompasses both the idea of a providential march of history and the narrative task of the *historiador*. *Ordenar*, in Zurara, means the providential determining of history, the manifestation of this determination through individual acts, and the informed and purposeful arranging of these acts into a narrative by the chronicler. In exercising the prerogative of *ordenança* (order), the chronicler, in the redaction of texts, creates a representation of a historico-political order promulgated through the vitality of the state and the will of God. We could say that Zurara, with this term, conflates historical determinism with the selective and narrative liberty of the chronicler who must construct the text by determining which events to include, which to exclude, which sources to use, and which to reject. This order, of course, always favors a European, monarchical perspective, and the exercise of selecting and ordering underwrites the authority of the chronicler's voice. Zurara's narrative order, metonymic of the state, is, by extension, analogous to the harmonic order of the world and of the turning of the celestial wheels, so the writing of history cannot be divorced from cosmic harmony and the infallibility of providence.

As the first chronicler of maritime expansion, it is not surprising that Zurara exemplifies the precept of *ordenar* with the orderly arrangement and movement of ships in a fleet as a manifestation of the power of the state and of the incontestability of supremacy. (From 1474 on, this maritime supremacy rested on the doctrine of *mare clausum,* that is, Portugal's territorial right to waters beyond its immediate shoreline.) Zurara's imbrication of the movement of ships with narrative is the obverse of the *discurso do naufrágio* of the shipwreck authors. Zurara, speaking of the departure of the Portuguese fleet from Lagos in *Guiné,* laments, "[a]nd since the story cannot be recounted in as good an order as necessary, because of the voyage the caravels did not make together, we will say what we can in the best way possible."[39] A dispersed fleet impugns the good order of political hegemony and therefore of historiography. Pages later, as a contingent of the fleet arrives at the Isle of Herons and is there reunited with other ships, there could be no more auspicious and happy moment, as such a restoration of order allows for the further and successful movement into African waters and, implicitly, the progression of the narrative:

> There was a great pleasure when those, arriving in sight of the Isle of Herons, saw the four caravels that were already there at rest. . . . And on approaching the ships at anchor they fired their cannons and guns as a signal of the joy that was in their hearts. . . . "Now then," said Lancelot, "since you're determined to leave, it is advisable for those of you who are very familiar with sailing orders [ordenanças] in such situations to recall them now, and that you help me arrange [ordenar] our departure so that we may proceed according to official protocol [ir ordenadamente]." And, putting aside differences of opinion, it was determined that they would leave in this manner. . . . that three boats would lead the caravels in which there were pilots who had already been in that land and knew the way.[40]

Shortly afterwards, as the caravels are on their way, the navigational order has been resumed (and the certainty of the narrative order as well) to such a degree that Zurara cannot resist adding a playful detail: "[a]nd before they arrived at the port in which they would disembark, they were ordered to maintain the caravels together; they were sailing so close together that men were jumping from one [ship] to the other."[41] Zurara's fleets, in these passages and elsewhere, are a requisite expression, in their ordered unity, of the realization of expansionist campaigns. They both are a symbol of military control and serve as the maritime analogue of historiography that will itself arrive to port in the form of royal recognition that will ultimately ratify it as the truth of history.

The integrated fleet as metaphor of the unified power of the expansionist nation and its role in the telling of history is overturned by the shipwreck narratives, where disintegration of order and the resulting chaos characterize seaborne Portuguese culture. A fleet's dissolution often acts as an opening image, as is the case with Amaral's *Santiago/ Chagas*:

> In the year 1601 the king, our Lord, ordered . . . six galleons to be prepared for sailing to India. . . . and because it was not possible to outfit so many ships to leave together at one time, they were dis patched as they were made ready. . . . However, since they did not depart in March, which is the natural time for this voyage, five returned once they reached the Equator.[42]

Or, Manuel de Mesquita Perestrelo, in the opening of the *S. Bento*, declares:

> All these captains, thus provisioned with what was required, left the port of this city of Lisbon on March 24, and followed their route for some days as a fleet, until, as time wore on, such varied things happened that it was necessary for them to disperse, each one seeing to his own situation on the voyage the best he could, for the salvation of the lives and merchandise for which he was responsible. The voyages of these ships I will leave aside, for it is not my intention to relate any other than that of Fernão d'Álvares.[43]

Francisco Vaz de Almada in the *S. João Baptista* relates in his second sentence how his ship lost the flagship—"on the seventeenth of July we separated from the flagship at night because we couldn't see its light: some say we separated intentionally by the design of the officials on board"[44]—and the story of the *S. Paulo* begins with its ship in distress even before it is out of sight of the Lisbon shore, its itinerary of undoing already in motion in the very geopolitical locus of stability and order.

These initial moments manifest failure not merely as the lack of a successful, round-trip voyage, but also as an active force that tears apart ships before they wreck, where absence presides over the voyages as a force of destabilization inherent, almost materially, in the ships as they are unable to maintain integrity as a fleet. The *Santiago/Chagas* under-stands "fleet" only in the loosest sense because the ships depart one at a time, and only as they become ready, and some are forced to abandon the outward voyage altogether. In the *S. Bento*, Perestrelo lets us know that disaster in the form of forced dispersal happens immediately, and this occasions a narrative restriction of focus as he tells us that he will only present the story of one ship. The moment of setting sail in ship-wreck narrative by definition is problematic, and mobilizes the first ex-perience of loss and abandonment. The display and exercise of power manifested by integrated fleets in the texts of Zurara and his followers have, in the shipwreck narrative, fallen apart, and the shipwreck authors track the experiences of individual, wayward ships.

If Zurara allows us to understand a company of ships as a potent en-actment of order and control, João de Barros and Diogo do Couto in their *Décadas* likewise each relate the India route and its ships to the very structure of empire. Yet Barros, staunch apologist of empire, writes voluminously about Portuguese India without narrating any shipwreck, so adamant was he about depicting the workings of Portuguese empire only in its favorable aspects. But the *carreira da Índia* for Barros lies at the center of empire, as he declares in the eighth book of the first *Decade of Asia*, because it constitutes one of the first conquests of empire. He writes:

> As the entirety of our *Ásia* is founded on navigations, on account of the fleets assembled each year for its conquest and commerce . . . it is useful, for a better understanding of its history, for us to give a gen-eral account of how, in those parts of Asia, spice was traded by navi-gation, along with all the other Oriental riches, until they came to our Europe, before we opened the route on the Ocean Sea.[45]

The India route, in Barros's vision, is one of the victories of West over East, carried out by fleets of ships. It is a tacit premise to the sub-jugation of the East, and to the conquest of the seas.

SHIP AND FRACTURE

An etymology: *naufrágio* < Latin *navis* [ship] + *frango* [to fracture]. In the morphological fabric of the word, a break, a fracture, breathes.

Let us repeat Barchiesi's question of 1959: "What is shipwreck?"

("Terminologia" 208). It is a physical wrecking, a breaking apart of the vessel, the death of a ship. It is the chaotic clash between human artifice and the natural world, as Sebastián de Covarrubias Orozco, the noted Spanish lexicographer, makes clear in his famous dictionary of 1611.[46] Barchiesi notes that shipwreck is a "providential accident" (208), a definition in keeping with how Amaral defines "disaster" in relation to the India route: disaster is blind bad luck, often triggered by human error or stupidity.[47]

But shipwreck, although it originates in the physicality of a ship, does not remain shipbound in its possible meanings or reach of influence. Shipwreck claims a figurative, symbolic, and metaphoric significance in the narratives it informs. In reading Álvar Núñez Cabeza de Vaca, the author of Spain's most well known shipwreck story *(Los naufragios),* Pranzetti argues that shipwreck is "that which underscores the border between an organized culture (the space of origin) and a disorganized culture (the space of conquest), where the surpassing of that border constitutes the move from a social state to a state of nature" (60). Gerbi defines shipwreck as "the catastrophe that destroys the prevailing economic and technical structure, without (by definition) taking the survivor's life" (247). And Rabasa asserts (also reading Cabeza de Vaca) that "shipwreck . . . marks the movement from order to chaos" (*Writing Violence* 34), that it marks "the transition to a primordial time signified by physical nakedness and the revelation that European civilization is a very thin veneer, easily forgotten" (50), and that it "entails a loss of material civilization, a transition to chaos and social anomie, but also a transition to a world where Western reason faces its limits and founders" (54).

In these definitions, shipwreck migrates from physical act to providential accident to metaphor, alike yet slightly different. In reference to the Portuguese narratives, Seixo finds that

> the symbolic loss of the ships, of merchandise and people, with all that is implied about the ideological thought that accompanies the odyssey of the discoveries, is . . . penetrated, in my opinion, by numerous ramifications of meaning that imbricate narrators, events, people, references, and weave together in a specific way the adventure of the Indias route. ("O abismo" 172)

The *navis fracta* (fractured ship), she continues, is the loss of what the ship holds, including "consciences and projects" (172–73), and represents the fracturing of communities (181).

The potential meanings of shipwreck, though, are not yet exhausted. In discovery-era texts, the ship never relinquishes its status as icon of European culture or the iterative nature of expansionist, ideological action. Shipwreck is hence the failure of empire and colonization, the moment when a series of power reversals begins (Merrim 88). We can think of it as a problematic moment in what Eduardo Lourenço calls the "nation-ship," a nation "having departed, from the very beginning, from a previous quay, outside of space and time, in order to navigate without end the apparent sea we call history" (xlv). The flow of history as traced over the seas by ships is precisely the idea we find countered in one of Francisco Manuel de Melo's writings on Portuguese political history of the seventeenth century. Poet, playwright, and historian, Melo (1608–66) epitomizes the aristocratic pursuit of letters and learning in restoration Portugal. His historical text, *Epanáforas de vária história portuguesa* (1660), contains five discrete books, one each dedicated to politics, tragedy, love, war, and triumph. The second one, on tragedy, narrates the shipwreck of the Portuguese armada off the French coast in 1627.[48] In the prologue to this *epanáfora*, Melo writes:

> Men who are lovers of reason should . . . maintain in their actions such an order that the harmony between them shows they are guided by a rational light; they should choose not just dignified tasks, but proper ones.
>
> It would appear that I ignore this entire proposition, or break it, inviting you now, at such a remove to read an account that, neither in its subject, or status, nor time could in any way be judged as in compliance with the exact observation I have proposed to you.[49]

The principles of order, harmony, and rationality Melo argues for in the prefatory remarks serve to emphasize how the presence of shipwreck in his book works against these very principles. Melo feels the need to justify his choice of material because the inclusion of an account of shipwreck ostensibly disrupts the precepts he has just identified—Melo, in short, knows that he must defend his decision to give a prominent historiographic place to shipwreck. He does so by claiming an Aristotelian tenet of mimesis: even tragic (or "sad") events give pleasure and are worthy of contemplation when they are represented in art. We must remember that our writer offers this justification in the context of a more extensive historiographic narrative. Melo is concerned because it is not just the presence of a tragic story he needs to defend, but the potential break the shipwreck story might cause in the overall flow of his collective narrative of five different books. The *Epanáforas* give us an instance of the incorporation of a shipwreck story within the flow of a larger historical text and the possible breach or disruption such a story threatens to realize. Melo's own historical circumstances are a reflection of his worry about disruptive chapters in a larger history, for he wrote in the years immediately following the Spanish occupation of the Portuguese crown (1580–1640). So it is that, in the prologular comments to the shipwreck story, the *Epanáforas* writer symbolically contemplates a disruption in the flow of Portuguese history and how his reader is to assimilate such a disruption under the nationalistic, guiding lights of harmony and reason.

With Melo's proposition of shipwreck as sense-defying in mind, it is possible to advance some further thoughts about the HTM texts. In shipwreck narrative, and its place in historical (and historiographic) trajectories, shipwreck is the movement from order to chaos (pace Rabasa), the fissure in systems of order and the attendant disaster or crumbling of signification as enacted on, through, and because of the body of a ship. A ship is at once a real and a figurative construct, and is meaningful only insofar as it is inhabited and steered under order(s)—shipwreck's first act of violence is to relate the ship and its passengers disjunctively. It effects a communal fracturation, in whatever sense we might understand community or an ordered and cohesive whole. Shipwreck is also the violence done to (maritime) linear forward movement and predictability; it is the reversal of perspective or epistemological frames; it is disorientation realized. If the ship is a symbol of empire and the full expression of maritime supremacy, of the uncontested ship of state, a shipwreck represents the wreck to trade and empire and the threat to thalassocratic might. The space of shipwreck motivates change and difference, but it is important to remember that this change and difference are not the premise of a utopic (re)configuration of reality. Shipwreck is the point at which an ethics of historiography as promoted by Fernão Lopes and Gomes

Eanes de Zurara reaches a breaking point and is no longer able to deliver the "natural" and correct record of overseas campaigns.

Shipwreck is thus a principle of loss and of senselessness as an iterative experience that causes the historiographic record to crash and splinter against its own regulated borders. In the HTM, the principle of shipwreck radiates lexically through each narrative in the ubiquitous expression "em pedaços" (in pieces). Everything, at one point or another, is rendered into pieces: ships, people, time, lifeboats, hierarchies, social groups, the prescriptive infallibility of the *pátria* in regard to the success of its expansion, and uncontested historiographic tradition. "Em pedaços," the syntagm that acts as a motific banner for the writers, tolls mantra-like in the shipwreckful imagination. Ultimately, "em pedaços" signals the telling of shipwreck as another action of disjunction—like the ship disjoined from its inhabitants—for there is an awareness that from the moment a narrative of shipwreck begins, it already contains and enacts a failure.

In considering the metaphorics of shipwreck in the Portuguese narratives, let's shift our attention momentarily to Álvar Núñez Cabeza de Vaca's account of the failed Pánfilo de Narváez expedition to America (1527), *Los naufragios* (The shipwrecks [1555]).[50] This narrative tells the story of Cabeza de Vaca's trek through the American wilderness over the course of several years (following the wreck of his ship) and his captivity by natives. Cabeza de Vaca's single text boasts many of the motifs we have studied so far, but there are differences between it and the elaboration of shipwreck in the more numerous Portuguese narratives. Perhaps the most striking difference is that, for all the disaster it contains, Cabeza de Vaca's narrative can be regarded as a story of building and renewal:

> the Spaniards are cast into wandering in atonement for the greed exemplified by their leader Narváez, from which journey the 'pilgrims' are rescued by God, who endows them with miraculous healing powers. . . . When Núñez tells his own shipwreck tale of rebirth into Indian life, he endows it not only with moral but also with exalted human and literary dimensions. (Merrim 87)

Symbolically important in *Los naufragios* is Cabeza de Vaca's nude or partially clothed body in the jungles of the New World, because this body represents a stripping away of European identity and a return to a utopian innocence.[51]

Beatriz Pastor Bodmer offers extensive critical commentary on the *Naufragios*, and focuses on Cabeza de Vaca's narrative as part of the "narrative discourse of failure," in which there issues forth a "demythification," a toppling of the idea of the New World as it was conceived by Columbus and Cortés.[52] A mythification presupposes an epic component; thus, demythification stands in opposition to an epic model (Pastor Bodmer 126). The narrative of failure, according to Pastor Bodmer's definition, "consistently undermine(s) an imperialistic discourse in which action is identified with conquest, man with the conquistador, and America with booty" (130); it involves, symbolically, "a destruction of the model of conquest" (133). We find many of the thematic units of this discourse in the Portuguese narratives: hunger, brutal necessity, suffering, hostile nature, or the threats posed by the natives.[53] Ultimately, Pastor Bodmer posits that "[t]he narrative of misfortune here simply sets the stage for the gradual process of self-definition of a new critical consciousness" (136), and thus finds a new narrative voice emerging from Cabeza de Vaca's account.

In a later study, José Rabasa *(Writing Violence)* argues that Cabeza de Vaca's text must be read as very much within the conquistatorial mentality and its attendant mode of narrative. Rabasa explains that a substratum of legal documents and colonial laws (32) underlies the text, noting that Cabeza de Vaca "outlines an ideal form of imperialism and casts himself as an equally ideal servant of the Crown" (ibid.), and that the *Naufragios* "has been singled out as one of the most accomplished narratives of the Conquest from a literary point of view" (45).[54] *Los naufragios,* in Rabasa's view, "is at once a story that transforms failure into success and a series of narrative loops whereby Cabeza de Vaca corrodes stock New World images" (52).

A key idea becomes apparent here as characteristic of Cabeza de Vaca's text and as one that distinguishes it fundamentally from the HTM narratives: however much movement from order to chaos there is in *Los naufragios,* however much failure it contains, or however much shipwreck may metaphorically represent a dissolution of the civilized world or a return to a more primitive state of being, Cabeza de Vaca's account is still a conquest text, redacted in the mold of conquistatorial narrative and power relations. Shipwreck functions as a premise to an inverted colonial encounter that nonetheless finds representation within a colonialist narrative boasting all the rhetorical trappings characteristic of such texts. The wrecks themselves claim little narrative attention and receive no prolonged, anguished elaboration, but instead provide a neat symmetry since they frame the narrative at both its beginning and its end. In this structural way, shipwreck initiates and provides closure to the text, cleanly sealing off its conquistatorial content and its submission to the crown as "an act of service" (Merrim 91).

Cabeza de Vaca writes his experience as a *relación,* a common prose genre of New World writing.[55] The *relación* establishes relations of textual authority between the writer and the Crown. Roberto González Echevarría studies the *relación* as typical of the Spanish sixteenth century in which "writing was subservient to the law" (45), and asserts that "[t]he *relación* pledges to be a textual link with the source of power through the maze of bureaucratic formulae that supplanted patrimonial authority" (56–57). Rabasa, in like manner, underscores the *relación* as a legal document when he notes that

> [t]he *relación* is both a form of historiography with its own generic constraints and a legal document whose style and contents were increasingly defined by laws and *ordenanzas* during the course of the sixteenth century. Whereas the *relación* would provide a truthful testimony on a set of particular events, a history . . . would draw out the universal significance of the events. (*Writing Violence* 86)

It is tempting to apply these same ideas to the Portuguese *relação,* that is, the textual (or generic) designation under which most of the shipwreck narratives appear, but it would be a mistake to do so because the Portuguese *relação* differs from the Spanish *relación* and in that difference we may find one of the crucial breakages the Portuguese shipwreck text enacts. The Portuguese *relação* is a much more flexible genre, both in its content and in its chronological span. It is a form of report that can boast wildly fantastic content, as the accumulated *literatura de cordel* demonstrates, and extends well beyond the period of discovery into the nineteenth century. The official Portuguese reports of discovery and conquest were often drafted under the rubric *carta* (letter), as was also the case in Spanish documents. But, as the generic designation of the shipwreck account, the *relação* is not addressed to the Crown and therefore exists outside of the bureaucracy of textual authority that informs Cabeza de Vaca's narrative.[56] The apologistic tone suffusing Cabeza de Vaca is not present in the Portuguese narratives, as these writers are not attempting to convert failure into success through formulaic rhetoric and established relations of authority. Because the shipwreck *relação,* then, exists outside the dynamic of textual links between the individual writer and the Crown since it typically is not directed to a monarch, we might think of it as an acephalic text. As a more or less independent genre, the *relação* claims no systematic link to centers of power, and the shipwreck narrative is not beset by an accountability influencing other modes of conquest writing. The shipwreck author writes from outside the discursive realm of power and appeals to no structure of authority in order to tell the tale of disaster—the shipwreck experience alone, not a preexisting relation to the state or the attempt to forge one through a text, confers authority to narrate. Shipwreck narrative positions itself obliquely in relation to the legitimacy of official discourse.

This generic independence represents one of the breaks of the shipwreck account vis-à-vis the official culture of historiography. There is a second type of independence that helps us understand why representatives of the official perspective of the Crown, such as Diogo do Couto or João Baptista Lavanha (D. João III's cosmographer), may be considered shipwreck authors in the terms I am outlining here. Diogo do Couto, the official chronicler of Portuguese India and keeper of the Goa archives, was himself an outspoken critic of empire—his *O soldado prático* is perhaps his most well known attack on the corruption of India officials. We should therefore not be too surprised to find Couto as the author of three shipwreck accounts: the *Águia/Garça,* one of the extant versions of the *S. M. da Barca,* and the *S. Tomé.*[57] All of these narratives, as Boxer points out ("An Introduction" 56–57; 65) were originally part of Couto's *Décadas.*[58] Couto, a consummate and prolific intellectual, opts to engage in shipwreck narrative and hence loosens the gridlocked claims of expansionist historiography as a way of criticizing them. At the same time, the highly intellectual Couto demonstrates his flexibility as a writer and the complexity of his narrative voice. Couto is a shipwreck writer in his capacity as an avowed critic of empire despite his redaction of the "official" *Décadas,* so shipwreck in his oeuvre responds to a tacit agenda of countering the hubris of expansion or its administration by exposing the corruption under which it operates overseas. It is possible to think of Couto's shipwreckful, narrative voice as that which allows him to refigure the edifice of historiography as one allowing for the incorporation of opposing and countering views.

But the shipwreck narrative acts as a disruptive text in part owing to the story of failure it tells and in part because it exists as a separate account, a discrete textual unit that claims no overarching frame narrative. This is one of the primary ways the shipwreck account of the sixteenth and seventeenth centuries can be distinguished from shipwreck-themed literature. As an autonomous text, the shipwreck narrative does not ally itself to a macronarrative to contextualize, explain, justify, or in any way provide closure or redemption to the disastrous experience. Unlike the poetry of Alfonso X or Berceo (in which the pilgrimage or frame of devotional travel prevents perdition and guarantees an ultimate redemption), or prose narratives that contain shipwreck episodes such as Fernão Mendes Pinto's *Peregrinação* (Peregrination [1614]) or Jerónimo Lobo's *Itinerário* (Itinerary) (c. 1640), the shipwreck narrative stands isolated on its own.[59] Thus, while shipwreck in Couto functions notionally as a break with the ideology of empire, Gomes de Brito, by extracting the narratives from their frame in the eighteenth century, visits a violence on Couto's texts that further consecrates their status as individual shipwreck narratives at the same time that he attempts to configure them as part of national history.

One final, defining characteristic of the shipwreck narrative remains for consideration, and that is the often prolonged description of a ship as it wrecks, as it is assaulted by nature or humans during a storm, or as it falls to pieces. Shipwreck writers linger over the intricate details of the destruction of a ship, and in so doing often freight well over half the narrative with the trials and distress of a ship or the particularities of its destruction. Writing a ship to pieces realizes part of the gradual rupturing or "disalignment" occurring throughout a shipwreck narrative. A slow breach plays itself out in these moments: like the sighting of seaweed, birds, or the color and run of the water in successful discovery or conquest texts that corroborate the certainty of the course, the breakup and disintegration of a ship reflects a falling away of familiar points of referentiality as the ship often provides the only available points of knowledge on a uniform and untrackable sea or in foreign, uncharted spaces. There is, in the shipwreck description, an active conjuration and engagement of unknowing within the text as part of the shipwreck story, a process of disintegration that stands in ironic contrast to all the sightings, plumbings, and compass points desperately invoked to specify position as the writer-survivor is forced to claim, eventually, "we're lost." Here empirical observations affirm that knowledge of the physical world is useless, even impossible, and serves no end. Perhaps this is why so many of the shipwreck authors emphasize the pragmatic qualities to be found in the shipwreck account, a kind of last attempt to restore the empirical imperative, the inscription of knowledge within a controllable context that grants a mastery over worldly phenomena.

If the detailed *descriptio* of the wrecking ship functions to carve out a kind of island within the text, there is also a cost to such a description from the perspective of chronology in the etymological sense of "ordering time" in that a suspension or breakdown of time occurs. Reflect on the following moment in the *S. António*:

> At the end of the three days which the storm lasted, when the weather began to improve, we rigged up a jury-mast in the forepart of the ship, which we made from some bits of wood from the half-deck which the seas had smashed, and which measured about two or three *braças* in length. And from the three remaining oars of the ship's boat we made a yardarm, and from a small spare sail (which was the only we had left) we made a makeshift foresail, and from some pieces of cords tied to each other we made the shrouds. When this was rigged up, it seemed ridiculous for us to try to navigate such a large ship with so small a sail. (*Further Selections* 134)[60]

In the *S. João Baptista,* Cabreira recounts a similar situation in which he had to make use of what was at hand to serve different purposes during a storm (Pereira 9:16), and other such instances may be found throughout the HTM.

What is noticeable here is that the ship functions as a closed system of referentiality. In the passage from the *S. António*, the duration of three days is juxtaposed to the recital of how some pieces of the ship were fashioned into others, how the ship, in essence, turned back on itself. This moment proposes a disastrous, useless referentiality. The redeploy-

ment of a ship's parts fails utterly: that is, the ship remains dead in the
water and cannot move forward, and Luís ascribes an absurdity to the
whole effort. I read this passage much as I do the prolonged descriptions
of disintegrating ships in that both kinds of instances—restructuring a
ship from its own parts and describing those parts in the process of
falling apart—create a kind of narrative bubble around the space of the
ship, in which further forward time stalls or becomes all but impossible.
To concentrate on the destruction of a ship suspends the motion of the
forward narrative and of locatability, effecting an erasure of historical
specificity. The description of one shipwreck, or of one ship breaking
apart, could be the description of any ship at any point on sea or on
land. Thus a pronounced emphasis on the ship's breaking body lifts the
narrative out of a local temporality and creates time and space islands,
something similar to Foucault's definition of heterotopias: they are "real
places . . . which are something like counter-sites, a kind of effectively
enacted utopia in which the real sites, all the other real sites that can be
found within the culture, are simultaneously represented, contested,
and inverted" ("Of Other Spaces" 24). In fact, Foucault here speaks of
boats, noting that "the boat is a floating piece of space, a place without a
place, that exists by itself, that is closed in on itself and at the same time
is given over to the infinity of the sea" (27)—the typical space, we could
say, of the shipwreck topography.

3

MANIFEST PERDITION I

MAROONINGS

*S*OMEWHERE IN THE WILDS OF AFRICA, Manuel de Mesquita Perestrelo, author of the *S. Bento*, plods along in the survival march through the "má terra" (terrible land) but keeps falling behind because his brother António's health is failing fast. Captain Fernão de Álvares Cabral accommodates the two as much as he can, often slowing the pace of the company's movement on their behalf and calling rest for the night earlier rather than later. One morning, though,

> the captain, seeing that . . . we were falling behind by quite a bit, waited for us to catch up to him and then remarked to us how well we could see the misfortune our sins had brought us, further noting that everyone was complaining to him for always waiting for us . . . so we should decide on what we were going to do, and if we could

we shouldn't lag behind; and furthermore, if António Sobrinho's strength wouldn't hold out and I was determined to stay with him, I should tell him this outright so that he wouldn't spend any more time dealing with things he was unable to solve and which placed all the others in manifest perdition.[1]

As Manuel and his brother lag behind, their detachment threatens the rest of the company with a "manifest perdition." A dangerous journey promises to become more so; a latent perdition threatens to become imminently realized. This passage from the *S. Bento* states a defining precept of shipwreck literature: perdition, and the dangers preceding and accompanying it, is continually realized or made manifest through the pages of the HTM. Shipwreck authors realize loss by narrating it. Manifest perdition happens when things break away from order, when the integrity of the whole begins to dissolve, when the ordered trajectory of the road *(caminho)* or the itinerary *(itinerário)* is threatened (and often disintegrates altogether) as a structuring device for negotiating and subordinating a space of displacement, a space inhabited as a result of the voyaging, traveling home culture, of the *império*. As the itinerant, narrating European subject, Perestrelo fractures the integrity of the march. The consequence of this might very well be death.

In this and the following chapter, I read select narratives in order to elaborate a poetics of the shipwreck text, that is to say, the way the experience of shipwreck finds figurative expression, and what the constituent images of this experience are. These analyses, focusing as they do on the internal constitution of the shipwreck account in its symbolic, metaphoric, and thematic complexities, trace the writerly preoccupations running through the chaotic narrative web of the HTM. The narratives of this chapter, the *S. João* and the *S. Bento,* grapple with the notion of how shipwreck makes things come undone—each narrative relates a series of maroonings caused by wreck. These maroonings, or moments of disorienting and unstable positionalities, affect the relationship to the world and to patterns of order. The *S. João,* the earliest extant and most famous of all the *relatos,* contains within it the disastrous seeds of all shipwreck stories to follow: in it we find the motifs, symbols, and ideas about shipwreck that will, in one way or another, travel through, and shape, other tales. Authors of later narratives will frequently refer to the wreck of the S. João, thus making it the mastertext of maroonings, the point zero of a disastrous intertextuality.

Manuel de Mesquita Perestrelo in his *S. Bento,* on the other hand, provides perhaps the most vivid account of the traumatic experience of shipwreck as one of a terrifying interiority, a trauma that will play itself out in the figure of Perestrelo the shipwreck survivor and shipwreck writer. Perestrelo's tale is a ghost story, the record of a trek through darkness and fear haunted by apparitions and the remains of a world in collapse. Perestrelo's tale tells us, repeatedly and in different guises, how edges or parameters escape him and his company and seem often to disappear altogether. Most borders—both real and psychological—necessary for organizing experience and providing some measure of safety, vanish. The angst-ridden desire to keep and re-create edges informs his narrative.

S. JOÃO: A MODEL OF PERDITION

The inaugural narrative of the HTM, this "storie altogether lamentable," as Camerarius calls the *Account of the S. João* in 1621 in the first English version of any Portuguese shipwreck narrative, is famous for its tragic humanity.[2] What will later become standard in shipwreck literature finds first expression here, where the narrative experience of shipwreck is constructed through a progression of ideas that take us from safety to danger, wholeness to fragmentation, control to chaos, possession to loss.

The narrative—and our analysis of it—begins with a prologue:

> The matter narrated in this shipwreck should make men very much fear God's punishments and become good Christians, and bring the fear of God before their eyes so His commandments will not be broken. For Manuel de Sousa was a noble *fidalgo* and a worthy gentleman, and during his time in India he spent more than fifty thousand *cruzados* in feeding many people and in doing good deeds for many others. He would end his life among the Kaffirs,[3] as would his wife and children, in such misery and want that he lacked food, drink, and clothing. He suffered so many hardships before his death that they seem incredible except to those who experienced them, including one Álvaro Fernandes, boatswain's mate of the galleon, who told me this story in great detail. I happened across him here in Mozambique in the year fifteen hundred and fifty-four.

Figure 6. Manuel de Sousa Sepúlveda and Leonor de Sá, from Deperthes, *Histoire des naufrages.*

And since this seemed to me a story which would stand as a good example and warning to all, I wrote the account of the trials and death of this *fidalgo* and his company so that those who wander over the sea may commend themselves to God and Our Lady, who intercedes on behalf of us all. Amen. (3–4)[4]

Through this prologular act, the anonymous author situates the *S. João* within the formal structures of the historiographic text, invoking in its course a number of topoi characteristic of the genre: the exemplarity ("bom exemplo") of the life of a *fidalgo* (nobleman or gentleman) possessed of exemplary qualities (principally *caritas*), the understanding of that life as an injunction to spiritual rectitude, and the authenticating presence of an eyewitness. The "heroic biography" to follow may also be read as a recrimination for sin and the pursuit of worldly goods because the overburdened ship, an icon of overseas mercantile culture, holds a wealth ripe to the point of rottenness. The homeward-bound vessel is a dangerous cornucopia, plentiful and deadly as it sails forth under the shadow of imminent destruction. A renewed sense of Christian humility that the *S. João* author asks readers to take away from this story rehearses the common practice in prologues to historical texts of directing the reading of the ensuing narrative in a moralistically didactic fashion. This lesson is reminiscent, within the Iberian shipwreck context, of the lesson Alfonso X seeks to impart in his *Cantigas de Santa Maria.*

Yet the ostensible and rote rehearsal of prologular topoi harbors within it the first maroonings that will unfold throughout the narrative. The lack of authorial self-naming stands in contrast to the naming of the informant, Álvaro Fernandes, the sole source of the story. The story of Sepúlveda, a Portuguese governor of India, exists under no authenticating pen of a named chronicler, only the hearsay of the boatswain's mate of the ship. The redaction of the account responds to no mandate from monarch or patron, participates in no overarching or ongoing narrative project, but is, rather, accidental—both the informant and his story are rescued like castaways, salvaged from the wreck of the ship. The author, at the moment of writing, is "here in Mozambique"; shipwreck has caused the locus of historical storytelling to shift away from the center of political power (the metropole) to the land of loss and wreck. To be lost in space threatens the story with its own disappearance, with sinking without a trace. The marooned story in Africa and its subsequent return to Portugal—a back-and-forthing of historiographic creation—and its lack of authorial identification allow the story to evade the linking of text to figures of power residing in the safety and certainty of the imperial seat.

Like all shipwreck tales, the *S. João* begins with a departure, and from this initial sentence the author elaborates a story of a violent, downward trajectory.[5] Setting sail in shipwreck narrative, as I have already had occasion to remark, is a priori a failed enterprise: the departure is the inaugural action of unaccomplishment. From this moment onward, we discover layers of disorder and chaos unfurling themselves before us like the sails of a doomed ship, and this negative expansiveness begins with the onset and then full fury of the storm. As the crew frantically attempts to relieve the distressed vessel, they engage in makeshift repairs of sails and of the ship, and it is during these repairs that the ship escapes the control of its crew and its directionality falters. Controlled, forward movement becomes difficult, if not impossible, and the wavering *discurso* of the ship anticipates the increasingly difficult project of maintaining the controlled, ordered progression of the company of survivors over land. The sea, the surface over which maritime itineraries are "written" or realized (thus rutters, portolan charts, or ships' logs are metaphoric tracings of the sea whose surface has been transferred to paper or parchment), resists, violently, the organizing principles and actions of the navigational mind; the sea's refusal to submit to the idea of itinerary is repeated by "safe" land, as the survivors are unable to inscribe, or maintain, a directionality over its eminently more traceable, stable surface.

Marooned on the coast of east Africa following the wrecks of the galleon and the lifeboats, the survivors, after an unsuccessful attempt to buy a cow from some natives who appear on a hill, prepare to march from their encampment on the beach in search of food.

> From this beach, where they wrecked at thirty-one degrees on the seventh of June in fifty-two, the company began to march in the following order: Manuel de Sousa with his wife and children, along with eighty Portuguese and one hundred slaves; André Vaz, the pilot, was also in this company, and he marched in the vanguard carrying a banner with a crucifix on it. Some slaves carried D. Leonor, the

captain's wife, on a litter. Directly behind came the master of the galleon, the sailors, and the women slaves. Pantaleão de Sá, with the other Portuguese and slaves (about two hundred people), marched in the rearguard. All together there were about five hundred people, one hundred eighty of whom were Portuguese. They walked in this manner for a month, experiencing many hardships and much hunger and thirst. (12–13)[6]

The arrangement of the survivors into a marching line symbolically represents the attempt to reestablish order after the chaotic experience of shipwreck; it constitutes an effort to reconstruct the order of class and status typical of Portugal, to unify a society on the verge of anarchy, marooned from the home nation and its structures of power and position. A vestigial, political order determines the placement of survivors in the line. Álvaro Fernandes's voice (or, more precisely, his voice through his anonymous mediator) marks latitudinal position and recites statistics related to the composition of the surviving company. The narrative voice clings to habits of precision, attempting to bestow some semblance of order on the survival march by indicating where it began, who was in it, and later, what distance was traveled in a day. The narrative strategy of indicating time, place, and position, although typical of texts that seek to establish a linear, forward movement as an analogue of an ordered world traversed by European subjects, here proclaims an absurdity: the company arranges itself into position in a situation where the exigencies of survival make such a protocol risible—they align themselves in a "meaningful" order in the middle of nowhere, the search for the necessities of survival affecting all equally and obliterating hierarchy. Yet, oddly, all are loath to abandon such order very quickly: when the company must ford a river, for instance, the minute everyone is safely on the other side, "they arranged themselves again into an ordered marching column" ("logo se puseram em ordem de caminhar" [203]). The marching column represents the adherence to a structure of order and knowledge, and for this reason threats to its dissolution are dealt with summarily.[7]

The protocols of authority and rank are displaced power structures of home culture that guarantee no success in negotiating survival. The cohesion of the body politic begins to crumble as the survivors learn that there is no necessary safety in the collective. If some members of the marching column fall behind, breaking off from the group to encounter certain death, all of the members are forcibly disbanded by the group of natives who, with promises of food and shelter, exploit Portuguese vulnerability.[8] These natives disband the Portuguese into separate units, divest them of their weapons, and even strip them of their clothes. The company depends on the disposition of the natives in order to survive, and cultural contact in the *S. João* and all shipwreck narrative proceeds as a negotiated, rather than imposed, encounter, thus overturning the relational dynamic of conquest texts. The forced dissolution of the company occurs decisively after the linear itinerary has been lost, after disorientation becomes more and more prominent: the survivors often find that they have been traveling in circles *(rodeios),* but remain unable to re-script their march narrative to their advantage. The overland survival march mimics the disorderly meanderings of the doomed ship.

The journey of experience over sea and over land detailed in the *S. João* is a journey of maiming the body politic and of dissolving markers of time, place, and controlled movement. The body of nation, order, and authority, symbolized by the ship, extends to Manuel de Sousa Sepúlveda's position as captain and head of that body. Before his ship wrecked, Sepúlveda was heading back to Portugal famous in his capacity as governor of the Indian city of Diu, a representative of the Portuguese exercise of supreme political power in the East. Yet, as the narrative progresses, his mental health deteriorates: he was "ill in the head" ("maltratado do miolo" [204]), the narrator observes, and "had lost his judgment" (20) ("andava muito doente e fora de seu perfeito juízo" [207]). His wife Leonor eventually takes over the command that is gradually slipping through her husband's fingers. His deterioration is substituted by Leonor's strength and responsibility:

> D. Leonor was already among those traveling on foot. A noblewoman, young and delicate, she marched along those harsh and arduous paths like any robust man from the countryside, on many occasions consoling others in the company and helping to carry her children. . . . It truly seems that Our Lord's grace was at work there, since without it a woman so fragile and so unaccustomed to hardships would not have been able to traverse such long and arduous trails, always suffering hunger and thirst. By now the company had

already gone more than three hundred leagues because of the detours. (19)[9]

Gender and patriarchal authority dissolve, or are inverted, in this passage. Shipwreck overturns the confines of Leonor's gender by imbuing her with a masculine physicality as she becomes like a "robust man of the countryside." She metamorphoses from delicate *fidalga* to stalwart marcher, and in so doing assumes a practical authority and decisiveness that would otherwise be denied her at home or if Sepúlveda were still in possession of his wits. The survivalist experience naturalizes the association between gender and political command precisely by inverting it in the figure of Leonor (much as the shipwreck authors will provide a de facto encomium to the shipwright's complicated craft by describing, in detail, a ship in the process of falling apart), an inversion that is part of the tragedy of the story. Only in the aftermath of shipwreck may Leonor be strong, but this strength is temporary and will eventually end in death.[10]

The deterioration of political structure in the wake of shipwreck happens initially in the figure of Sepúlveda, whose inability to act as the head of the company is emphasized by the somatic affliction of Sepúlveda's own body in the form of persistent headaches, necessitating, at one point, that his head be swathed in towels. The metaphoric, gendered body of Aristotle's polis ails in the wake of shipwreck as it is decapitated by Sepúlveda's madness.[11] Sepúlveda symbolically loses his own body and the power to control it as a consequence of shipwreck and this imperils all the survivors. As authority transfers from Manuel to Leonor, her gendered body gains symbolic importance. On it, the destruction of shipwreck will be enacted not once but twice. Leonor's woman's body, as we know, is also a maternal body, and in this her afflictions across the sands of Africa trace a palimpsestial narrative over the medieval experience of shipwreck in Alfonso's *Cantigas de Santa María.* In the *S. João,* as in all shipwreck narrative, a ship's obligations to its passengers are in many ways maternal in nature: it contains and holds them and should see to their safety. The ship's natural space—expanses of limitless water—invokes a maternal, womblike world. When a ship wrecks or breaks apart, either at sea or in sight of the shore, it abdicates this maternal responsibility by forcing passengers and cargo from its holds in the manner of a terrifying and abortive birth. At one point in the *Santiago,* after the ship has wrecked, it in essence wrecks again:

> On the first and second days after the wreck . . . everybody was going about bound with two or three ropes to be tied on to the rafts, and, after winding the ropes many times round their waists they wound them as many times again round their necks, in order to be able to move more freely. It was such a sad sight that they seemed thus all condemned to death with nooses round their necks. On this same day one of the ship's sides broke open and, as if it was giving birth, threw out the boat with a third part missing. (Ley 271–72)[12]

The ship's expulsion of the lifeboat "a modo de parto" ("like a birth")[13] contrasts—or should we say complements—the sad spectacle of the survivors girded with noose-like umbilical cords. In the *S. Paulo,* during a terrible storm at sea,

> they saw with their own eyes the elements conjured against them, the waves so furious and promising them, once their souls were departed, to be the graves of their flesh; and without a doubt there was no one there, however courageous or boastful, who didn't at that moment wish to be even the smallest insect on land, since nature seems to ask each to return to his ancient mother, the land, from which our first father, Adam, was formed. But men of the sea are very similar to women at the time of birth, who, with their strange and tremendous pains, swear that if they escape from that moment they will never copulate or join with a man ever again.[14]

The gender-bending experience of storm and imminent wreck is so extreme that the sailors become like mothers in labor while the primal, nonsexual mother (dry land) has been displaced from the scene of danger.

In the *S. João,* Leonor's anguished inability to provide for her children corresponds to the galleon's inability to protect the travelers and precious items it encloses in its wooden womb—this tale is rather like a *mater dolorosa* on the outskirts of the world.[15] Leonor's body, shipwrecked once with the other S. João passengers, experiences shipwreck again at the hands of the Africans. All types of *perda* (loss) are visited on her, as she is attacked (like a ship in a storm), disrobed (like the sails that are torn by the wind or ripped from the yards), and cajoled by the natives and her husband (like the attempts to steer a wayward ship). Her naked, humiliated body finally commits itself to the sand like a broken ship to the depths of the sea, never to rise again.

To read the ship as exclusively feminine, though, is to overlook the phallocentric symbolism of the ship's body and the destruction caused by wreck, especially as it is enacted on the mast. Christine Arkinstall interprets the meaning of the mainmast in Cristina Peri Rossi's *Descripción de un naufragio*, a poem with symbolic preoccupations similar to ones in the *S. João*, by remarking that it "represents the claim propounded by imperialism that it protects those members of its sociopolitical body that permit it to function," a protection that is a "phallocratic definition of boundaries and appropriation of bodies" (427). Throughout all shipwreck narrative, the dismasting of a ship signals the moment the vessel is irrecuperably lost or damaged. This is the moment, then, when the masculinist enterprise of imperialism receives a definitive blow, and breaks; if the ship surrenders its maternal protection, it also abdicates its patriarchal imperative grounded in imperialism (or commerce).[16] Thus, in the gendered readings that ships and shipwreck invite, the mast is a phallic symbol of power—when a ship is dismasted it is also un"man"ned, triggering the gender inversions working their way through wreck's aftermath. Sepúlveda's abandonment of command is a surrender of the prerogative of male power, of course, and it is one that will not be recuperated in the space of this narrative until Álvaro Fernandes, the accidental chronicler, restores a phallocentric control over the shipwreck experience by recounting it. Leonor herself authorizes the telling (and therefore control) of the *S. João* to revert to male control. Just before she dies, Leonor

> said to André Vaz, the pilot: "You can all see what we have been brought to. We will not be able to move on, and will find our end here because of our sins. Leave here in order to be saved, and commend yourselves to God. If you should reach India, or in time, Portugal, relate how you left Manuel de Sousa, me, and my children." (23)[17]

The rescuing of the entire story of the S. João by a man's voice contrasts with the reference to the unrecorded story of Leonor's death supposedly narrated by three female slaves in Goa.[18]

But back to Leonor's body. She and the ship, like Mary, are intercessors: whereas the ship mediates between East and West, Leonor must

Figure 7. The dismasted ship in a woodcut from the 1601 edition of the
*S. António, Naufragio, que passou Iorge Dalbuquerque Coelho, Capitão
e Governador de Pernambuco.*

mediate between her demented husband and the other survivors, between the harsh landscape, the abusive treatment by the natives, and her
children. The native tribes of Africa—referred to generically in shipwreck accounts as *cafres* or "Kaffirs," are both friendly and hostile, more
often bent on taking advantage of Portuguese castaways and inflicting
cruelty on them as not, as many of the writers claim. (As a female body
under African control, Leonor adumbrates the experiences of women in
nineteenth-century American barbary captivity narratives.[19] Although
we do not find in the *S. João* the depiction of sexual advances on the
women by the natives as we do in the barbary tales, the situation of the
female Portuguese shipwreck survivor is comparable to that of the white
female captive in the North American tales as discussed by Haberly.)[20]
Leonor's captive, female body issues perhaps its most pointed symbolic
statement when, in a final act of forced subservience and humiliation,
the *cafres* strip Sepúlveda of his clothes and then proceed to Leonor, who

violently defends herself against such an affront until her husband convinces her to submit by reminding her of the truth of Job 1:21 that "they were born naked" ("lhe lembrava que nasceram nus" [209]). These actions initiate the sequence of events ending in the death of Leonor and her children, and of Sepúlveda:

> It is said that D. Leonor would not allow herself to be stripped, defending her body by fists and blows since it was her nature to prefer being killed by the Kaffirs than to find herself naked in front of everyone. There can be no doubt that at that instant her life would have ended had it not been for Manuel de Sousa, who pleaded with her to let herself be stripped. He reminded her that they were born naked and that God wished her to be, too. . . . Once naked, D. Leonor threw herself on the ground immediately and covered herself with her very long hair. She made a hole in the sand and buried herself in it up to her waist; she never again would rise from the sand. Manuel de Sousa asked an old nanny of hers for her torn shawl so that D. Leonor could cover herself with it, and the nanny gave it to him. Even so, D. Leonor never again rose from that place where she fell after finding herself naked. . . . Manuel de Sousa, though he was not in his right wits, did not forget that his wife and children needed to eat. Limping from a wound in his leg inflicted by the Kaffirs, he went into the forest in this battered state to find some fruit for them. When he returned, he found D. Leonor weak from hunger. . . [and] one of his children dead, and buried him in the sand with his own two hands. The next day Manuel de Sousa returned to the jungle, again in search of fruit, and this time when he returned he found that D. Leonor and the other child had died. . . . They say that when he found D. Leonor dead, Manuel de Sousa did nothing but send the slaves away and sit down beside her with his face in his hands for about half an hour, without crying or saying anything. . . . Then, he rose and began to dig a grave in the sand with the help of the slave women. All the while, never speaking a word, he buried her and the child. Once this was done, he turned and followed the path he had taken when searching for fruit. Without saying anything to the slaves, he went into the jungle, never to be seen again. (23–24)[21]

There is much of note in this finale to the *S. João*. It directs the experience of shipwreck, in which gender inversions figure prominently, to a negative end. Leonor must defend her own body by blows, in so doing appropriating a masculinist code of honor because Sepúlveda's surrender of Portuguese arms to the *cafres* earlier on constitutes the final straw for her. Her husband is tragically unable to protect his wife's honor like a man; "[y]ou surrender your arms, and I give myself up as lost along with all these people"(21),[22] Leonor proclaims on that occasion. But her own appropriation of this code fails as she can no longer survive the re-gendered body shipwreck has forced her to occupy.

But just as important is the grave on the beach. The land swallows Leonor and her husband, a symbolic defeat (Adamastor's ghost hovers presciently over this scene) of the Portuguese by Africa. And it is a de-feat that happens in silence. There is a gradual loss of speech on the part of the company's leaders (Manuel and Leonor) that, coupled with the digging of the grave, suggests a decline in, or loss of, narrative sub-jectivity. In losing the ability to speak, husband and wife lose the ability to narrate themselves, and from this perspective Álvaro Fernandes's telling of the story through the anonymous author is all the more sig-nificant: he speaks (indirectly) because Sepúlveda and Sá no longer can, nor could they in the final days before their deaths. Sepúlveda's own si-lence throughout most of the narrative, particularly after he loses his mind, is all the more noteworthy given the last time we hear him speak. As the arduous overland march is about to begin from the encampment on the beach, the captain addresses the survivors:

Friends and gentlemen: You clearly see the state we are in because of our sins. I truly believe mine alone are enough to account for our dire travails. But God is so merciful that He granted us a great favor by not allowing us to sink with our ship, inundated as it was by water below-deck. It will please Him Who was served in rescuing us from that danger to deliver us to a land of Christians. To those who might die of hardships on this journey, may their souls find salva-tion. You well understand, gentlemen, that the days we spent here were necessary for the convalescence of our sick. And now, God be praised, they are well enough to walk, so I have called you together so we may decide what path we are to take in order to reach salva-tion. Our plan to build a boat, as you saw, was struck down since we could not salvage any materials from the ship to make it. So, gentle-men and brethren, as your lives are concerned as well as mine, it would not be right to do or decide on anything without everyone's consent. The one boon I ask of you is that you do not abandon me or leave me, if, on account of my wife and children, I am not able to walk as quickly as the best of you. Thus united will God in His great mercy help us. (12)[23]

Sepúlveda speaks with authority for the final time, and this reasoned speech stands in contradistinction to the silence he will enter irrationally. So it is that Sepúlveda's speech is more than just a "mere rhetorical construction" (Zurbach 217) inherited from earlier textual models; it functions centrally as the speech act that precedes Sepúlveda's silence and heralds his demise. It reflects, as Zurbach notes, a "profoundly negative" (218) environment in which silence implies the loss of ability to direct and lead, to control, that is, the "narrative" of overseas action.

Sepúlveda's silence reflects an anxiety about narrative subjectivity. In standard expansionist texts, however displaced a subject is from the home culture, narrative agency is not impeded. Controlled itinerancy and narrativity work together forcefully and underlie the full expression of expansionist sovereignty. In the transferral of political power from Manuel to Leonor, Leonor assumes a subjectivity, an agency, typically reserved for men alone. The inclusion of her spoken words in the *S. João* is the by-product of her new, temporarily empowered position to tell the story of the survivors and that consecrates her role as subject in this narrative. Yet, like Manuel, Leonor as speaker in the text falls into silence. The grave of her body is the grave of subjectivity, in one sense, because the historical actor, the figure of European hegemony, is incapable of narrating in the first person his, or her, story. The narrator mentions repeatedly the sterility of the landscape and establishes it as a driving motif of shipwreck survival and authorial inadequacy: "where they suffered such great sterility, as can't be believed or written."[24] This sterility, this "alien land" ("terra alheia") is a landscape of negativity, of power and order overturned and undone.

S. BENTO: LITTORALLY SPEAKING, OR, THE ANXIETY OF EDGES

Swinging from vines, then pole-vaulting from rock to slippery rock, Manuel de Mesquita Perestrelo and the survivors of the wreck of the S. Bento cross a dangerous river in the interior of Africa. "So it was that

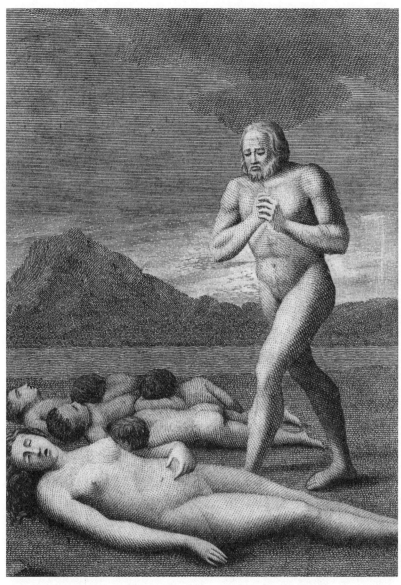

Figure 8. Manuel de Sousa Sepúlveda and Leonor de Sá, from *Factos memoráveis da história de Portugal* (1826).

we were crawling on our backs and stomachs given the danger and lay of the land, when it pleased Our Lord to put us safely on the shore of the river,"[25] Perestrelo writes in a narrative permeated by an anxious, insistent regard to borders and to their location and dissolution, to the safety and danger of limits and edges as they block, impede, and facilitate survival with almost chimerical unpredictability. Perestrelo's *S. Bento,* a protracted account of survivors fighting their way through the same unforgiving landscape that received Manuel de Sousa Sepúlveda's family and passengers, charts a course of alignments with and against borders and liminal spaces as the determining characteristic of shipwreck and its consequences.[26] In this the *S. Bento* manifests, in often terrifying and unsettling terms, the disorienting blow to reality and perception shipwreck causes and the troubling task of rendering it as narrative.

More than any other HTM author, Perestrelo explores the interior world of the psyche where the exterior realities of shipwreck, survival, and ceaseless wandering serve to emphasize the tortured perambulations of the aware and perceiving mind. He anticipates rather remarkably Kristeva's seminal thoughts on abjection and horror in which the idea of the border plays a defining role. "How can I be without border?" Kristeva asks. "It is thus not lack of cleanliness or health that causes abjection but what disturbs identity, system, order. What does not respect borders, positions, rules" (4), she continues, unknowingly describing the Portuguese shipwreck experience. Perestrelo and company progressively move into the territory of Kristevan abjection as they scratch for food, hunt out latrine spaces like pack animals, or struggle through waist-deep mud. Julia Kristeva: "The abject confronts us, on the one hand, with those fragile states where man strays on the territories of the *animal*" (12). Manuel de Mesquita Perestrelo: "And thus some [of us] went around without finding any sign of intelligence in others, as if everyone were irrational beasts that were grazing there, carrying only instinct and frightened eyes scouring the countryside to see if they could find a plant, bone, or vermin (one that wasn't poisonous) to grab hold of."[27]

In one sense, all shipwreck literature renders a narrative attempt to come to terms with a traumatic incident (or series of incidents) in which the narrator or survivor emphasizes a personal and individual reckoning of shipwreck or an impersonal and collective one. In other words, the lone narrative voice of the shipwreck writer shifts, in perspective and focus, from narrative to narrative, between a memoir-like account in which personal experience of danger and safety emerges as the principal concern to a more "representative" authorial posturing in which the narrator endeavors to come to terms with shipwreck as a brutal visitation of nature or divinity on a Portuguese collective—be that collective one of Christians, subjects of the crown, or citizens of a seafaring nation. The conjunction of trauma and narrative—or better, of narrating subject—dominates Perestrelo's account, as his repeated use of the word *imaginação* (imagination) demonstrates. This story of looking within begins on board, at night, during the terrors of a storm-tossed ship: "as men who, in a few hours, expected to give an account of our well or poorly spent lives to Our Lord, each began to come to terms with his own conscience, confessing quickly to some clerics in the company."[28] After the wreck, the survivors are thrown into further, miserable introspection as they are pounded by rain:

> As soon as night fell, we huddled together underneath some trees, each of us retreating into thoughts about his own fortune and thinking of those things that were most painful. And so that even in that paltry shelter we should not find relief, it rained so much that night that, our barely clothed bodies being unable to tolerate the cold, we got up; so it was that in the dark we ran from one place to the next, this activity acting as relief from the afflictions caused by the cold and the little sleep and the fear created by our own imaginations, all these things making us greatly desire the return of daylight.[29]

The traumatized narrating subject is thrown into relief as survivors attempt to find and plot parameters; even after Perestrelo has returned to the safety of his native land (where he writes his account), fear and suffering grip his pen. He recounts shipwreck by invoking the world out of order, an image that then leads to a reflection on avarice and expansion:

> And truly it was a strange confusion by which misfortune brought these things to pass, and the memory of it might suffice to prevent poverty from being considered so great an evil, to fly from which we forsake God, our neighbour, country, parents, brethren, friends, wives, and children, exchanging peace and pleasure for such hardships as we suffered here. And so long as we live the fear of poverty

induces us to brave seas, fires, wars, and all other perils and hardships
which cost us so dear; but not to oppose on every point the just ex-
cuses of those who are tormented by necessity, I will cut short the
thread of my discourse . . . for I was carried away by the memory and
dread of what is here represented, and return to my purpose, which
is to write only the true facts concerning the events of this narrative.
(Theal 1:222)[30]

This reflection on maritime campaigns is part of an interruption or digression within the main narrative (one occasioned by the horror of the
chaos caused by wreck) to which Perestrelo now returns.[31] By first di-
gressing, or breaking off from, the main thread of the text, then in turn
breaking off the digression, Perestrelo emphasizes the magnitude of the
shipwreck memory and its disruptive potential on narrative and chronological linearity. The underlying principle of order in historiographic
narrative here finds itself stressed to the point of breaking in the mind of
a narrator who is concerned with both the "truth" and the interiorized,
individual experience of shipwreck as opposed to an official vision of
seafaring and expansion.

We observed in the preceding chapter that one of the symbolic
meanings of the ship is empire and maritime supremacy, a seaborne icon
of home culture and of the expansive itinerancy of the sovereignty of
the king. Sailing under the king's orders is tantamount to transporting the
authority of monarchical power to the seas and the lands beyond it. The
steerage of a ship, then, represents a fluency, a forward-moving and controllable expression of the state's political and cultural expediency—a familiar way, that is, of seeing, perceiving, and negotiating reality. All is
right with the world when ships sail and are navigated according to plan.
The "direct" or "right" course ("rota direita," in Perestrelo's words) is a
navigational analogue of epistemological certainty; to navigate "on
course" means not simply to follow the correct or predetermined route,
but to maintain a hold on a politically or culturally informed template
of perception and experience. Consequently, when Perestrelo says of his
ship during the description of the storm at sea that "never again could it
be navigated correctly" ("nunca mais se pôde navegar direita" [225]), he
also marks a break, a veering off, a breach in the orderly patterns of
movement and of tracking movement that work equally to shape an or-

derly record of what is encountered on an itinerary. This moment of *desandar* (wandering) initiates the conflictual relationship to borders suffusing this narrative. The S. Bento, now sailing alone (recall that it was part of a fleet that broke up in the introductory paragraphs), charts a haphazard course across the water, one that is "outside of all order and usual navigation" ("fora de toda a ordem e navegação costumada" [223]). Certainty is dissolving under Perestrelo's remembering pen, and after the wreck the ship's passengers chart haphazard courses through the jungles of Africa. These courses characteristically move along the "edge of the sea" ("à borda do mar") or the "edge of the river" ("à borda do rio"), and are not so much routes as random vectors the survivors follow to find food, shelter, or villages of natives with whom they might trade. In these blind meanderings where the "certain path" ("certa trilhada") is almost always a deception or an illusion, the itinerant European is frequently forced to abandon the prerogative of determining a marching path (an exercise of order-making and cartographic determination) and surrender it to potentially dangerous natives. "We decided to wait for the Kaffirs . . . so that they could show us a way to a village,"[32] Perestrelo observes in resignation at one point. The power to make a route as a sign of superiority appears later as the company decides to head to the beach as a strategic move to defend itself from possible attack, but is defeated: "but as soon as the Kaffirs understood this, they placed themselves in front of us with their bows drawn, telling us we would not go except where they would guide us."[33]

The nightmarish wandering through the jungle, the disorienting *caminho* on land and the increasing impossibility of tracing and remembering paths, ones that move along and then away from edges, begins, as it did in the *S. João,* over water. After the harrowing experience of a storm at sea, land is sighted, but contrary to the relief that might be expected at such a juncture, the land rises darkly and menacingly like Adamastor before the passengers of the S. Bento:

> The next day dawned and we were a league from land . . . as soon as day broke and we saw ourselves close to the steep mountains and jagged rocks of that strange and barbarous land, there was no one who wasn't relieved at the sight, given the danger we had just been

through, but at the same time wasn't terribly afraid, present as it was in everyone's mind how covered those expansive and unknown jungles must be with the Portuguese skeletons of those who had sailed in 1552 on the S. João with Manuel de Sousa Sepúlveda.[34]

The approach to the strange and barbarous land triggers a memory of the experience of Sepúlveda and his company, who found within it both shelter and tomb. Perestrelo calls on the sepulchral motif present in the poignant end of the *S. João,* dramatically and gravely resuscitating the bodies of Sepúlveda's expedition before our readerly eyes with the "ossadas portuguesas" ("Portuguese skeletons") scattered among the forests. The coast Perestrelo and company approach is first and foremost a cemetery, a space of fear and uncertainty that promises to render deathly reminders about shipwreck to the passengers on the S. Bento who seek safety and the means of survival therein. Perestrelo and company approach the border of land "com grande receio" (with great fear), a state of mind opposed to the reasoned exercise of skill as a means of survival.

Fear eventually overwhelms the entirety of the S. Bento company, one so pervasive it occasions a hallucinatory, phantasmagoric negotiation with the real world even before the ship reaches shore:

> A sailor . . . began crossing himself and calling on the name of Jesus in a loud voice; and when some asked him what was the matter, he pointed out a huge wave off the starboard that was quite some distance away but was taller than all the other waves, saying that in front of it he saw a large gathering of black figures, which could be nothing other than demons. With all this commotion everyone rushed to the ship's sides to see such a terrifying thing, and then the wave hit us astarboard with such force and weight that it almost sunk us at once.[35]

The hull of the ship is the dividing line between order and the chaos of the abyss, symbolically significant as the marker between rational thought and fear. It is not surprising that all on board verify the presence of the dangerous, worldly wave and the presence of otherworldly demons accompanying it with bodies pressed tightly against the sides of the ship, straining against the confines of the logical. Later, the supernatural world makes another appearance, this time in the form of phantasmal voices in the dead of night:

> That night, after we had settled down to sleep, like the night before and all the rest we spent in this place, in the dead of night we clearly heard loud screams coming from the place where the ship had broken apart, saying "To port, to starboard, up there," and many other confused words we couldn't understand—these voices sounded like us in the storm when, waterlogged, we were about to run aground. What that was can never be known for certain, but we suspected that either we were hearing things that had thundered in our ears continually during that time, or there were evil spirits who delighted in pursuing us (something that Our Lord, in his mercy, wouldn't permit). But whatever it was, the sure thing is that it happened, or appeared to happen: at first, every person thought that only he heard that terrifying noise, and knowing there would be difficulty in others accepting this as true, eventually everyone was asking everyone else if they heard the same thing. We all confirmed that yes, everyone heard it, and agreed that given the hour, darkness, and storminess of the nights, it was one of the two things I already mentioned.[36]

The shipwreck moment re-presents itself as ghostly voices heard in the night. Auditory apparitions, in fact, form part of the repertory of shipwreck literature topoi tracing back to works such as the *Aeneid*, book 3, where Aeneas's men hear monstrous murmurings at night as they hide in the woods, or the spectral voices accompanying Saint Elmo's fire in the sea voyage to the east in the medieval *Relación de la embajada de Enrique III al gran Tamorlán* of Ruy González de Clavijo. Yet Perestrelo's ghosts, in the context of a narrative preoccupied with the disruption shipwreck causes to a narrating subject whose own trauma intrudes on the structures or borders of the historiographic text, function as more than a mere topos. The phantasmal requires Perestrelo to undergo a process of verification about the reality or truth of the experience that is inconclusive. The subjective imagination impedes the perception and authoritative representation of the world, and Perestrelo's "frightful sound" ("espantoso som") invokes a fearful reverse side of the marvelous and the exotic that permeates discovery and conquest texts.[37] *Espanto* (fear) disrupts the narrator's relationship to phenomenal reality in that certainty cannot be recuperated even at a later moment of writing—indeed, the impossibility of certainty is a theme in Perestrelo's text and seems to be its very point.[38] The episode proposes that one of the destructive aftereffects of shipwreck is that language itself has lost cogency, that speaking (or, more generally, an instance of discourse) has become spectral and phantasmal, devoid of referentiality. The "palavras confusas" ("confused words") are a speech act without a speaker. They emanate from the site of breakage, that is, the place in the water where the ship broke to pieces. The border between wholeness and fragmentation is marked by ghostly speaking or vestiges of language, the eerie cries in the night that seem not only unbelievable but cast doubt over the possibility of representing, through language, an experience that defies rationality. Language has washed ashore like the pieces of a wrecked ship. It has become, to a certain degree, stranded on the shore like the survivors.

And it is the shore, or the littoral, to which I now turn, that geographical space of liminality present in virtually any narrative about travel over the sea. Perestrelo narrates a distressed relationship with the shore throughout his account as a locus that oscillates between acting as a space of safety and shelter and as one of danger and death. The littoral, the shore, or the beach is the point of contact between sea and land that is composed of elements of each; it imposes a dual and unresolvable signification on the shipwreck survivors. It acquires a pronounced resonance in shipwreck narrative because survivors find themselves, at every turn, out of place: they find safety neither on water nor on the land; the sea does not allow an itinerary to be traced over it, and the land confounds the attempts of its negotiation or refuses to align itself with what is already on maps. Immediately after the S. Bento's wreck, the "fralda do mar" (seashore) both receives the survivors and acts as the space for the first deception visited on them. Camp is moved, as Perestrelo tells us, to the bank of a nearby river, and survivors are shuttled across in rafts (jangadas); they sleep on the "borda do rio" (bank of the river), and, in the initial attempt to trade for food, "we all were deceived in thinking that the interior must be more populated than the shore of the ocean, given the little that the Kaffirs have to do with it."[39] As they march through the "uncertain and dangerous path" ("incerto e perigoso caminho") by following the footprints of elephants, the survivors keep returning to contemplate the wrecked ship from the vantage point of

the shore; they hold a fascination for the spectacle of the disaster that marooned them:

> with our minds occupied in this anguish and our eyes filled with
> tears, we couldn't take a step without on several occasions going back
> to look at the skeleton of that beautiful and ill-fortuned ship of
> which there weren't even two boards left nailed together. Everything
> was smashed on those rocks. Still, as we contemplated it, it seemed as
> though we beheld relics and a piece of this, our dear homeland, from
> whose shelter and company (which was the last service we desired) we
> were unable to separate ourselves without great emotion.[40]

This passage, in which the ship is regarded in all its violent wreckage
at the same time it is cherished as a relic, construes the ship in discordant terms that foreground its problematic symbolic value. The nostalgic perception of the ship as Portugal that Perestrelo sketches asks us to
read the ship as his homeland, a once-steadfast vessel now ruined and
scattered among the rocks of the shore. With it lay its attendant structures of value as "shelter." If we keep in mind the authorial issues that
consistently affect Perestrelo's telling of the wreck, then we can understand the conflicted relationship with the S. Bento's skeleton as a sorrowful fascination with the tradition of orderly writing the *pátria* represents and which is undone by shipwreck. The ship is hence a figure of the
archive (a point I will return to in the next chapter),[41] a system or tradition of knowledge and writing. The emphasis on the nostalgic state of
mind links this writing dissonantly to memory and the past—that is, the
founding notions of historiographic discourse.[42]

Perestrelo takes care to remark that the departure from, or abandonment of, such a symbol is one attended by great emotion. The lens of
emotion highlights Perestrelo's own subjectivity as a presence in his tale:
he wants us to remember that his own psyche is the filter through which
we learn this story, and in so doing emphasizes the individual presence
at the scene of shipwreck as that which determines the shape of the
story. This individualistic, subjective relationship with the world as that
which generates a text reminds us more of the plaintive medieval lyric
than it does the disinterested detachment of the narrators of official historiography. The presence of the individual narrating subject is signaled
in the title with the expression "que se achou no dito naufrágio" ("who

was present in said shipwreck"). The historiographic rendering of shipwreck announces itself from the outset as a product of a specific (and
traumatized) narrating subject.

The liminal space of the beach, on which the symbolic separation
from country as a body of order (including textual order) occurs, is also
a space of anti-arrival, the point where a failed voyage is finally consum-
mated, the disastrous counterpoint of the departure from the home
country that official texts unilaterally script as auspicious and aprioristi-
cally victorious. The beach is at once life-giving and funereal: Perestrelo
remarks on the "such longed-for sand" ("areia tão desejada") (285) as the
locale where rest and convalescence might be found. Only pages earlier, a riverbank had served as receptacle for the bodies of dead companions, bodies deposited on the sand by the tide and occasioning a collective "mournful cry which echoed among the caves of the shore" (Theal
1:243).[43] The cry on the beach articulates the disorder and death that
shipwreck causes and might be understood as the emblematic utter-
ance, beyond words and language, that speaks for all the loss and inversions visited on the company. It signals a preoccupation with the disposition of the (dead) European body as a body outside the confines or
parameters of official movement and prescribed displacement. The
bodies from the S. Bento that are buried gesture, metonymically, to the
dead or crippled body of Portugal in the form of the wrecked ship. This
metonymic association, in line with my earlier argument of the ship as
archive, allows us to link the burial of the S. Bento bodies to the death
of narrative agency in the S. João.

The anxiety about burial in the S. Bento points to the dissolution of
another border—that of nature's capacity to embrace and consume a
body after death as a finalizing act of closure. It is this shocking inability
of nature to accommodate the dead that we find in the S. Bento, where
even the possibility of burial does not provide relief from a relentless ig-
nominy continually enacted on the European body in the landscape of
shipwreck:

> Those who were still alive were so weak and weary in mind and body
> that the most their strength and charity could compass was to place
> the dead bodies in a shallow grave fenced with stakes, wherein we
> left them badly covered. This gave rise to another misfortune not less

than that of hunger, which was that as the place where we dwelt with
the [Kaffir] king was in the midst of a large and ancient thicket
where there were many tigers, lions, and other wild animals, these
[fell on their prey first] by eating the flesh of those who were thus
badly buried. (Theal 1:274)[44]

The inability to provide proper burial recalls the lack of shelter resulting
from the wrecked ship, and these bodies must now be subjected to the
savagery of wild animals, where tigers "are the sepulchres of our bodies"
("sepulturas de nossos corpos" [305]).

The littoral in the *S. Bento,* therefore, particularly the delimited space
of the beach, acts as the stage on which bodily instincts find satisfaction
or not, and where lifeless European bodies reach the end of the voyage.[45]
These "unnatural" dispositions of the body on the beach mirror the death
of the necessary artificiality of hierarchy, as in the following instance:

But as fortune never begins with little, to all these disasters another
was added, which, though it could not make things blacker than
they were, was still a source of much grief, coming as it did from
men who were bound to him [the captain] for benefits bestowed
upon them; and this was that the greater part of the company were
seamen, of whose good qualities few authors had then written, and
these from day to day gradually lost all sense of fear and shame, and
being gathered in one body headed by the boatswain (although he
had no hand in their ill-doing), they grew so undisciplined that they
made absolutely no account of Fernão d'Álvares, but rather each
time he reprehended their disorders (which were not few) they an-
swered that he should not dare to reprove them, for he was no longer
their captain, and they owed him no obedience. . . . Seeing this, the
ship's master, who came from this kingdom and bore him a special
hatred . . . determined to attempt his diabolical and inhuman act.
(Theal 1:240)[46]

In the end, the mutiny does not happen, but its threat is nonetheless significant as a diabolical potential equaling, or surpassing, the magnitude
and severity of the wrecked ship—in fact, mutiny is made possible by
the destruction of the icon of the home country. It is this order-on-the-
edge that the beach represents, and as the survival party moves away

from it into the interior of Africa, any system of order teeters on the brink of disappearance. And it is precisely this departure from the beach that mobilizes the anxiety of negotiating the courses of rivers. Rivers function as the natural dividers and organizers of space, the multiarmed backbone of cartographic representation. A labyrinth of rivers weaves through the *S. Bento*: while they serve to provide food or wood for boats, they also mark an acute moment of the disjunction between the space of shipwreck survival and the previously documented representations of this geographical space. The rivers in shipwreck narratives are often unknown, or appear to follow different courses than they do on the maps. They are part of the landscape that may lead to nowhere; they are the cartographic, organizing principle that may impcdc organized movement. They flow, like the passage of time from one day to the next, but do not deliver directionality or the certainty of a safe end to wandering.

4

MANIFEST PERDITION II

GOING UNDER

*T*HE *S. JOÃO* AND THE *S. BENTO*, as we saw in chapter 3, harbor within their respective stories of the trials and consequences of shipwreck narratives of maroonings, or shifts, away from established paradigms of order, the mechanisms of historiographic production, gendered power relations, the navigational route (*rota* or *caminho*) as the presiding trope of epistemological certainty in structured campaigns of displacement underlying expansion or conquest, or the organizational function of the border in negotiating geographical space or delimiting the real or chronological linearity in historiographic texts. We now turn to a series of symbolic and metaphoric presences suffusing shipwreck narrative that, in conjunction with the ideas in chapter 3, work to define a poetics of the shipwreck narrative—that is, the motific and notional precepts that inform the narrative representation of shipwreck. These symbolic and metaphoric constructions are founded on the body and its signifying potential. The body in water, the reconfigured body of ships, the textual body, and shipwreck as an embodiment of the unnatural will steer this chapter's readings.

S. PAULO AND SANTIAGO: BODIES IN WATER

A multitude of bodies swirls through the shipwreck accounts: human bodies, boats' bodies, the bodies of culture, text, and nation. As the image through which shipwreck writers most persistently enact and represent breakage, bodies wash up before us sometimes whole, but most often in pieces, a product and producer of disaster. Constitutive of the preoccupations of shipwreck authors are people and ships, two kinds of bodies that merge metaphorically, each an icon of the other intertwined in a tight and unbreakable bond of symbiotic referentiality.

The shipwreck(ed) body that boasts a range of figurative meanings always appears originally in water, and characteristically suffers a violent disarticulation. The assault on the physical integrity of the body happens in a historico-cultural context that distinguishes these bodies from their medieval ancestors (such as the compositions of Alfonso X). The Portuguese bodies in water float in a sea whose symbolic connotations have changed. The advent of Christian imperialism in the fifteenth century is largely responsible for this shift. The systematic practice of Iberian expansion depends primarily on the agency of water; imperialism mandates that travel over and across water is essential, not incidental, to the realization of empire and therefore to the survival of its textual culture. Such maritime travel beats at the very heart of expansionist epistemology and symbolism, as inseparable from it as the notion of destiny itself. Negotiating the sea, then, claims primacy as the agent of a divine agenda that is realized through a complement of political, economic, and cultural imperatives. In Os Lusíadas, to take a supremely representative example, water and seafaring structure the episodes of the poem and demarcate the coordinates of its epistemological journey. Camões repeatedly presents the acquisition of new knowledge and the realization of prophetic and mythic nationalism through the agency of ships over water. His poetic personages come to know the world through boats, and this links the voyages of Os Lusíadas centrally to the actions of divinity. "Water . . . is Knowledge: one of the faces of God, one of his primordial manifestations" (18), notes Centeno. This aquatic episteme pervades the canonical texts of conquest, so the distressed body in water cannot help but echo symbolically the associated ideas of water, cohesion, power, and control.

The violence that definitionally oversees the committal of a body to water in shipwreck literature resolves, negatively, a latent dilemma about the symbolic meanings of ships: a seaborne ship is a figure of ambiguity because, on the waves, it is at once in its natural element and at the mercy of one of its fiercest enemies.[1] Likewise, people in water may either sink or swim, and the submersion of the human body reflects an aspect of the expansionist mentality that placed aquatic ability undecidedly along a continuum of natural/unnatural, civilized/barbaric. In Camões's watery poem, for instance, Portuguese sailors remain shipbound while traveling over sea, with one important exception: the frolicking in the water with the nymphs on the Isle of Love in canto IX. In *Os Lusíadas,* water is a sacred element, the home of gods or deities such as Neptune/Poseidon or the Tágides. Tellingly, it is only under the supervision of nymphs and Tethys that the weary homebound sailors may come into auspicious contact with water.[2] The sailors' harmonious habitation of the sea emerges as a definitive sign of their apotheosis, their transcendence of the worldly and of the circumstances of time and place. Natation, for Camões, is the sport of gods.

Thus, symbolically water is sacred, and therefore highly regulated and restricted, an unnatural place for humans who nonetheless do succeed in crossing and inhabiting it—and only barely, as Camões often reminds us as water deities balk and rebel at its violation by sending storms to trouble Vasco da Gama's fleet. The human form in water also foregrounds the civilized/barbaric binarism (one of the many binarisms on which conquistatorial ideologies were built), because natatorial ability is, in expansionist thinking, also a "barbaric" skill.[3] Swimming is a talent of the barbaric other, of either the Old or New World. A passage from Linschoten's *Itinerary* (1595) contains a representative articulation of this in a chapter on the "Arabians and Abexiins dwelling in India," people "infected" with the sect of Mohammed who are often hired by Europeans as ship hands: "[t]hese people are so serviceable and willing [to do any thing], that if there chanceth but a hat, or any other thing, to be blown over, or fall into the water, they will presently leape, cloathes

and all [into the sea], to fetch it again, for they swimme like fishes"
(268).[4] From this perspective, violent truck with the sea, even to the
point of death, ironically stands as a mark of superiority. In the *Santiago,*
a narrative in which Portuguese passengers swim frequently, Cardoso
also tells the anecdote of a slave swimming recreationally among the
ruins of the ship, shipwreck having thus caused the erasure of a marker
usually distinguishing barbarians from Europeans.[5]

With these general remarks in mind, I wish to turn to the *S. Paulo*
and the *Santiago,* stories that both vividly enact the drama of loss on the
bodily form. The metaphoric equation between humans and ships re-
lies, in part, on the fact that both can sink. The sea collapses the distinction between human and artificial bodies, granting each buoyancy (usually life-sustaining) or condemning each to destruction under its waves.
Even the ocean itself is a body, a pulsing, thumping, eternally moving
being, nature's most immediate ambassador in the lives of sailors and
passengers; its own mutability reflects the mutations of spirit, mood,
and necessity of those subjected to it on a daily and vital basis.

The *S. Paulo,* the most evocative account of storms, dismemberment, and trials at sea, and the *Santiago,* a story with a prolonged and
detailed description of the continuous building and rebuilding of lifeboats, everywhere depict the body as it slips "debaixo da água," or under
the water. The goings-under of the waterbound body are charged with
interpretive possibilities, ones that relate to the writing and reading of
shipwreck narrative. The bodies appear in two gradations of commitment to the water: they are either partially or fully immersed. Wrecked
ships may not sink entirely, as the masts of the S. Paulo that protrude
above the water, or the remains of the Santiago sighted at dawn, demonstrate. Humans participate equally in this subaqueous limbo. Some victims of the Santiago cannot sleep because "they always were in water up
to the waist, at the very least, without ever being able to sleep, because if
someone dozed off a wave would come along and hit him in the face to
keep him alert."[6] This erosion of the distinction between human bodies
and the artificial bodies of ships that submersion in water initiates—an
erosion, we could say, of received notions of knowability and the reckoning of the world into categories such as animate/inanimate or subject/
object—gains emphasis as these partially submerged bodies appear as
signs of an unfolding referential estrangement. The "desastre da per-

dição" ("disaster of perdition") causes the pieces of the S. Paulo and the Santiago to be misperceived by the passengers, the once-familiar now uncertain:

> Day began to break and many now said that they saw land, and some affirmed it was the mainland. But when it was quite light they saw that they were altogether mistaken, since what had seemed land and trees were the lids of the ship's hatchways all broken up, and barrels and boxes which had been carried away and had struck at that point because it was shallower. (Ley 269)[7]

Cardoso sketches a scenario of the "scattered remains of the beautiful structure which their ship had been" (Ley 270)[8] as a backdrop to the frenzied attempts of its inhabitants to see to the "salvation of bodies" ("salvação dos corpos"). The terror augments until the "people in the middle of the ocean" ("gente no meio do mar") eventually constitute what Cardoso deems "the most horrible spectacle of the shipwreck"—the disconsolate screaming, then drowning, of those refused admission to the overburdened lifeboats:

> At this point the most horrible sight of the whole shipwreck was seen, for both those on the rafts and those on the rocks, hoping to find refuge in the boat, left them and came naked, up to their chests in water, crying out all night because of the coldness of the water and their unbearable agonies. Nothing could be heard except sighs, groans, and pitiful supplications. They shrieked to those in the boat to help them. (Ley 274)[9]

This moment of primal agony recalls Elaine Scarry's assertion that "[t]o witness the moment when pain causes a reversion to the pre-language of cries and groans is to witness the destruction of language" (6). The gesture toward the dissolution of language suggested by the screaming bodies in water resonates forebodingly in the context of expansionist culture. Shipwreck's potential to trigger a reversion to a prelinguistic state in essence construes the European body as bestial, as having crossed the divide separating civilized, language-bearing subjects of the Crown from the barbaric objects of imperial action. Cardoso's testament to language's failure is made all the more disturbing because of the ideological implications. Moreover, he sketches an unsettling portrait of the agency by which this dissolution happens, for the state of bestiality into which the Portuguese body is placed happens at the hands of other Portuguese. Cardoso's screaming bodies in water announce the failure of the European to maintain a position of uncontested *subject*ivity in the expanses of the ocean. That the abandonment of the privileged subject position—that is, the descent into bestiality—happens from within, at the hands of other Europeans, suggests why Cardoso considers this to be the most horrible of all the aspects of shipwreck.

The agency by which bodies enter water has other connotations as well. The *Santiago* is especially rich in details about the scramble of shipwreck swimmers to enter a few overcrowded lifeboats. There is the instance of the young boy who eventually takes a place in the lifeboats, but only after being made, in a remarkable gesture of cruelty, to grab the blade of a sword, which leaves a deep gash in his hand. The overcrowding of these boats requires that a kind of kangaroo court be established within the very boats to decide which occupants are to be thrown overboard. These "executions" depict an especially harsh pathos as the condemned plead for their lives, usually unsuccessfully, and find themselves tossed into the water under the threat of the sword. As the Portuguese body turns on itself, it delivers a fatal blow not only to the (symbolic) integrity of Portugal—for, as we have already remarked, ships and their passengers are floating icons of the home kingdom—but to the possibility of heroic self-identity. The shipwreck experience forces a breach in the possibility of a return to identity after prolonged experiences of change and displacement. Jackson's study on the binary of utopia/otherness as one underlying a Portuguese quest for self-identity in the overseas voyages helps us understand how shipwreck might represent a gap in such a quest:

> A voyage that reenacted classical quest motif . . . began by affirming the self in order to reunite it with its mythic origins after rituals of exile, sacrifice of the body, and loss of identity. . . . the body reconstitutes itself . . . after having been dismembered by the voyages, implying the return of a changed and rejuvenated hero. (Jackson, "Utopia and Identity" 187)

According to Jackson, we may glean "the values of empire through the vicissitudes of the body" (191). Shipwreck aborts a ritual return or recuperation because there is no return of a hero—in those narratives that do boast of a heroic figure, such as Paulo de Lima in the *S. Alberto* or Manuel de Sousa Sepúlveda in the *S. João,* these heroes die in the space of shipwreck exile, undergoing no rejuvenation, no change, and no return. Any return of surviving bodies to Portugal (even the metaphoric body of the nation) is accidental, and thus points to the "loss of being" Jackson argues for as constituent of Portuguese voyages ("Sinkings" 151).

It would be wrong, however, to imply that the attempted, symbolic recuperation of the body does not occur at all in shipwreck narrative. The narratives do record several instances of terrified crew and passengers submitting relics to the sea in the hope of reaching safety, so the texts do narrate attempted, spiritual recuperations. The submersion of relics to the water is at once prayerful and sacramental—it is an act of supplication for release from danger—and a symbolic "resacralization" of the primal, godly element that has become so treacherous because of the profanity visited on it as the vehicle for the pursuit of earthly goods. These holy bodies in water, in the context of empire and the Portuguese missionary activity in the East, resonate strongly with stories such as the transferral and reputed incorruptibility of the body of Saint Francis Xavier, whose corpse underwent a series of disinterrals and maritime voyages. Xavier's body not only famously resisted putrefaction but was miraculously impervious to water, a relic that became the object of a fetishistic fascination.[10]

The religious symbolism of the body allows us to inscribe the ubiquitous presence of wounds and disease within an attempted program of salvation that is very much reminiscent of the medieval devotional lyric. Recall the moment in the *S. João* when the survivors are washed ashore: "[t]he rest came to land as God pleased: some on top of the waves, and some under, and many were wounded by the nails and wood" (10).[11] The wounded bodies of the survivors suggest a christological symbolism: like Christ, these victims receive wounds inflicted by wood and nails. These quasi stigmata offer perhaps an escape valve from the annihilation of shipwreck that would allow for a redemptive reading. Ships become the weapons that mediate between the divine and the human; Scarry argues: "The relation between God and human beings [in the Old Testament] is often mediated by the sign of the weapon. [They are] differentiated by the immunity of the one and the woundability of the other" (182–83). The wounding of the shipwreck body opens an ambiguity that the shipwreck authors struggle to resolve in their narratives with the frequent insistence on shipwreck as a retribution for sin: these bodies are hurt, but are they redeemed? They are punished, but are they saved?

Just as disposition in water allows for a metaphoric fluency between bodies, so does the ubiquitous motif of the dismembered body of ships and persons. Ships break apart as storms assault them, in turn seriously maiming or killing their passengers. Pieces of ships float through the narratives, as do pieces of people. Hostile natives do their part to render (Portuguese) bodies into pieces; disease and sickness, in some cases, do theirs. The broken, ill, or dismembered body serves as a vivid and gruesome enactment of a world rendered to pieces. The shipwreck authors so relentlessly present bodies under siege that this motif defines shipwreck narrative just as much as *naufrágio* itself does.

Dismemberment serves to establish the equivalence between human and ships by positing that both suffer violence and malady in almost identical terms: both kinds of bodies become disabled or injured; both must be tended to and healed to the greatest degree possible (quick, makeshift repairs on ships, or the cutting away of potentially dangerous masts or yardarms, are equivalent to the ministrations to the sick and dying); both may die or disappear. And, much as shipwreck writers take pains to depict a vessel in the process of wrecking or falling apart, so we find similar instances of human bodies flying to pieces before our eyes. A case in point is this passage from the *S. Paulo*:

> The seas were running very high, causing the ship to pitch heavily, and as the look-out man on the maintop was preparing to come down without due care and attention, the ship gave a sudden roll which threw the poor grummet off the maintop and he fell on one of the yardarms and from there into the sea, just at the feet of a man who was standing by the gunwale and was nearly knocked into the sea by the falling body, and who was injured in the leg by it. The victim's head was smashed to pieces on the yardarm where his brains were left embedded. . . . Three days later another similiar accident occurred, this time to the look-out man on the fore-top. . . . he fell from the top into the sea, grazing one of the flukes of an anchor . . .

[which] had taken all the skin off the top of his head and it hung like a friar's hood from his occiput. (*Further Selections* 63–64)[12]

Legs, arms, heads, hands, feet, partially digested "fishbitten corpses"— the systematic, narrative articulation of disarticulation is so prevalent that we can posit a shipwreckful poetics of dismemberment. This litany of fragmentation, of the bodies in bits, was common to classical epic, as Quint's study proves.[13] For instance, Quint finds in Lucan a correlation between narrative structure and the broken body: "[t]he narrative disunity of the *Pharsalia* corresponds to a body in pieces" (141). His examination of dismembered bodies and corpses in this and other texts rests on the thesis that "epic violence (is) a drive to dismemberment and formlessness" (147), a politically motivated process demanding that in order "[t]o portray history from the perspective of the lost republican cause and to counter the unifying historical fictions and narratives of imperial ideology, both bodies and poems must fall into pieces" (ibid.).

It certainly would be feasible to suggest that the shipwreck narratives— at least those written by learned authors—are heir to a symbolic signification of the body in its political overtones, keeping in mind that the shipwreck tales do not purport to be records of epic achievement or explicit promotions of a political positionality of their own. Quint's argument configures the body within an ideology whose poles are two competing political systems—empire and the lost republican cause[14]—or, as is the case with his examination of Alonso de Ercilla's sixteenth-century *La Araucana,* within a story of winners or losers. However, the ideology of empire in the HTM and its exercise of power comes under de facto attack, with no "other side" vying for primacy as exemplified in the *Aeneid/Pharsalia* opposition. It leaves an ideological void, one that questions the possibility of the reversal of loss and perdition, of renewal issuing from the space of the wreck. The body in pieces in shipwreck narrative is a disintegrated body with little or no potential for reintegration. The Portuguese shipwreck body is always a body in pieces and not a body in parts, according to the distinction advanced by David Hillman and Carla Mazzio in their work on the body in early modern Europe.[15] Bodies, then, suffer a fragmentation and are denied the possibility of restorative reassembly. Shipwreck's bodies in pieces, scattered among the oceans and sands of Africa and the East, imagistically forge a messy openness in the shipwreck narrative that confounds closure and the more programmatic, hermeneutic sealing-off of mainstream historiographic accounts. The dismembered body—much like the natant body we considered earlier—represents a lack of fixity and stability of its originating structure of authority and knowledge, that is, the body of imperial order and power. Fragmented, dispersed bodies are disenfranchised ciphers wandering, often randomly, through space.

CONCEIÇÃO: THE CONVERTER'S CRAFT

Liquidity binds bodies together: ships and humans suffer equally in water, and liquidity itself is a figure for the facility with which different kinds of bodies enter into a web of interreferentiality. Liquidity underlies the mutability, or transformability, that shipwreck sponsors, the shifting alignments triggered by wreck and the spaces of survival. This is one of the predominant subtexts of the *Conceição*, a story structured motifically by the constant building and rebuilding of lifeboats, a multiplication of small crafts fashioned from other crafts, where objects enter into new and unexpected use.[16] In the *Conceição*, Manuel Rangel presents a convertibility in the wake of disaster—a disastrous convertibility, we might say, endemic to shipwreck and its narratives.

The word *convertibility* gestures toward Greenblatt's assertion that "the whole achievement of the discourse of Christian imperialism is to represent desires as *convertible* and in a constant process of exchange" (*Marvelous Possessions* 71). The convertibility Greenblatt locates at the heart of (New World) imperialistic discourse surfaces negatively in the shipwreck narrative in that it marks the failure of desire as a facilitator of imperialism rather than as its consolidation. The desire for gold motivating the *carreira da Índia* voyages turns back on its passengers in unexpected and deadly forms. Monetary desire gives way to necessity, and this experience—in itself a transformation—transforms the role of material wealth. The transformation empties out systems of economic value, the inevitable result of the futility of greed *(cobiça).*[17]

A number of the transformations and transfigurations of shipwreck originate in the demands of survival: the search for food, shelter, and protection from danger. Such moments dismantle any preexisting notions of order or worth and effect radical revaluations of goods and circumstances. A characteristic moment appears in the *S. Alberto* as the ship is on the verge of sinking:

> The danger subsequently increasing, they threw overboard every-
> thing on the gun-deck and in the spice-holds, so that the sea was
> covered with untold riches, most of them thrown away by their very
> owners, to whom they were now as hateful and despicable as they
> were formerly beloved and esteemed. (*Tragic History* 111)[18]

Shipwreck converts valuable cargo into its opposite, and the decisive first step in this transformation is the consignment of the payload to the surface of the sea. The riches of India are rendered "superfluous" in the literal and figurative senses of the word: they both "flow over" the surface of the water (superfluous < Latin *superfluus*, "running over") and are now uselessly extraneous items, the demotion from their original status finalized by the waves. The owners themselves toss the precious com-modities overboard, and in so doing sever a referentiality necessary for any economy—the items no longer index a value of exchange. Two forms of currency—water and money—clash here, the former disem-powering the latter. Proprietarial relationships to signifiers suffer disas-ter. There is an economy, and an economy of signification, that sinks with the ship. "The sea was now covered with boxes, lances, barrels, and many other things which appeared in this mournful hour of shipwreck" (Theal 1:219–20),[19] writes Perestrelo. Often, these formerly esteemed items will be vomited up by the sea onto the beach—that problematic, liminal space of antiarrival that receives the devalued spoils of empire.

After this sinking of signification, an alternate valuation emerges, a reversal of worth that proposes that value is not an inherent quality of material goods but rather a function of circumstances. Rich silks and brocades, for example, are humbled into service as tent cloth:

> in a few hours there might be seen a superb lodging made of rich car-
> pets, pieces of gold cloth, and silk, put to a very different use from
> that for which they were made, and for which they were intended by
> their owners, who had earned them with the pains by which such
> things are acquired. (Theal 1:223)[20]

Scenarios of resignification such as this one point not only to the futility of the pains required for amassing wealth, but also to the start of a process in which recyclability of materials instantiates an unavoidable tautology of meaning prompted by shipwreck.

Several moments in Manuel Rangel's narrative of the *Conceição* illustrate best these circular fluencies. Even though Rangel narrates an arrival in Cochin at the narrative's end, his writerly concern throughout is the seemingly endless building of lifeboats, rafts, and skiffs, and the search for food on an island in the middle of the sea. The hunt for sustenance, a capitulation to an irrational impulse, finds a counterpart in the building of lifeboats, which is here presented, counterintuitively, as another irrational activity:

> And since God provided us with wood and sustenance, we determined, together with some of the sailors who remained there, to make a boat in which sixty or seventy people would fit. And they right away decided to go back to the ship in a raft they had made of an antenna, to get wood. . . . As the raft was made the ship was undone, and never again was a plank or board of it seen. . . . And even though the sailor who was in charge of building the larger craft had never held an axe in his hand, it appeared that God was visibly walking among us, helping us and showing us how to make the boat.[21]

The specialized knowledge of boatbuilding is miraculously granted to the survivors, as they understand it, from on high. Yet the divine provenance of the shipwright's craft does not prevent the fact that the boats built by the survivors soon return to pieces. There ensues a flurry of exchange as boat parts are reappropriated to serve as housing material on land, then return to the water newly assigned to duty as the skeleton of yet another vessel. The fluidity of transformation, as people and objects move from water to land to water, realizes a spatial limbo, where neither water nor land grants safety. Pieces of boats are used for tent stakes, then are conscripted into service as part of the architecture of another boat; masts serve as beacon posts on land, then serve once again as masts. A *batel* (boat) is made, then falls to pieces and serves to make an *esquife* (skiff). The skiff then disintegrates and its pieces are used to make another *batel*. Even the tools by which recycled boats are made mutate form, like the saw made from a sword (342).

ÁGUIA/GARÇA: BOOKISH BOATS, OR, BOATISH BOOKS

At one moment in the *Santiago*, as the beleaguered survivors of the ship reach the African village of Luranga at a time when so many are falling sick from lack of food and exhaustion, a trading contract is drawn up by Gaspar Ximenes (saved from being thrown overboard earlier by his younger brother Fernão) with some Moors for the purchase of food. This contract is written in blood: "he gave a written promise that he would comply, a promise written with the blood of one of the tenders of the sick."[22] In the metamorphoses characteristic of shipwreck, a trickle of blood issues from a body and becomes ink. The human body—the alter ego of a ship (and vice versa)—has become a pen, a stylus, an inscriber. The body produces a text as its means of salvation: the bloody text will do its job as a trading treaty and bring food and sustenance back to its origin. The blood sacrificed will be returned as vital substance. The bleeding body-text is valuable only insofar as it responds to the brutally concrete demands of survival in that its reading produces food.[23]

Bodies produce texts, so texts are another form of body, undergoing the same fortunes as ships and people. Like humans, texts may be temporarily held captive by the natives of Africa in the dynamics of negotiation and exchange typical of postdisaster sociology. In one narrative, a native brings the survivors of the Santiago letters from other Portuguese that inform them of their imminent rescue:

> [H]e brought them letters from Fernão Rodrigues Caldeira and another Portuguese and orders to take them away from there. Then he gave them the letters. One was for Diogo Rodrigues Caldeira, brother of Fernão Rodrigues, and the other for them all. (Ley 281)[24]

The letters are metonymic representations of their writers, so the text of the letter is tantamount to the bodily—and welcome—presence of other Portuguese. The native's role as medium is significant, because the successful delivery of the documents depends on the goodwill of the natives, as do so often the lives and sustenance of Portuguese castaways. Hence the Portuguese are surrendered into the hands of non-Europeans after shipwreck, as is their system of writing. Perhaps for this reason, Cardoso prefaces the delivery of the letters by noting how overjoyed the Portuguese were to see the native: "[t]his caused them all as great a

pleasure as if they had seen a Portuguese" (Ley 281).[25] This pleasure is
surely linked to the native's role as an unwitting restorer of a textual
community. The role as facilitator of Portuguese writing grants him the
aura "of a Portuguese." But these victories are as tenuous as the food
supply—Portuguese textuality hangs, as it were, by a thread of blood.

Threats to the culture of text production, like other breakages in
shipwreck narrative, are only partially realized. For if we find the draft-
ing of letters in the *S. Tomé* or the *S. João Baptista* to bespeak a preoccupation with textual productivity,[26] we also find instances like the
following in the *Águia/Garça*. The sister ships are traveling together, and
the Garça gets the worst of a storm. The imperiled passengers board the
Águia:

> After all the people in the *Garça* had been saved, Francisco Barreto
> drew up a certificate worded as follows:
>
> 'The great ship *Garça* was lost after getting as far as the Cape of
> Correntes, in twenty-five degrees Southern latitude, and she foun-
> dered through shipping much water. I, together with the gentlemen
> and other people in my own ship, saved everyone in theirs, and we
> are now continuing our voyage to Portugal with the same difficulty.
> We ask for the love of God that all faithful Christians who may learn
> of this, through this boat reaching some place where there are Por-
> tuguese, to commend us in their prayers to Our Lord, that He may
> give us a good voyage and bring us safely to Portugal.'
>
> This certificate was placed in a tube which was tightly closed and
> caulked, and they made a tall cross in the boat, to which they tied it,
> so as to keep it out of the water; and then they let the boat drive
> whither the waves would take it. God granted that it fetched up in
> the roadstead of Sofala, where Bastião de Sá was then captain, as they
> subsequently learnt when Francisco Barreto returned to winter at
> Moçambique for the second time. (*Further Selections* 42)[27]

The salvation of passengers generates a moment of textuality, one
that recalls the ludicrously formal request for help sent as a note between
the two ships we saw in chapter 2. This episode mobilizes a remarkable
image of the text released from official moorings: the text as a ship is
sent on an aimless journey, with no guarantee of its arrival. The routeless
ship may not reach any port, and the text that is part of its very architec-

ture may not reach any reader. The shipwreck crisis produces a way-wardness that implicates maritime directionality with the redaction of a text: both manifest necessitated losses of control. The ship left to the waves and the potentially readerless text recall the letters delivered by the African natives: if they reach their destinations, they will only do so accidentally.

The image of the boat-text literalizes a latent metaphoric reciprocity of ships and text that informs all HTM narratives. If a ship is a place in which texts are generated, it is also physical structure comparable to a book. Like a book, it organizes texts (*escritos* in the parlance of the ship-wreck authors) within a set of concrete enclosures where meaning, through writing, is sought and constructed. The confines of a ship are analogous to the function of the covers of a book or codex as demarca-tors of a locus of sense making. When shipwreck authors dedicate con-siderable narrative space to describing the (attempted) repair of ships, they in fact describe the incessant attempts to make meaning: to restore a ship to the control of the helm, to right it as it sinks in the middle of the ocean or in view of the shore, to patch its broken limbs and dress it again with sails are attempts to "make the ship mean" in the way it was intended, to grant the seaborne ship an active and supervisory role in the construction of a forward-moving discourse in both its navigational and narrative valences. The repairs effected on each ship of each succes-sive narrative could be thought of as the efforts to reinstate the logic and directionality of narrative lost—or threatened—in previous narratives. It is possible to read the skill of carpenters and caulkers as akin to the skill of the bookbinder who manufactures a physical object in which various *escritos* come together and are occupied by readers. There is even a simi-larity between the raw materials of books and ships: each is made of boards and cords, iron (bosses and nails); there is paper and writing in each. Sails perform a locomotive function in that they move the ship in a certain, controlled direction, much as the arranged leaves or signatures of a book suggest a certain movement through them. Both canvas and leaves are sewn together, the canvas into arrangements of sails, the leaves (paper or parchment) into quires.

Hence we can read book and ship as enclosures created and main-tained by communities, be they a maritime or a readerly community, or both. As icon of Portuguese (or European) culture in which writing is central, we could think of the ship as a figure of the archive as Roberto González Echevarría argues for it in *Myth and Archive*.[28] For González Echevarría, the archive is a repository of knowledge and the secrets of the state, an accumulation of (legal) texts, a preservation of an order of writing and reading (24); more important, it is "the process whereby texts are written" (ibid.). We might understand the beleaguered and wrecked ship as a symbol of the archive in these terms in that it represents the power and knowledge of the metropole exercised through a highly regulated redaction of texts and documents. As ships break apart, so does their authorizing and originating home culture, its power structures now disabled and useless—and this includes its historiographic discourse foundering and sinking like a ship's passengers and cargo.[29] In this reading, the boat-text sent on its way in the *Águia/Garça* may be understood as a salvage effort to retain, or minimally restore, the ship as the repository of (discursive) authority. The manuscript is sent on a haphazard journey outside of legislated, navigational action in which a ship's route is prescribed in the sailing orders or *regimento*. The manuscript in a tube is a remnant of the once-powerful Archive of the State, a source and repository of power created through navigation and writing.

The *S. Bento* sketches a vivid scenario in which the order of the archive can be read as in ruins in the broken and wrecked body of the ship. In chapter 3, recall that we observed how the S. Bento in pieces, viewed from the shore by Perestrelo and his fellow survivors, elicits an affective response because "it seemed as though we beheld relics and a piece of this, our dear homeland, from whose shelter and company . . . we were unable to separate ourselves." We also observed that this wrecked ship represents the disastrous rending to pieces of the archive. So it is that the shipwrecked vessel is the wrecked vessel of historiography, of textual authority. With the wreck of this discursive vessel also occur the wrecks of the vessel of the Crown, the vessel of hegemony and maritime supremacy, the vessel of economic and evangelical prerogative—all these ships sink and splinter on the shores of the HTM.

THE BREAKING OF WAVES

It is possible to regard the assault that a wrecked or disabled ship symbolically visits on the tradition of authority and knowledge via the archive as an inflection of the ancient idea of seafaring as an unnatural

vocation. Blumenberg ascribes a violence to seafaring owing to a violation of natural boundaries:

> the ancient suspicion that underlies the metaphorics of shipwreck:
> that there is a frivolous, if not blasphemous, moment inherent in all
> human seafaring, on a par with an offense against the invulnerability
> of the earth, the law of *terra inviolata,* which seemed to forbid . . .
> radical alterations of the relationship between land and sea. (10–11)

He concludes that the "metaphorical and the real events of transgressing
the boundary between terra firma and the sea beyond blend into each
other, like the metaphorical and the real risks of shipwreck. What drives
man to cross the high seas is at the same time what drives him to go beyond the boundary of his natural needs" (28–29).[30]

This transgression of the boundary of "natural needs" lies at the heart
of shipwreck narrative, recording as it collectively does the pursuit of
wealth born of rampant *cobiça* (avarice). Avarice is the characteristic
moral failing precipitating the dangers of the India route, and shipwreck
authors issue stern condemnations of it without cease.[31] Scientific writer
Pedro de Medina, in his *Regimiento de navegación* (1563), claims that sailing breaches a divinely ordained separation between land and sea, because "God created land for man and the sea for fish."[32] Although
Medina acknowledges that ships and navigation are a triumph of artifice
over nature, the fact remains that seafaring is not a natural phenome-
non. Humankind casts itself into a habitus not properly its own.

The violation of natural boundaries as motivated by unnatural greed
is one way the shipwreck authors rationalize the senselessness of shipwreck and repeated maritime disaster. In the *S. Tomé,* passengers wallow
in a maritime circle of hell, in a morass of divine retribution that speaks
to the presence of a wrathful deity:

> In short, everything was against them, until the ship refused to answer
> the helm and broached-to, without sails, since they were all torn. . . .
> All this night they passed in great trouble and distress, for everything
> they could see represented death. For beneath them they saw a ship
> full of water, and above them the Heavens conspired against all, for
> the sky was shrouded with the deepest gloom and darkness. The air
> moaned on every side as if it was calling out "death, death"; and as if

the water which was entering beneath them was not sufficient, that which the Heavens poured on them from above seemed as if it would drown them in another deluge. Within the ship nothing was heard but sighs, groans, shrieks, moans, and prayers to God for mercy, as it seemed that He was wroth with all of them for the sins of some who were in the ship. (*Tragic History* 57–58)[33]

The miseries and travails following wreck witness humans at odds with the natural world; in so many instances, nature itself seems to take revenge for having been violated. Manuel de Mesquita Perestrelo chronicles a relentless battle against the natural world, one where wild animals threaten the passengers at every step (and such animals do not even respect the sanctity of the dead, for they devour bodies placed in too shallow graves), or the inhospitable jungle disorients and terrifies the members of the survival march. Perestrelo speaks of their *caminho* as a "persecution," and wonders about offenses against God while the raw landscape hinders his and his companions' progress. Or, in the *S. Paulo* and the *Santiago,* beautiful coral cuts into human flesh and wounds it like poison.

The brutalities inflicted on the body constitute one form of "natural" retribution, but these are secondary compared to the mortal dangers confronting the soul as narrated in the *S. António,* dangers that appear to be a palimpsestial rehearsal (if an inadvertent one) of the mortal dangers of the devotional *cantigas.* At one point, the starving survivors ask permission of Captain Jorge d'Albuquerque Coelho to eat the bodies of the deceased. This degree of desperation is exacerbated when the survivors contemplate suicide when the captain refuses the request:

So greatly were we suffering from hunger, that some of our comrades went up to Jorge d'Albuquerque and told him that they were only too well aware that people were dying from pure starvation, while those who were still alive had nothing whatever to eat; and that since this was so, would he give them leave to eat the bodies of those that died, since the living had no other resource left. When he heard this appalling request, Jorge d'Albuquerque was pierced to the soul and his eyes streamed with tears, on seeing the state to which their misery had brought them. And he told them very sorrowfully that their request was so utterly unreasonable that it would be a

great sin and blindness to allow such a bestial desire. . . . And the
perverse enemy . . . began to employ a new and unexpected ruse
against us. . . . Seeing that neither the wildness of the waves nor the
fury of the storm had availed to finish us off, he planted a hellish
conviction in the hearts of some of our people, that since there was
no hope of them being saved or delivered from that dire peril, we
would all have to die anyway. Convinced by this evil counsel of the
faithless foe, some of them decided that since there was no chance
whatsoever of being saved . . . in order to avoid prolonging the
agony they would scuttle the ship, so as to go to the bottom more
quickly and thus end their lives and their sufferings together. (*Further Selections* 146–47)[34]

The anguish and terror of the storm-tossed ship lead the homeward-
bound colonists to consider extreme and abominable actions. The company is cast into the realm of bestial desire and taboo; their experiences
provide access to the forbidden, to the unnatural, to the perverse. The
imminent descent into cardinal sin links the *S. António* to the tradition
of understanding navigation as a violation that is simultaneously an act
of authority and knowledge in expansionism and a transgression of limits.[35] Yet Afonso Luís, the *S. António*'s author, also implicitly invokes the
unnatural as part of the repertoire of expansionist binarisms. One of the
dangers of early modern Iberian navigation is that it allows admission
into the realm of the infidel. Francisco Vaz de Almada warns that the
land of the infidels (in this case Sofala, in Africa) can contaminate the
Christian who lingers in its precincts, that "not only is the body put at
risk but also the soul, by remaining in the land of infidels where their
evil customs and ceremonies may find their way in."[36]

5

AN ILLUSTRIOUS SCHOOL OF CAUTION

ORTUGUESE SHIPWRECK LITERATURE, for all the disaster and loss of life it relates, reveals itself as remarkably vital in that it is born twice. First, the individual pamphlets appeared in the shops of booksellers; then, Gomes de Brito marshals many of them together in his anthology and gives them life again in 1735 and 1736 under the rubric of history. The *História Trágico-Marítima* marks the arrival, once and for all, of shipwreck and its textual incarnation as a cultural institution in Portugal. Gomes de Brito's anthologizing act, occurring as it does in its own historical circumstances, has a determining and lasting effect on the reading of shipwreck owing, in large part, to the dedication to volume 1 and the Inquisitional permissions for publication *(licenças)* printed in both volumes. The licenses, redacted by Inquisitional censors (some are formulaically short, others are more extensive), stand as the first, systematic critical response to shipwreck narrative, and allow us to glimpse how, when texts travel through time, they also travel through ideologies.

THE CURIOUS COLLECTOR OF SHIPWRECKS

When Bernardo Gomes de Brito sat down to organize his collection in the early years of the eighteenth century, he worked at a time when Portuguese life was undergoing significant change under D. João V, the long-reigned monarch (1706–50) who, buttressed by the wealth of the trade with Brazil, effected material and cultural modifications in Portugal guided by a desire to elevate his country to a greater international status by emulating and importing foreign ideas. (This importation was largely accomplished through the *estrangeirados,* or "foreignized people," Portuguese who lived abroad and returned to Portugal to implant models of knowledge, culture, and politics acquired elsewhere.) The king's nationalistic vision was based on a studied internationalism;[1] part of his agenda for the revivification of Portuguese culture included the founding of the Royal Academy of Portuguese History in 1720. The academy's mission, according to a decree of December 8, 1720, was to "write the ecclesiastical history of these realms, and after that everything that pertains to them and their conquests."[2] It had as its objective "solely historiographic activity" (Castelo-Branco 183). Under the favor of the king, this official historiographic institution sought to narrate anew the national past as it "proposed to restore the actions and deeds of the Portuguese to the notice of the world."[3]

With this in mind, let us turn to Gomes de Brito's dedication to D. João V in volume 1 of the HTM:

SIRE

Since Your Majesty, by your royal magnificence, became august protector of history in establishing your illustrious Academy, it is clear you permitted the fortunate historians of this century the glory of seeking your royal protection. Of such a boon I now avail myself so, with these tomes, I may place at Your Majesty's royal feet historic fragments which, by the good fortune of being dedicated to you, lose their pitiful horror. So I achieve for those vassals of the Crown (who now serve Your Majesty under a better star) the happiest port in their shipwrecks, if one not for the benefit of their lives, then for their memories. May Heaven prolong Your Majesty's life for the good fortune of this monarchy.[4]

Although Gomes de Brito wants his shipwreck project to be regarded as part of the larger historiographic renovation promoted by the monarch, his connection (if any) with the Royal Academy remains unclear. Perhaps he aspired to membership, with the HTM serving as his entry bid.[5] Even if this was not true, the presence of the king and the academy in the dedication serves an important end in the reading of shipwreck. The shipwreck tales, in Gomes de Brito's editorial vision, represent a lack of cohesion, a fracturing ("these historic fragments"), and now find integrity or wholeness as the narratives change their status from independent stories to episodes in an organized and more expansive historiographic enterprise. The act of dedication to the historical vision of the academy attenuates or erases the horror of shipwreck by rendering it as part of the official, collective memory. The shipwreck narratives' fragmentary, and fragmenting, nature is countered by reading them through the lens of the academy's integrative historiographic project. Gomes de Brito's dedication, and the arrangement of the narratives within his volumes, overturn the disruptive potential of shipwreck narrative by reinscribing it into the mastertext of Portuguese history. In this the editorial decision to arrange the narratives chronologically is important ("in which are chronologically written the shipwrecks that the ships of Portugal experienced after the Navigation to India was put into effect")[6] as it imposes a rigidly temporal frame and sequencing to them. By making them, collectively, a chronistic text (in the etymological sense of an arrangement and writing of time), Gomes de Brito neutralizes the narratives' recalcitrance to categorization and makes them obey the state-controlled march of history.[7] Even the proximity of the word *naufrágios* to the name of the monarch on the title page[8] stabilizes shipwreck by metonymic association with the Crown, and recuperates shipwreck as a uniquely Portuguese contribution, as it were, to history. To read shipwreck narratives under the symbolic and corporate figure of the king is to bestow a directionality on them by bringing them to a structured community of readers with monolithically nationalistic designs. Allying the narratives with a royally sanctioned institution of history, it might be argued, completes the round trips envisioned by the passengers of the India route forcefully aborted by disaster. The double qualifier "trágico-marítima" (tragic-maritime) inscribes this book within a tradition of universal, archetypal experiences, thereby conferring a transcendence on the narratives that minimizes or obliterates their potential to stand as records of (national) failure.

One of the mechanisms allowing for the conspicuous presence of shipwreck within the flow of national history is the notion of the curious. Among the five licenses *(licenças)* printed in the HTM's volumes,[9] two make mention of curiosity as a defining trait both of Gomes de Brito and of his work. Manuel de Sá refers to the "curious labor" ("curioso trabalho") ([§iv^a]) of the collector of shipwrecks as inaugurating "an illustrious school of caution" ("huma ilustre escola de cautelas") ([§iii^b]), and Francisco Xavier de Santa Teresa mentions the "praise-worthy curiosity of Bernardo Gomes de Brito" ("louvavel curiosidade de Bernardo Gomes de Brito") ([§§^{a}]), dubbing him some lines later the "curious, and untiring, collector of these accounts" ("curioso, e incançavel Collector destas Relaçoens") ([§§iii^a]). "Curious" and "curiosity" signal the passage of the narratives into the mentality of the late Baroque and early Enlightenment periods. For Tabucchi, "curious" means "'bizarre,' 'unusual,' 'erratic'" (30), as well as the "desire to know" (39). Yet "curious" designates not solely a desire for knowledge but also an object of knowledge, and this bears on how the inquisitors reshape the status of shipwreck within an emergent rejuvenation of the past.

In the Middle Ages, *curiositas* was an impediment to knowing. It was associated with the workings of memory as an agent of disorder and randomness, a "mental fornication" (Carruthers 83) that undermines the "mental maps and organizing structures" (ibid.) necessary for efficient cognition,[10] whereas in the Renaissance, curiosity came to be allied with wonder or the marvelous. Something that was curious combined fascination and the impulse to knowledge—something that was curious made the mind work. This is the sense described by Knauff:

> "Curiosité" and "curieux" are terms which carry a double meaning even in 17th-century usage, referring either to a desire to know or to learn something; or to a strange, wonderful and unusual occurrence or thing, the object of gawking or of collecting. "Curiosité" is both

an attitude, a tendency displayed by a subject, and directed towards others; and it is a descriptor for objects situated entirely outside the subject. (273–74)

Gomes de Brito's collection of shipwrecks in an anthology (a bookish *cabinet de curiosité*) reveals the editor's efforts to control strange and terrifying phenomena. Shipwreck, because it is such a characteristic part of the Portuguese past, is especially apt for exercising a desire for knowledge, and for bringing together uniquely Portuguese objects of knowledge.

Curiosity as an impulse to knowledge or as an inherent quality in an object of knowledge (shipwrecks, or a book of shipwrecks) identified by the inquisitors reappears in a tome less than a decade after Gomes de Brito's volume I was published (1735) in the work of another anthologist. In the prologue to his *Anno historico, diario portuguez, noticia abreviada de pessoas grandes, e cousas notaveis de Portugal* (Historic year, Portuguese calendar, and abbreviated notice of great people and notable things from Portugal) (1744), an encyclopedia in which the notable events of Portuguese history are narrated according to the days of the month, Francisco de S. Maria declares:

> I offer to the desire of the curious, I expose to the mordacity of critics, this volume that contains the first four months of the historic year and the first 120 days of the Portuguese calendar. . . . Here the curious reader will find many and various items on which he may exercise the intellect, and impart, in not a useless fashion, their application. . . . The tragic, bellicose, and political events of the past are also the rule by which present and future events should be measured and regulated. Signs from heaven, plagues, fires, shipwrecks are other such admonitions for our edification so that we will fear similar punishments.[11]

Here, the function and effect of curiosity is to incite the mind and to instruct it within the overarching frame of national history. In this instance curiosity resides with the reader and not with the object of knowledge and is understood as intellectual desire. The inquisitors in their *licenças* implicitly support Gomes de Brito's claim that his anthology erases the horror of shipwreck by ascribing the stories, and their collector, with the (edifying) label of "curious"; shipwreck, by its strangeness, promotes a drive to know and scrutinize the past in its unique and eccentric particularities.

Now let us turn to the fact of collection itself. The curious editor's grouping together of accounts that first appeared as discrete, printed units forms part of the campaign to inscribe shipwreck within the monarch-centered canon of Portuguese history and writing. The pamphlets, under Gomes de Brito's hand, collectively constitute, and participate in, a historiographic frame narrative through a chronological principle of arrangement. Gomes de Brito creates an encompassing order for the narratives that was lacking when they first appeared as *folhetos* and thus allows for a directed reading. The narratives' incorporation into the rational, historiographic structure of empire is comparable to the marching order of Sepúlveda's plodding column in the *S. João* in that the sequencing of texts is tantamount to placing them on a symbolic march.

The printing press, and the book as a physical object, each contribute to the fashioning of shipwreck and shipwreck narrative as monuments of national history. The printing press works as an agent of the common good, facilitator of the "bem público" continually espoused by the shipwreck authors as they claim a didactic (practical or religious) use for the narratives, and now, as a book shipwreck becomes part of the consolidation of D. João V's vision of national, historiographic recuperation. Shipwreck narratives in the eighteenth century do not simply form part of the march of Portuguese history—to a large extent, they define it.

As ephemera, the shipwreck pamphlets were subjected to the vicissitudes of time and circumstance, much like the doomed ships in their pages, always hovering on the brink of extinction. Gomes de Brito, by imposing a codicological form on them, imposes a recoverability and a perpetuity unavailable to the single, unprotected *folheto*. By situating the pamphlets within a different sector of print culture, the HTM anthologist invests the narratives with a trackable itinerary and domesticates them in that he unifies a company of dissonant and disperse voices under his editorial hand and confers a definitive shape on the narratives through uniform typography, a title page, a table of contents, and sequential pagination. Francisco Xavier de S. Teresa declares in his *licença* that "this book, after being printed, will without a doubt serve as a better rutter for all the navigators in the seas of India."[12] The loss of

directionality endemic in the *discurso do naufrágio* is here startlingly restored by the printed book of shipwrecks. As the individual pamphlets
testify to the disoriented meanderings of shipwreck, to the loss of itinerary and route, the printed book bestows once again a *caminho* on the
seas of wreck. The inquisitor proposes, ironically, that a book of shipwrecks will guide and take sailors to where they want to go.

So it is that the physical attributes of the book work toward anchor-
ing these stories of waywardness, loss, and the instability occasioned by
wreck and disaster. The codex permits the narratives to come into contact with a different reading public, under different circumstances. The
authorizing presence of the Inquisition in the two volumes reflects
Gomes de Brito's already inquisitorial stance toward shipwreck narrative. As he assembles the narratives, he exerts power over them from
above, coercing them into his own ideological project. In the action of
the anthologist, the ship-as-book metaphor is completed: Gomes de
Brito's books reconstitute the integrity of the ship-text, making it whole
again once and for all. The editor runs an ideological thread through the
narratives as the binder runs a cord through the quires. Shipwreck narrative is henceforth a state-authorized book, the terrified passengers and
crews having at last found a "happy port" ("felis porto").

A HAPPY PORT

When Gomes de Brito claims in his dedication that the vassals of the
crown of yesteryear have now found a home, he implies that the shipwrecks have been restored definitively to the state, that their disruptive
potential to the smooth flow of national history is now gone. The shipwreck narratives serve as examples, if tragic ones, of Portugal's historic
and heroic past. Gomes de Brito's anthology inducts shipwreck literature into the historiographic canon. The licenses written by the Inquisitional readers and printed in the HTM confirm and elaborate on this,
and are the topic of our final comments.

The *licenças* printed in the HTM are, as I remarked earlier, the first
series of critical articles written on Portuguese shipwreck narrative that
reflect the preoccupations of their authors working within a given cultural and historical milieu. Even a cursory reading of the licenses reveals
that the inquisitors were enthusiastic and perceptive readers of shipwreck narrative, and their texts are learned, and frequently eloquent.

This is not to say, of course, that there is no ideological agenda motivating the readings put forth in the licenses and the granting of the imprimatur; quite the contrary, since Inquisitional censorship during the life of the Royal Academy of Portuguese History worked from within the academy's very bosom (Ribeiro 170) and hence was a mouthpiece of the state. But the Inquisition committed no greater sin in this regard than any other ideologically driven institution, so perhaps it is better for us to consider it, in its role as an arm of the monarchy, as a promoter of ideologies and political agendas as well as a suppressant. Although it would be wrong to deny that the readers of the Inquisition did not want to assure that shipwreck be read in a predetermined manner, it would also be wrong to view their work as the product of frenzied, zealous ideologues writing outside the bounds of reason and accountability. If this had been the case, the vision of shipwreck promulgated by the licenses would not have survived over the centuries, a vision that influences the reading of shipwreck down to our own day.

Such a vision is based on shipwreck survival as an exemplification of heroism underwritten by the horrors detailed in the stories of individual wrecks. Writes Manuel de Sá: "Of the tragic events to be read in the accounts of these unfortunate ones, there is much that glorifies the heroism of those magnanimous spirits."[13] He then invokes the Baroque conceit of the theater of history, noting that "this book . . . in the theater of history plays a truly tragic role."[14] José da Assunção shares Manuel de Sá's perspective on the hero-making experience of suffering by acknowledging the "indomitable men, of whom special mention is made for us in the present history."[15] He adds the further distinction that virtue is increased in the face of adversity and adduces a number of citations from Latin authors to this effect. Francisco Xavier de S. Teresa joins in the spirit by declaring that the Portuguese shipwrecks supersede the experiences of such figures as Ulysses, Francis Drake, Thomas Candish, or even Portugal's own Fernão Mendes Pinto, author of the *Peregrinação*: "if we reflect on it well, the storms that caused the horrible shipwrecks exceed in their horror the events of all those memorable storms that Virgil describes [here follows an enumeration of classical tempests]."[16] The aggrandizement of Portuguese shipwrecks against the background of antiquity resuscitates a Renaissance practice, now in the service of an Enlightenment excavation of the past. History, heroism, and tragedy:

this triumvirate of ideas will inform HTM criticism from the eighteenth century on.

On a general level, the tragically heroic aspect of shipwreck, besting as it does centuries of precedents, is recognized in the tales themselves. Yet it is the repeated preoccupation on the part of the inquisitors, implicit in their licenses, of the disruptive potential of the collective pages of shipwreck within the imperial (or national) historiographic mastertext that defines the licenses' signal contribution to shipwreck criticism; that is, the inquisitors hint at an understanding of shipwreck narrative that I have elaborated in this study but it is one they attempt to neutralize. Although Manuel de Sá and his fellow inquisitors tacitly acknowledge the disruptive or problematic chapter in national history shipwreck narrative represents, their intent is to effect a harmony and cohesion among the texts, to bring them safely and in a controlled fashion to the shore of a seamless exemplarity by dint of a national suffering and heroism (overseen by stern and merciful Providence) that allows Portuguese history to surpass grand moments of the classical past. They endeavor, ultimately, to gloss over the breaches and ruptures of shipwreck, to steer these unruly narratives to a "happy port" under a "better star." The task the inquisitors set for themselves is reminiscent of Foucault's comment on the function of discontinuity in discursive fields of knowledge: "discontinuity is one of those great accidents that create cracks not only in the geology of history, but also in the simple fact of the statement; it emerges in its historical irruption; what we try to examine is the incision that it makes, that irreducible—and often very tiny—emergence" (*Archaeology of Knowledge* 28). The inquisitors identify, and try to suture, the incision.

The notion of shipwreck as a divine warning, and the benefit to be derived from heeding it, appears in the prologue of the *S. João* and reappears in all of the *licenças,* including the ones scattered through the third volume.[17] However brutal the realities of shipwreck may be, in the end they yield a "sweet lesson" ("suave lição"), in Júlio Francisco's words—the lesson of God's mercy to survivors, the "expressions of His ire, [that] are also gifts of His love" (José da Assunção).[18] The sweet lesson of providential grace acquired by reading Gomes de Brito's narratives in the safety of our armchairs puts us in mind of the safety of the spectator position that underlies Blumenberg's philosophical excursus on Lucretius's shipwreck metaphor. For the Inquisition, reading (and therefore writing) about shipwreck mollifies the horror of disaster.

> This second volume of the *Historia Tragico-Maritima* . . . which Mr. Bernardo Gomes de Brito curiously proffers and intends to make manifest to everyone through the printing press, becomes credible (through this publicity) as a mirror, in which each and every one of those who live in the tempestuous sea of this world contemplate themselves every day. (José da Assunção)[19]

The stories speak to all readers and prompt contemplation by serving as a metaphor for worldly and daily life. This ratification of shipwreck would not be possible, according to José Troyano, were it not for the narratives' collective presence manifested by the volumes of the HTM, a bringing together that Troyano likens to a scene in the *Aeneid*:

> These [authors] left us Portuguese shipwrecks printed on the leaves of this book, as the ancient shipwrecked [sailors] did on the bitter leaves of the olive tree where, in testimony of their gratitude, they hung the remnants of their shipwreck, as Virgil observes: *Haply here had stood a bitter-leaved wild olive, sacred to Faunus, a tree revered of old by mariners, whereon, when saved from the waves, they were wont to fasten their gifts to the god of Laurentum and hang up their votive raiment.* What other thing do we read in the bitter leaves of this book, the olive tree made symbolic, than the remains of a shipwreck.[20]

The HTM is an offering to God, like the votive gifts in Virgil's poem. There could be no more cogent statement about the significance and symbolic ramifications of anthologizing the shipwreck narratives. Although Troyano in his comments may speak to the value of the narratives as proper "literary" works (Tabucchi 34), his *licença* ultimately seeks to heal the rupture in historical certainty effected by the narratives. He begins by insisting on the wholeness and cohesion the HTM confers on the originally independent and autochthonous stories. Additionally, Troyano recognizes, as Gomes de Brito does in his dedication, that the narratives are fragments *(despojos)*, but are made whole by the form of the book and the public scrutiny the codicological form invites. Both the Mantuan's tree and Gomes de Brito's books serve as frames for display, as organizational principles by which the apparent arbitrariness of

wreck and survival is overturned by a volitional act of ordered arrangement. The inquisitors echo the desperate belief voiced by the shipwreck
authors that shipwreck is ultimately out of the hands of humankind and
that the mystery of death and disaster is an unknowable part of the divine will. In this sense God is a shipwreck author also, the primordial
impetus behind the shipwreck narrative enterprise as Ecclesiasticus proclaims and as José da Assunção infers by referring to God as the "com-
piler of this volume" ("compositor deste volume").

But this acknowledgment of the divine hand really does not move
beyond what any of the shipwreck writers themselves say. In this reading
the tales are more like parables than historical documents until the
inquisitors demonstrate the benefit of historical hindsight. True, these
accounts boast a tragic exemplarity, they are "funereal spectacles," but
most important—and here surfaces the key ideological notion—they
are now a consecrated part of the prophetic march of Christian imperialism. The inquisitors explicitly bring the shipwreck stories into the center of expansionist policy from the troublesome margins surrounding
such a policy that the narratives created and inhabited until the eighteenth century. Virgil's olive tree, in this light, is an apt comparison because it grows in a canonical text of Roman imperialism. The end, the
happy port of the shipwreck stories, is absorption into a seamless history.
Júlio Francisco writes:

> As the events that compose this book are so pitiful and so unhappy
> in their wide variety, and the desire that the spirit immediately feels
> at the beginning of any one of them to see the end to which it ulti-
> mately comes, all of this makes this book's lesson so sweet and so
> pleasing that it permits no interruption; even the brief time it took
> me to read (the book) seemed briefer still given the sweetness of its
> lesson.[21]

Francisco's sweet lesson is one that is also "very useful" ("utilissimo") in
that it allows seafarers to conceive of a "holy fear of death" ("santo temor
da morte"). But the Horatian precept has a further application: in addition to the sweet usefulness that all shipwreck narrative delivers, a usefulness that either incites a holy fear of death or provides solace about
the mysterious presence of God's guiding hand, there is also a readerly
recuperation and smoothing over of a disruptive and disrupting past.

Reading the assembled narratives from start to finish is a relatively brief activity, one that stands in ironic contrast to the considerable chronological span represented by the various accounts. Shipwreck collapses chronology when the narratives of it exist as a book, and this collapse erases rupture. Francisco tells us that he was unable to put the book down and would admit of no interruption during his reading of it; his is a smooth readerly voyage that contrasts with the chaotic experience of shipwreck, and it is one that supplies the *fim* or end to narratives that inherently lack closure. Hence Francisco's uninterrupted reading nullifies the power of the narratives to enact an interruption in the general reading of history. Francisco grants an equation between voyage and text via reading: that is to say, because the reading of the text is successful, issuing forth a sweet and useful lesson in uninterrupted fashion, so the voyages contained in the pages of the HTM are successful as well.

THE MINISTERS OF MEMORY

*T*HERE IS A DARK KNOWLEDGE that Joseph de Cabreira, captain of the N. S. de Belém and author of the story recounting her wreck, wishes his readers to acquire: how to shipwreck. He writes his tale more with haste than with care—"almost a draft" ("quasi em borrão")—as he races against the clock to write the account requested by officials in Madrid (Cabreira writes as Philip II is king of Spain and Portugal) before it fades entirely from memory. Acutely aware of the passing of time, his shipwreck pen reaches back to his past to trace, in fading yet still discernible lines, "such barbarous climates, with so few hopes of life" ("tão barbaros climas, com tão poucas esperanças de vida" [Pereira 10:9]).

Cabreira's words to his reader join the multitude of voices running through the shipwreck stories, voices that call out, plaintively, like

Perestrelo's lament on the beach, before time threatens to silence them. They cling to the shipwreck story like a survivor to a plank. It is what they bring home, what they offer to posterity. Perestrelo, for his part, offers the "voyage, shipwreck, exile, and end" ("viagem, naufrágio, desterro e fim" [219]) of his captain and his company. He, along with the other authors, forms a choir of existentialists who contemplate experiences of extremity, their contemplations now classic texts in that they are always the same and forever new. "Remember me" seems to be the dying echo of the voices in the wrecks in Gomes de Brito's books.

And what of Gomes de Brito's books? The remaining volumes of the *História Trágico-Marítima* that Gomes de Brito had reputedly prepared but never saw the light of print remain, probably, lost to us for good. We can speculate, as some have done, on why the curious collector of shipwrecks never published them: Was he weary with the bureaucratic processes and delays of the Inquisition and publication? Was his anthology his failed bid to become a member of the Royal Academy of Portuguese History? Whatever the answer, Gomes de Brito's shipwreck project shipwrecked. Two pieces of it floated across the oceans of time to us, with a third, similar piece not far behind. So we take them from the water and we read.

NOTES

PROLOGUE

1. For an encyclopedic survey of the presence of the S. João story in Portuguese letters through the twentieth century see Martins, *Naufrágio de Sepúlveda* 54–168; in addition, consult Ares Montes, Barchiesi, "Un tema portoghese," Duffy 44–45, Garcia, Miraglia, Moser, "Dois dramas," Pinho, and Pögl. Pagliaro studies a seventeenth-century Latin text printed in Italy recounting the exemplary story of Manuel and Leonor. Notable reincarnations of the story are Camões (see chapter 1), the allegorical epic by Corte-Real, the eighteenth-century tragedy *Successos de Sepulveda* attributed to Nicolau Luís (for brief comments on this play, see Barchiesi, "'Os sucessos de Sepúlveda'"), and Francisco de Contreras's *Nave Trágica de la India de Portugal* (1624), dedicated to Lope de Vega (for comments, see Abad). The *S. João,* as well as several other of the Portuguese narratives, appear on premodern lists of books about Portuguese expansion

and exploration. For further information, see Rogers's bibliographic study *(Europe Informed)* of four of these inventories.

2. On the *carreira da Índia*, see Ames (esp. ch. 4); Boxer, *From Lisbon to Goa, Tragic History* 1–30, *Portuguese Seaborne* 205–20, and "Some Second Thoughts"; Cortesão; Diffie and Winius, esp. 198–206; Godinho, ch. 9; Guinote, Frutuoso, and Lopes; Matos and Thomaz; Russell-Wood, *Portuguese Empire,* ch. 2, and *Portugal and the Sea* 42–55. In addition to the mercantile aspects of empire, the Portuguese presence in India and the east was also vigorously missionary; see Alden for an in-depth study of the Jesuits abroad. Pérez-Mallaína provides numerous details about daily life on board sixteenth-century ships making the regular voyage between Spain and the Americas (the *carrera de Indias*); also see this author's *El hombre frente al mar* for Spanish interpretations of New World shipwrecks. For a listing and synopsis of *carreira da Índia* ships between 1497 and 1653, see the modern edition of a British Library manuscript (without indication of date) by Maldonado.

3. McAlister further notes that the "richest component of Portugal's Old World empire was the *Estado da India*" (251).

4. Blumenberg's monograph traces a history of the shipwreck metaphor in philosophical thought.

5. See, for instance, Deperthes, Huntress (*Narratives of Shipwrecks* and *A Checklist*), and Neider. For a catalog of American shipwreck narratives of the seventeenth and eighteenth centuries, see Donahue 120–34. Donahue and Lincoln offer studies of the English-language narratives.

6. See Calvo-Stevenson, ch. 2, for a treatment of classical and Christian shipwreck stories.

7. See Margarido, "Une incursion," for comments about the pamphlets from the perspective of textual criticism.

8. The biographical information on Gomes de Brito is scant: Barbosa Machado's brief entry in his *Bibliotheca Lusitana* (1741) provides us with the editor's birth date (May 20, 1688), the names of his parents, and the observation that he "didn't attend the schools, as nature had bestowed on him a good memory and sound understanding" ("naõ frequentou as escolas, como a natureza o dotasse de feliz memoria, e boa comprehensaõ" [532]). Silva adds that Gomes de Brito was still living in 1759 (*Diccionario* 377). Barbosa Machado claims that another three volumes of the HTM were ready for the press, but, so far as can be ascertained, these remaining volumes were never printed. According to Francisco de S. Maria's *Anno historico* (1744), a historical compilation almost exactly contemporaneous with the HTM, the first shipwrecks of the *carreira da Índia* were suffered by four ships of Pedro Álvares de Cabral's fleet in 1500 (2:114).

9. I consider this third volume as fully situated within the shipwreck narrative enterprise, regardless of its editorial provenance, so it should be understood that my use of "HTM" includes the third-volume narratives. For a representative discussion of the "apocryphal" nature of the third volume, see Boxer, "An Introduction" 74–77.

10. Duffy (36–39) offers general comments on Portuguese eighteenth-century string literature. For a collection of ship and shipwreck-related texts of this type, see Palma-Ferreira. Cesariny's anthology contains examples of Portuguese string literature of all kinds through the nineteenth century.

11. "gloriar a heroicidade daquelles espiritos magnanimos" (Tabucchi 29). Tabucchi reprints the licenses from the first and second volumes.

12. "Ó mar salgado, quanto do teu sal / São lágrimas de Portugal! / . . . / Quem quere passar além do Bojador / Tem que passar além da dor." The English translation is that of Zenith, *Fernando Pessoa* 278.

I. A SHIPWRECKFUL SHIP

1. For studies of the cultural and literary aspects of the Learned Monarch's reign that was characterized by a fluency between Christian, Muslim, and Jewish intellectuals, see the studies by Márquez Villanueva.

2. I use Mettmann's edition and numbering of the texts. The "shipwreck" *cantigas* are 9, 33, 36, 112, 172, 236, 267, 313, 339, and 383. According to Snow ("'Cantando'"), "[the 360 Marian miracle tales] of the *CSM [Cantigas de Santa Maria]* derived initially from Latin prose versions of Marian miscellanies which served Alfonso and his collaborators for their subsequent transposition to verse and to the Galician-Portuguese language" (62–63). On Alfonso as the sole author of the *Cantigas,* see Snow, "Alfonso" 124.

3. "Sedia-m' eu na ermida de San Simion / e cercaron-mi as ondas, que grandes son: / en atendend' o meu amigo, / en atendend' o meu amigo! // Estando na ermida ant' o altar, / [e] cercaron-mi as ondas grandes do mar: / en atendend' o meu amigo, / en atendend' o meu amigo! // E cercaron-mi as ondas, que grandes son, / non ei [i] barqueiro, nen remador: / en atendend' o meu amigo, / en atendend' o meu amigo! // E cercaron-mi as ondas do alto mar, / non ei [i] barqueiro, nen sei remar: / en atendend' o meu amigo, / en atendend' o meu amigo! // Non ei i barqueiro, nen remador, / morrerei fremosa no mar maior: / en atendend' o meu amigo, / en atendend' o meu amigo! // Non ei [i] barqueiro, nen sei remar, / morrerei fremosa no alto mar: / en atendend' o meu amigo, / en atendend' o meu amigo!" (translation in Fowler 84).

4. For readers who wish to consult this rich poetic corpus firsthand, see Brea. English translations of many of the poems can be found in Fowler, Jensen,

and Zenith *(113 Galician-Portuguese Troubadour Poems)*. For a compilation of criticism on the Galician-Portuguese lyric, see Wright.

5. Henrique Dias, at the conclusion of the *S. Paulo* (235), paraphrases this psalm as his authority for maritime suffering as punishment for sin.

6. "La bendicta Virgen es estrella clamada, / Estrella de los mares, guiona deseada, / Es de los marineros en las cuitas guardada, / Ca quando essa veden, es la nave guiada" (9).

7. "La Gloriosa me guie que lo pueda complir, / Ca yo non me trevria en ello a venir" (12).

8. In this and following translations of Alfonso's *Cantigas* I use Kulp-Hill's texts, except that here I insert the first line of the refrain systematically throughout the translation as indicated in Mettmann's edition. I have also modified Kulp-Hill's translation of "en mui gran coita" (l. 23 of original, l. 15 of translation), "in grave danger," to read "in great affliction." The original text of the *cantiga* is: "Esta é da nave que andava en perigoo do mar, e os que andavan en ela chamaron Santa Maria de Vila-Sirga, e quedou logo a tormenta. // *Ali u todo-los santos | non an poder de põer | consello, pono a Virgen, | de que Deus quiso nacer.* // Ca razon grand' e dereito | é de mais toste prestar / sa graça ca d'outro santo, | pois que Deus quiso fillar / sa carn' e fazer-se ome | por nos per ela salvar, / e feze-a de vertudes | font' e deu-lle su poder. / *Ali u todo-los santos | non an poder de põer.* . . . // E poren dizer-vos quero | dela un miragr', e sei / que loaredes seu nome; | aynda vos mais direi: / connoceredes de certo | que sabença do gran Rei, / seu Fillo, de pran á ela | por tal miragre fazer. / *Ali u todo-los santos | non an poder de põer.* . . . // Aqueste miragre fezo, | assi com' aprendi eu, / a Virgen Santa Maria | de Vila-Sirga con seu / poder; e parad' y mentes | e ren non vos seja greu, / ca eu de loar seus feitos | ei sabor e gran prazer. / *Ali u todo-los santos | non an poder de põer.* . . . // Hũa nave periguada | andava, com' aprendi, / pelo mar en gran tormenta, | e quanta gent' era y / estavan en mui gran coita; | e, assi com' eu oý, / a nav' era ja quebrada. | Des i o mar a crecer / *Ali u todo-los santos | non an poder de põer.* . . . // Começou tan feramente | e engrossar cada vez, / e volvendo-s' as arẽas; | des i a noite sse fez / cona tormenta mui forte, | negra ben como o pez, / demais viian da nave | muitos a ollo morrer. / *Ali u todo-los santos | non an poder de põer.* . . . // E porende braadavan | e chamavan Sennor Deus, / e San Pedr' e Santiago, | San Nicolas, San Mateus, / e santos muitos e santas, | outorgando que romeus / de grado seus seerian | se lles quisesse valer. / *Ali u todo-los santos | non an poder de põer.* . . . // Todos en perigoo eran | e en gran coita mortal, / e ben cuidavan que fossen | mortos, non ouves[s] y al; / mais ũu crerigo que era | y, pois viu a coita tal / e oyra dos miragres | da Santa Virgen dizer / *Ali u todo-los santos | non an poder de põer.* . . . // Que ela en Vila-Sirga | fez e faz a quantos van / y mercee e ajuda | pedir das

coitas que an, / des i das enfermidades | son ben guaridos de pran, / o seu corp'
e os da nave | lle foi logo offrecer. / *Ali u todo-los santos* | *non an poder de
põer.* . . . // E diz: "Varões, chamemos | ora de bon coraçon / a Virgen Santa
Maria | de Vila-Sirga, e non / se faça end' om' afora, | e peçamos-lle perdon, / ca
a ssa vertude santa | no-nos á de falecer." / *Ali u todo-los santos* | *non an poder de
põer.* . . . // E os gẽollos ficaron | como poderon mellor, / e o crerigo dizendo:
"Madre de nostro Sennor, / pois guaan[n]as de teu Fillo | perdon ao pecador, / a
nossos erros non cates | por mercee; mas doer / *Ali u todo-los santos* | *non an
poder de põer.* . . . // *Te* queras de nos, coitados, | e valla-nos o teu ben / e a ta
virgĩidade, | per que ss' o mundo manten. / Acorre-nos, Sennor bõa, | pois poder
ás end' e sen, / ca sen ti no-nos podemos | desta coita deffender. / *Ali u todo-los
santos* | *non an poder de põer.* . . . // Pois que tu en Vila-Sirga | aos cegos lume dás
/ e ressuscita-los mortos | pela vertude que ás, / acorre-nos, Virgen santa, | ca
non cuidamos a cras / chegar; mais tu esta coita | nos podes toda toller." / *Ali u
todo-los santos* | *non an poder de põer.* . . . // O crerigo, pois diss' esto, | os ollos a
ceo alçou / e logo de mui bon grado | "Salve Regina" cantou / a onrra da Virgen
Madr'; e | hũa poomba entrou / branca en aquela nave, | com' a neve sol caer. /
Ali u todo-los santos | *non an poder de põer.* . . . // E a nav' alumeada | aquela ora
medes / foi toda con craridade; | e cada ũu enpres / a fazer sas orações | aa
Sennor mui cortes, / des i todos começaron | o seu nom' a bẽeizer. / *Ali u todo-
los santos* | *non an poder de põer.* . . . // [E] o mar tornou mui manso, | e a noit'
escrareceu, / e a nav' en otro dia | en salvo porto prendeu, / e cada ũu dos da
nave, | assi como prometeu / offerta a Vila-Sirga, | e non quise falecer. / *Ali u
todo-los santos* | *non an poder de põer.* . . . // E da offerta fezeron | ũu calez mui
grand' assaz / que o crerigo adusse | a Vila-Sirga, u faz / a Virgen muitos mira-
gres, | assi com' a ela praz. / E porende lle roguemos | que nos faça ben viver. /
Ali u todo-los santos | *non an poder de põer.* . . .*"*

9. The relation of *coita/tormenta* (affliction/storm), *door* (pain), and *mar*
(sea) as premises for Mary's intervention underlies other shipwreck *cantigas*,
such as 339, which begins: "For she gives aid in trouble and grief and pain to the
one who calls on Her and comes to the rescue in storms at sea, about which I
wish to relate a miracle" (Kulp-Hill 412) ("Ca acorre en coit' e en pesar / e en
door a quena vai chamar, / e acorre nas tormentas do mar; / ond' un miragre
quero retraer").

10. Kolve's chapter 7, "The Rudderless Ship and the Sea," a densely illus-
trated study of textual and iconographic images of the ship as church, offers
many points of contact with Alfonso's poems. Goedde reminds us that "[f]rom
late antiquity the Ship of the Church was among the most familiar nautical
metaphors" (39).

11. "Mais pela costeira do gran mar d'Espanna / *ind'* aquela nave con mui

gran companna, / levantou-s' o mar con tormenta tamanna. . . . // Levantou sas
ondas fortes feramente / sobr' aquela nave, que aquela gente / cuidou y morrer. . . . // E o mercador eno bordo da nave / estava enton encima dũa trave,
/e hũa onda vẽo fort' e mui grave / que lle deu [no] peit', e no mar foi deita-
do. . . . // A nav' alongada foi, se Deus me valla, / del hũa gran peça pelo mar,
sen falla; / mai-lo demo, que senpre nosco traballa, / quisera que morress' y
log' affogado. . . . // El andand' assi en aquela tormenta, / nenbrou-sse da
Virgen. . . . // "Nenbra-te, Sennor, que t'ei eu prometudo / d'ir aa ta casa, *est' é*
ben sabudo; / mas tu dos coitados esforç' e escudo, / val-me, Sennor, ca muit'
and' atormentado."

12. "e rogaron / a aquel cuja nav' era | que as levass', e punnaron / d'entrar
mui toste na nave. | Mais foi tan grand' a pressura . . . // D'y entrar, e en queren-
do | sobir per hũa escaeyra / do batel e[n] essa nave, | sobiu a filla primeyra- /
mente, e depois a madre | cuidou a seer arteyra / de sobir tost', e na agua | caeu
con sa vestidura."

13. This miraculous passage through water as proof of Mary's intercession
also appears in Berceo's shipwreck:

> . . . [T]hey saw a traveler come out of the sea,
> it seemed that he was a wretched pilgrim.
>
> When he came to them, it was on the shore,
> all knew him, he was the one who had jumped,
> they all crossed themselves, "How, in what way
> did he remain alive in the sea one whole hour?" . . .
>
> The pilgrim said . . .
> "When I tried to jump out of the big ship,
> for it was clear it was going to sink,
> I saw I could not save myself from death;
> I began to say, 'Help me, Holy Mary!'. . .
>
> She was swift, She brought a good cloth,
> it was a cloth of value, never did I see its equal;
> She threw it over me, She said, 'No harm will come to you;
> believe that you fell asleep or lay in a bath.'" (Mount and Cash 111–12)

(Vidieron de la mar essir el un peregrino, / Semeiava que era romeruelo
mesquino. // Quando vino a ellos, que fué en la ribera, / Conocieronlo todos
que el que salió era; / Santiguaronse todos; como por qual manera / Fincó en el
mar vivo una ora sennera // Disso el peregrino. . . . // "Quando de la gran nave
quisse fuera salir, / Ca parecie por oio que se querie somir, / Vedia que de

muerte non podía guarir: / ¡Valme Sancta Maria! empecé a deçir // . . . Luego fo ella presta, adusso un buen panno, / Panno era de precio, nunqua vid su calanno: / Echómelo de suso, disso: 'Non prendrás danno: / Cuenta que te dormiste e que ioguist en vanno.'") (141–42).

14. *Cantiga* 112: "for they saw that the ship was full / of water mixed with sand" ("ca viron a nave chēa / d'agua volta con arēa); 236: "one day the galley chanced to break to pieces on a rock" ("mas un dia foi assi / que sse foi en un penedo l a galea espeçar"); 339: "[the ship's] bottom split open, and it filled with water" ("hūa nave . . . / pelo fondo s'abriu / assi que muita d'agua foi coller").

15. "Ca ouve gran tormenta, l que o masto foi britado / e a vea toda rota; l e el se viu tan coitado / que prometeu [que] se vivo l ao porto arribado / fosse, que romeu en Salas l vel a santos seus altares."

16. My thanks to David Haberly for this formulation.

17. See Kolve's figure 138 (310) for a fifteenth-century painting depicting Christ crucified on the mast and crossbeam of a ship. Goedde observes that "we . . . encounter in patristic theology an identification of Christ with Odysseus, for in his voyage to eternity Christ was willingly nailed to the mast of his ship (mast and yard form a cross), just as Odysseus was tied to a mast to escape the Sirens" (39).

18. This vertical vectoring of space is everywhere apparent in the miniatures of the *Códice rico*: for instance, the numerous long, tall columns surmounted by Romanesque arches that frame individual scenes of so many *cantigas,* or spears held upright literally pointing to heaven, or the upward sweep of the walls of buildings. The *Códice rico* illuminator in this way works the salvific trajectory of each *cantiga*'s story into the visual field. Of relevance is Burke's observation: "Ancient and medieval thought took this sublunary world as an image of that which is above. This vertical mirroring that occurs between heaven and earth would also have a kind of horizontal counterpart below—this earthly realm would be itself a place of reflections. The medieval sense of hierarchy in effect lent itself to such a presentation" (19–20).

19. "E tivemos todos nestas miserias, que fora castigo de Deos apartarem-se as naos inimigas de nós, porque tinhamos por cousa nunca acontecida vir uma nao sem leme, nem vellas de tāo longe em partes tāo tormentosas a porto algum. No que se vio ser manifestamente milagre da Virgem, como acima digo" (Pereira 9:12).

20. "E vendo Nuno Velho a veneração que faziam à Santíssima Cruz mandou a um carpinteiro que de uma árvore que junto dele estava (ditosa e bem nascida naquela Cafraria, pois de um ramo seu se fez o sinal da nossa salvação) fizesse uma Cruz. . . . Triunfo foi este da Sagrada Cruz digno de se festejar à

imitação dos de Constantino e Heráclio, porque se aqueles cristianíssimos e devotos emperadores libertaram a verdadeira de seus inimigos . . . esta (imagem daquela) foi . . . levantada e arvorada no meio da Cafraria, centro da gentilidade, da qual hoje está triunfando. E pois que abraçado com este doce madeiro se salvou o mundo do seu naufrágio, quererá Deus Nosso Senhor alumiar o entendimento destes gentios, para que abraçando-se com esta fiel Cruz que lhes ficou se salvem da perdição e cegueira em que vivem" (Águas 2:162–63).

21. "fomos a um mato, e em nome de nossa Senhora da Natividade benzemos as arvores, fazendo-lhe todos voto de que se nos trouxesse a salvamento a qualquer porto da outra banda do Cabo de Boa Esperança, de lhe vendermos o navio, e o procedido delle traze-lo a este reino para as freiras de Santa Martha" (Pereira 10:43).

22. "Pero dexemos las velas, que en el son más de culpar que la madera de los árboles . . . pues dellas se haçen los navios é másteles y entenas dellos" (13:245).

23. The presence of the *Libro de los naufragios* in Oviedo's text is problematic for critics. On the one hand, Calvo-Stevenson suggests that it establishes "a sense of closure for the otherwise open-ended *Historia*" (171); on the other hand, Kohut finds it to be fundamentally incoherent, manifesting an "ambiguous and even contradictory formulation of [Oviedo's] intentions" (367) that seems to stand in ideological opposition to Oviedo's (official) historiographic position (371).

24. "En tormenta vivimos; muramos en puerto" (13:247).

25. "Antes, em vossas naus vereis, cada ano, / Se é verdade o que meu juízo alcança, / Naufrágios, perdições de toda sorte, / Que o menor mal de todos seja a morte!" I provide canto, stanza, and sometimes verse numbers following the citations of the English translation. These are identical in the original (the Portuguese edition of the poem cited is that of Ramos).

26. "Outro também virá, de honrada fama, / Liberal, cavaleiro, enamorado, / E consigo trará a fermosa dama / Que Amor por grão mercê lhe terá dado. / Triste ventura e negro fado os chama / Neste terreno meu, que, duro e irado, / Os deixará dum cru naufrágio vivos, / Pera verem trabalhos excessivos. // Verão morrer com fome os filhos caros, / Em tanto amor gèrados e nacidos; / Verão os Cafres, ásperos e avaros, / Tirar à linda dama seus vestidos; / Os cristalinos membros e preclaros / À calma, ao frio, ao ar verão despidos, / Despois de ter pisada, longamente, / Cos delicados pés a areia ardente. // E verão mais os olhos que escaparem / De tanto mal, de tanta desventura, / Os dous amantes míseros ficarem / Na férvida e implacabil espessura. / Ali, despois que as pedras abrandarem / Com lágrimas de dor, de mágoa pura, / Abraçados, as almas soltarão / Da fermosa e misérrima prisão."

27. "Que eu polo rosto angélico apertava, / Não fiquei homem, não, mas mudo e quedo / E, junto dum penedo, outro penedo!"

28. "Converte-se-me a carne em terra dura; / Em penedos os ossos se fizeram; / Estes membros, que vês, e esta figura / Por estas longas águas se estenderam. / Enfim, minha grandíssima estatura / Neste remoto Cabo converteram / Os Deuses; e, por mais dobradas mágoas, / Me anda Thetis cercando destas águas."

29. Three recent studies (Banks, Lipking, and Quint [ch. 3]) consider the ambiguities of interpretation prompted by Adamastor, in particular as they relate to the forces of nature and the African subaltern.

30. Adamastor's momentary release from his telluric prison to speak with extraordinary travelers has a Dantesque flavor to it in an engraving illustrating a 1776 French translation of the poem (see Figure 5).

31. See chapter 3 for further analysis.

32. Thanks to Nicola Trowbridge Cooney's seminar essay for suggesting this point.

33. Leonor's nudity and death negatively prefigure the vital—and orgiastic—happiness experienced by the Portuguese sailors on the Ilha dos Amores (Island of Love) in canto IX. Notes Quint: "Adamastor and his dire prophecy are . . . symbolically connected to the ending of the *Lusíadas* and the celebration on Venus's island of love. But the relationship . . . is one of inversion" (119).

34. I owe thanks to K. David Jackson for this suggestion about the classical gods and their significance in the Baroque: "The dynamics of a system of signs in opposition, in which everything exists in relations to its opposite, where there are dialectical tensions of symbolic forms, belongs to the age of voyages and to the aesthetic of Mannerism and the Manueline Baroque" (*Builders* 19).

35. "Ó glória de mandar, ó vã cobiça / Desta vaidade, a quem chamamos Fama! /. . . . / Que castigo tamanho e que justiça / Fazes no peito vão que muito te ama! / Que mortes, que perigos, que tormentas / Que crueldades neles esprimentas! / . . . / Fonte de desemparos e adultérios, / Sagaz consumidora conhecida / De fazendas, de reinos e de impérios! / Chamam-te ilustre, chamam-te subida, / Sendo dina de infames vitupérios; / Chamam-te Fama e Glória soberana, / Nomes com quem se o povo néscio engana. // A que novos desastres determinas / De levar estes Reinos e esta gente? / Que perigos, que mortes lhe destinas, / Debaixo dalgum nome preminente? / Que promessas de reinos e de minas / De ouro, que lhe farás tão facilmente? / Que famas lhe prometerás? Que histórias? / Que triunfos? Que palmas? Que vitórias?"

36. There is a moment in the *S. Paulo* reminiscent of the Velho's speech: "forty leagues at sea from the coast of Guinea, our hardships began and the dire

predictions and opinions of the quarrelsome fishwives of Lisbon, as well as the sayings of others, came to pass" ("quarenta léguas ao mar da costa da Guiné . . . tiveram princípio nossos trabalhos e se começaram a cumprir em nós o prognóstico e juízo das regateiras de Lisboa e ditos das gentes") (Águas 1:173).

37. Margarido reiterates this oppositional relationship between shipwreck and empire by placing *Os Lusíadas* and the *História Trágico-Marítima* in a "dialectical relation" ("Une incursion" 247). For Margarido, heroism and shipwreck constitute "two opposed readings of the symbolic truth of the sea" ("Os relatos" 992). Soveral likewise recognizes shipwreck literature as containing an overall "disgrace," but for him it is ultimately ennobling in nature, that with which "glory is bought" (399); for Soveral, shipwreck literature forms part of the "literature of a heroic bent."

38. "Este receberá, plácido e brando, / No seu regaço o Canto que molhado / Vem do naufrágio triste e miserando, / Dos procelosos baxos escapado, / Das fomes, dos perigos grandes, quando / Será o injusto mando executado / Naquele cuja Lira sonorosa / Será mais afamada que ditosa."

39. "That is, our poet, as he was returning from China where he had gone to serve as overseer of the dead, was wrecked at sea and came to the shore of that country, rescuing this poem (which he was carrying with him) from the shipwreck" ("Esto es, que nuestro Poeta viniendo de la China, adonde avia ido por Proveedor mayor de los difuntos, se perdió en el mar, i salió en esta tierra, salvando del naufragio este Poema que traia consigo") (2:544) . For examples of this type of "biographical" reading, see Freitas and Henry H. Hart (143–48). Stegagno Picchio studies this episode as part of the "mythification" of the life of Camões, and argues that "shipwreck is the existential metaphor of the entire Camonian corpus" (262). One of Camões's sonnets is also purportedly based on the event (for a comment and an English translation, see Greene 144–45). On the possible relationship between shipwreck and Camões's poem "Sobolos rios que vão," see Moura ("O texto e o naufrágio").

2. THE DISCOURSE OF THE SHIPWRECK

1. Thanks to Sara Lipton for this citation.

2. "e todavia deixaram-se por então ficar. E nós também o faremos aqui, por continuarmos com a outra embarcação em que ia o capitão Estêvão da Veiga" (Águas 2:114).

3. "com tudo entre este laberinto de pareceres, e guiado de melhor discurso, mandei lançar o batel fóra" (Pereira 10:25).

4. "y para esto pensé de escrevir todo este viaje muy puntualmente, de día en día todo lo que yo hiziese y viese y passasse, como adelante se veirá" (16–17).

5. "E porque querer escrever nossos infortúnios e acontecimentos de cada dia (pois não passou nenhum que os não tivéssemos) seria um grande processo e causaria mais fastio ao leitor que contentamento (já que as cousas compridas, como afirma o Poeta, costumam ser desprezadas e tidas em pouco, e agradar as breves), não tratarei mais que com a maior brevidade que em mim for possível as cousas notáveis que nos aconteceram, assim na viagem como na perdição, e os dias em que foram, usando de toda a verdade que me assiste, pois em o que meu engenho e palavras faltarem, ela só bastará para lhes dar ornamento e decoro; porque o caminho que a nau fazia todos os dias, e os rumos a que governava, e em que alturas, deixo ao que compete o tal ofício, que são homens do mar e que têm seus roteiros por suas partidas e graus, pois não sou desta profissão, e era tão noviço no mar, por ser esta a primeira vez que fora do Reino saí, que nem os rumos da agulha sabia" (Águas 1:173–74). The reader will note that I have supplemented Boxer's translation with the additional material present in the HTM version of this narrative.

6. "hallarán las conquistas de la Nueva España claramente como se han de ver. Quiero volver con la pluma en la mano, como el buen piloto lleva la sonda, descubriendo bajos por la mar adelante, cuando siente que los hay" (28).

7. "la orden del camino é navegacion que se haçe desde España á estas partes, y del cresçer é menguar de la mar é su fluxo é refluxo, é del nordestear é noruestear de las agujas de navegar, é otras particularidades convenientes al discurso de la historia" (1:38).

8. For a discussion of the Portuguese literary Baroque, especially in poetry, consult Silva, *Maneirismo e barroco*. Seixo also makes relevant observations about the HTM and Mendes Pinto's *Peregrinação* in "Maneirismo e barroco."

9. Silva presents a series of antitheses typical of the period; see *Maneirismo e barroco* 335–41.

10. "E contudo, dada a esta desordem a melhor ordem que foi possível, e aparelhadas as ditas naus de suas cargas e coisas necessárias, partiram para este Reino" (218).

11. "a qual achámos toda coberta de corpos mortos, com tão feios e disformes gestos que davam bem evidentes mostras das penosas mortes que tiveram, jazendo uns por riba, outros por baixo daqueles penedos, e muitos de que não apareciam mais que os braços, pernas ou cabeças, e os rostos estavam cobertos de areia ou de caixas ou de outras diversas coisas. . . . E verdadeiramente que era uma confusa ordem com que a desventura tinha tudo aquilo ordenado" (235).

12. "Nestas suspeitas . . . se gastou este dia com nossa vigia, assim dos inimigos como a dos uns dos outros, muito suspeitosa e muito ambígua de ser certa

ou não ser; pois não havia ali quem se cresse nem confiasse de si mesmo; até que ao outro dia, em rompendo a alva, o Padre Manuel Álvares chamou e convocou a todos, e diante de um altar que feito tinha, com um retábulo de Nossa Senhora, começou a fazer prudentemente, com palavras dignas de tal varão e a tal tempo necessárias, uma amoestação e breve fala, para reduzir a todos à concórdia e unanimidade, dizendo: 'Caríssimos Irmãos em Cristo, trago-vos à memória aquele santo dito do Evangelho, que *Omne regnum in se divisum desolabitur,* e com a concórdia é tão certo que as cousas pequenas e mui mínimas se fazem muito grandes e duráveis, e com a discórdia as cousas muito grandes se desfazem e diminuem, e tornam em nada; devia-vos, Irmãos, de lembrar que todas as outras naus que se perderam no cabo de Boa Esperança, como foi o *Galeão,* e *S. Bento,* e outras muitas, uma das cousas que destruiu e totalmente matou a gente delas foi a discórdia que entre si houve . . .'" (Águas 1:213). As in the citation in n. 5., here too I have added the translation of material present in the HTM account to Boxer's translation.

13. In a typological study of the shipwreck image, Landow makes a distinction between "traditional" shipwreck (i.e., premodern, a definition that oddly does not take into account expansionist narratives) that testifies to the presence of God, and "modern" shipwreck, testifying to God's absence. Álvares's sermon functions as an attempt to write a divine outcome for the shipwreck, to make it part of what Landow calls "the basic structure of the divinely sponsored, continuous, meaningful pilgrimage to God" (20).

14. In this the non-HTM version of Manuel Álvares's narrative of the S. Paulo is especially revealing with its inclusion of several pen-and-ink sketches of scenes of wreck (see Álvares, *Naufrágio da Nau "S. Paulo"*) and the author's insistent references to the "pintura" (painting or iconographic representation) of the shipwreck. Álvares seems to be saying that only through the interplay of words and images can the enormity of the terror of shipwreck be comprehended. Shipwreck thus cannot be contained by any one form of representation.

15. For studies of this aspect of India ships, see Martins, *Teatro quinhentista,* and Moura, "Teatro a bordo."

16. "D. Henrique, cardeal neste Reino de Portugal, que neste tempo governava, mandou uma galé para que trouxesse a nau pelo dito rio acima, como fez, e se pôs a dita nau defronte da Igreja de S. Paulo, que ora é freguesia, e por espaço de um mês ou mais que ali esteve ia tanta gente vê-la que era cousa espantosa, e todos ficavam admirados vendo seu destroço, e davam muitas graças e louvores a Nossa Senhora por livrar os que nela vinham de tantos perigos como passaram" (Águas 2:46).

17. "*Ama.* A nau vem bem carregada? / *Marido.* Vem tão doce embandeira-

da! / *Ama*. Vamo-la, rogo-vo-lo, ver. / *Marido*. Far-vos-ei nisso prazer? / *Ama*. Si, que estou muito enfadada. / *Vão-se a ver a Nau, e fenece esta farsa*" (116).

18. Until Boxer, "Jorge de Albuquerque Coelho," it was commonly believed that Bento Teixeira Pinto was the author of the *S. António.*

19. "Uma só cousa quero contar para se poder ver o muito trabalho que sofremos e a que estado nos chegou este naufrágio, que saindo Jorge de Albuquerque com alguns que o acompanhámos em Belém, e encaminhando em romaria a Nossa Senhora da Luz, pelo caminho de Nossa Senhora d'Ajuda, sendo sabido na cidade, dos parentes e amigos, que era chegado ali, D. Jerónimo de Moura, seu primo, filho de D. Manuel de Moura, e outras muitas pessoas o foram logo buscar, e sabendo que era já desembarcado e aonde ia e que caminho levava, foram após ele; e chegado o primo a nós outros, que íamos juntos, nos saudou, perguntando-nos se éramos nós os que nos salváramos com Jorge de Albuquerque, e dizendo-lhe que sim, nos perguntou: 'Jorge de Albuquerque vai diante ou fica atrás ou tomou por outro caminho?' E Jorge de Albuquerque, que estava diante dele, lhe respondeu: 'Senhor, Jorge de Albuquerque não vai diante nem fica atrás nem vai por outro caminho.' Cuidando D. Jerónimo que zombava, quase se houve por desconfiado, e lhe disse, que não gracejasse, que respondesse ao que lhe perguntava. Disse-lhe Jorge de Albuquerque: 'Senhor D. Jerónimo, se virdes Jorge de Albuquerque conhecê-lo-eis?' Disse ele que sim. 'Pois eu sou Jorge Albuquerque e vós sois meu primo D. Jerónimo . . . aqui podeis ver, e julgar o trabalho que passei.' E criando-se ambos, e não havendo mais que um ano que se deixaram ver, e sendo muito amigos, e conversando muito tempo, o desconhecia de maneira que nem com isto o pôde acabar de conhecer. Foi então necessário a Jorge de Albuquerque mostrar-lhe sinais na pessoa, por onde com muitas lágrimas o abraçou, espantando-se de quão dessemelhado vinha ele, e assim vinham todos os mais" (Águas 2:47–48).

20. It is interesting to compare the impossibility of the return in the *S. António* with the impossibility of the return as noted by Jackson in Fernão Mendes Pinto's *Peregrinação* (Peregrination): "As a whole, the *Peregrination* can be understood as another epic voyage on symbolic oceans, more intimate than heroic. It relates the experience of a common Portuguese traveler, carried here and there by the waves and through lands of a strange and unpredictable world, without the benefits of protection by mythological gods, a shipwreck in life. In his search for being, through the great maritime peregrination, the navigator-author lives a surrealism, or other nature, which paradoxically for him is a hard reality. From this textual voyage-memoir, once begun, there is no possible return home, nor even a fictional exit, for almost no reader exists or existed capable of sharing the experiences or accompanying Mendes Pinto's voyage as difference,

much less prepared to understand the text as the intimate historiographical re-lation of a distant and unknown reality, unless through false literary forms whose practiced deceptions were well known" (*Builders* 31).

21. For further studies on the structural patterns of shipwreck narrative, see Araújo, Carvalho ("Acerca dos 'relatos de naufrágio'"), Jorge, and Seixo ("O abismo" 165 and "Concepção" 74); on the "thematic structuralism" of (mostly non-Portuguese) shipwreck narratives, see Milanesi; for a study of the various kinds of "discourse" as exemplified in the *S. Tomé*, see Kreutzer. In a related vein, Landow elaborates a typology of the "literary iconology" of shipwreck based mostly on nineteenth-century paintings and English and American litera-ture. Also see Seixo, "Les récits de naufrages," and Martins, "As funções do nar-rador." Two doctoral theses provide readings of shipwreck in contemporary lit-erature and in Spanish-American colonial writings. See Burch for a study of contemporary shipwreck literature through the combined lenses of postmod-ernism and postcolonialsm with an argument for "postcultural survival stories." Calvo-Stevenson addresses shipwreck in Spanish-American texts contemporary with the activity of the Portuguese writers.

22. In this I vary with Lanciani, who finds the precursor of shipwreck narra-tive in medieval travel literature, especially the voyage of St. Amaro ("Uma história trágico-marítima" 107–12).

23. Seixo ponders "to what degree [shipwreck narratives] accommodate, or trouble, the imperialist perspective" ("O abismo" 183); Lanciani notes that the narratives reveal the "dramas of the sea" through an "optic that is no longer im-perialist and glorifying" (*Sucessos* 54).

24. A similar view is expressed by Lepecki in her discussion of the *S. João*: "the narratives of the *História Trágico-Marítima* completely serve ... the politics of conquest and navigation, in that the textual segments *shipwreck-privation-death* are necessarily less important (in the specific case of the first account *[S. João]*, but also in many other passages) than the *moralizing* and *exemplary* segments" (cxv).

25. "Da acção com que a navegação de Guiné, Brasil e do Oriente pertence mais à Coroa de Portugal que a outra alguma" (Of the action through which the navigation of Guinea, Brazil, and the East pertains more to the Crown of Por-tugal than to any other). This chapter includes the remarkable transcription of the words spoken by Christ to Afonso Henriques, first king of Portugal, on the battlefield of Ourique in which the Son of God issues an imperial mandate to Por-tugal. (Amaral's narrative contains a list of books on maritime expansion, studied by Rogers *[Europe Informed]*; it is also one of the narratives reprinted in an eighteenth-century counterfeit edition.) This passage of the Gospel according to

NOTES TO CHAPTER 2 137

Melchior Estácio do Amaral imaginatively reiterates the authority granted to Portugal to expand overseas and "subjugate the Saracens" and the enemies of the faith in the series of papal bulls issued in the fifteenth century. For a transcription, with English translation, of many of these bulls, see Davenport.

26. "Senhores fidalgos e cavaleiros, amigos e companheiros, não deveis de vos entristecer e melancolizar com irmos demandar a terra onde levamos posta a proa, porque pode ser que nos leve Deus a terra onde possamos conquistar outro novo mundo e descobrir outra Índia maior que a que está descoberta, pois levo aqui fidalgos e cavaleiros por companheiros com quem me atrevo a cometer todas as conquistas e empresas do mundo, por árduas e dificultosas que sejam" (360).

27. In a footnote to the "greater India" mentioned in Barreto's speech, Boxer observes: "A thinly veiled allusion to the allegedly gold-rich 'empire' (in reality, tribal confederation) of Monomotapa—a will-o-the-wisp which led many Portuguese to their deaths in the interior, including Francisco Barreto himself in the expedition up the Zambesi in 1573" (*Further Selections* 33 n. 2).

28. "Tanto que foi manhã, lançou a nau Garça uma manchua ao mar com quatro marinheiros e o escrivão da nau, que se chamava João Rodrigues Pais; e veio à nau de Francisco Barreto com um escrito do capitão para ele, que dizia assim: 'Senhor, cumpre muito ao serviço de Deus, e d'el-Rei Nosso Senhor, chegar V. Senhoria cá, e pela brevidade desta veja o que cá vai. Beijo as mãos a V. Senhoria" (366).

29. Madeira notes that the shipwreck text is a "hybrid" (267), and that its discourse is "difficult to classify . . . [it is] without definition and without a definitive shape" (268).

30. For an overview of the various kinds of texts written during the expansionist sixteenth and seventeenth centuries, see Jackson, *Builders* 28–37, Lach, *The Century of Discovery* 181–204, and Rogers, *Quest* 185–93. Also see Rebelo.

31. Of note is Rabasa's explanation of *counter*-: "I prefer the prefix *counter*- to *anti*- because it does not necessarily suggest a position outside colonialism, but one attempting to work its way out from within" (*Inventing A-m-e-r-i-c-a* 21).

32. The shipwreck narratives therefore participate tacitly, if not overtly, in what Hart identifies as the "tradition in European culture of what might be called an alternative critique, of opposition from within to the imperial expansion of Europe, most notably to the western enterprise that Columbus proposed and then achieved" ("Review Article" 533).

33. "Houve grande dúvida se era este o baixo da Judia se outro. Não falta quem sustente ser este o baixo da Judia. As razões que por esta parte há são as seguintes . . . dizem que o baixo em que se esta nau perdeu está na mesma altura

que o da Judia . . . e que não há tal baixo como este situado nas cartas antigas de
marear, que agora por novo baixo se quer escrever. . . . Os que dizem não ser
este o baixo da Judia movem-se por razões mais urgentes, que são as seguintes . . .
três dias antes da perdição, se viram muitas aves . . . ao domingo se viram
muitas mais aves destas; e à segunda-feira, que foi o dia em que se a nau perdeu,
quando veio a tarde já havia muito poucas, havendo se ser pelo contrário se este
fora o baixo da Judia, porque são tantas as aves nele. . . . Finalmente, vistas as
informações que há do baixo da Judia, e cotejadas com o que se viu neste baixo
em que se a nau perdeu, não há maior despropósito que quererem à força de
contenção fazer de ambos os baixos um só. . . . Respondem a isto que é erro das
cartas . . ."(Águas 2:58–59).

34. Such is the case in the *S. Bento* when an astrolabe is traded for goats and
cakes (251). The devaluation of the astrolabe as another sign of failure is in keeping with Arkinstall's interpretation of its function in Peri Rossi's *Descripción de
un naufragio*: "[the astrolabe is] an instrument which enabled a ship's position
to be plotted by measuring the altitude of heavenly bodies—other worlds which
constitute a topography of seemingly fixed coordinates against which one's place,
and hence identity, may be constructed. Above all, the astrolabe constitutes an
excellent metaphor of patriarchal reasoning that makes the other's supposedly
natural distance from man the guiding principle of society" (437).

35. "Em a primeira *Década,* como foi o fundamento dêste nosso edifício de
escritura, em algũa maneira quisemos imitar o modo que os arquitectores tēem
nos materiais edefícios" (3).

36. Barros was only able to complete four of the Asian *Decades,* published
in 1552–63.

37. See Russell's biography for a wealth of information on this figure.

38. Rebelo notes that the "protocols of reading the history of Portugal" during the expansion mirrored biblical hermeneutics in that they obeyed an
already known authority (76). See Barreto for a study of Zurara's historiography
as "transitional" between the Middle Ages and the Renaissance.

39. "E como quer que a estorya se nom possa recontar em tã boa ordenãça
como compria per razom de vyagē que as carauellas nom fezerō todas jũtamēte.
Diremos o que podermos naquella milhor maneira que se poder dizer" (194).

40. "Grande prazer ouue antre aquelles quando chegando aa uista da Ilha
das garças. vyram as quatro carauellas que ja hi jaziam de repouso. . . . E em
chegãdo aos nauyos que jazyam ancorados armauõ seus troōs e suas collobretas
cõ as quaaes fazyam seus tiros en sinal do prazer de seus coraçoões. . . . Hora
pois disse lançarote tēedes determinado todauya partyr he bem que vos outros
que ja vistes muytas ordenanças perteecētes a tal caso vos nembrees dellas. e que
me ajudees a ordenar nossa jda como vaamos ordenadamente. E leixãdo aquy as

desuairadas tençoões que antre elles ouue. finalmente foe determinado que saissem per esta guisa. . . . que fossem ante das carauellas tres batees. nos quaaes saissem pillotos que ja fossē em aquella terra e que soubessem o caminho" (203–5).

41. "E āte que chegassem ao porto ōde auyā de desembarcar teuerō ordenáça de se juntarē todas as carauellas. Jndo tā juntas que os homeēs saltauom de hūas nas outras" (208).

42. "No ano de 1601 mandou el-Rei Nosso Senhor que . . . se aprestassem seis galeões para passarem à Índia. . . . [e] porque se não puderam aprestar tantas naus para saírem juntas em uma maré, as foram lançando assim como se puderam aviar. . . . Porém, como não partiram em Março, que é a natural monção desta carreira, tornaram a arribar cinco da Linha" (479–80).

43. "Aparelhados assim todos estes capitães do que lhes cumpria, partiram do porto desta cidade de Lisboa, em . . . 24 de Março . . . e seguiram sua rota alguns dias assim em conserva, até que andando o tempo, sucederam tão diversos acontecimentos que foi forçado apartarem-se uns dos outros, ajudando-se cada um do caminho que melhor lhe parecia . . . para salvamento das vidas e fazendas que levavam a seu cargo: cujas viagens particulares deixo de contar, por não ser meu intento tratar mais que de Fernão d'Álvares" (217).

44. "[a] dezasete de Julho nos apartámos da nao capitania de noite por se lhe não vêr o farol: outros dizem, que porque o quizeram fazer os officiaes" (8).

45. "Como tôda esta nossa *Ásia* vai fundada sôbre navegações, por causa das armadas que ordinàriamente em cada um ano se fazem pera a conquista e comércio dela . . . convém, pera melhor intendimento da história, darmos ũa gèral relação do modo que se naquelas partes de Ásia navegava a especiaria com tôdalas outras orientais riquezas, té virem a esta nossa Europa, ante que abríssemos o caminho que lhe demos pera êste nosso Mar Oceano" (301).

46. "SHIPWRECK. the reducing of a ship to pieces against a rock or running into the sand, in such a way that the ship breaks open and wrecks . . . the same thing is to be sunk by the waves" ("NAUFRAGIO. el hacerse pedazos el navío, dando en alguna roca o encallando en el arena, de modo que se abre y desbarata . . . lo mesmo es ser hundida con las olas" [773]). Thirty years after the publication of the HTM, Cândido Lusitano's poetic dictionary defines shipwreck adjectively rather than substantively: "SHIPWRECK. Fatal, dire, lugubrious, sad, funereal, deadly, lamentable, deplorable . . ." (NAUFRAGIO. Fatal, funesto, lugubre, triste, funereo, mortifero, lamentavel, deploravel . . .) (61). Rafael Bluteau defines shipwreck much as Covarrubias did: "ruin, loss of a ship by storm, wrecking to pieces against the shore" ("ruina, perda do navio por tormenta, dando á costa em escolhos" [111]).

47. See *Santiago/Chagas,* ch. 12, "On the cause, and disasters, of why many

Indiamen were lost" ("Da causa e desastres por que se perderam muitas naus da Índia").

48. For a French translation of this second *epanáfora,* see Boisvert. Also see Belardinelli for further critical comments.

49. "Devem os homens amantes da razão . . . guardar em suas acções uma tal ordem que a própria harmonia delas mostre serem guiadas pela luz racional; não só escolhendo as obras dignas, mas as competentes. Toda esta proposição parece que ignoro, ou quebranto, convidando-vos agora, e de tão longe, a ler uma relação que nem pela matéria, nem pelo estado, nem pelo tempo, se julga em alguma parte conforme à precisa observação que vos tenho proposto" (13).

50. This is the title of the 1555, and most widely circulated, printing (see Cabeza de Vaca; an English translation is called *Castaways*). There was, however, an earlier version (1542), titled *La relación que dio Álvar Núñez Cabeça de Vaca de lo acaescido en las Indias.* See Adorno and Pautz for this first version with an English translation and accompanying scholarly study.

51. See Glantz; Pranzetti remarks on the "loss and search for [an] identity" (58), of a "social and economic identity impossible in the mother country" (73).

52. Pastor Bodmer's use of the term *mythification* is apparently synonymous with *fabulous* or *legendary.* Both *demythification* and *failure* operate in her argument as the inverse of this.

53. "Taking several forms, including hunger, cold, sickness, and thirst, necessity transforms the epic action of the discourse of mythification into the desperate wanderings of the shipwrecked" (Pastor Bodmer 121), "the action of the discourse of failure becomes a struggle for survival" (126).

54. Basing their comments on the 1542 version, Adorno and Pautz state: "Thus . . . [its] value . . . deepened with the passage of time as it offered a glimpse of the 'ideal conquest'" (3:115). Pastor ("Silence and Writing") sketches a gradual transformation of Cabeza de Vaca that happens throughout the text, in which he seems to adopt a more peaceful vision of conquest near the end. Yet, Pastor observes, "It would be an error . . . to assume that this transformation and the narrative discourse in which it is expressed implies a radical rejection of the colonial perspective and all of its forms of domination. . . . it [does not] cancel a project of colonial character" (142).

55. "The legal report, or *relación,* written from obligation on the part of the narrator to inform the Crown of new developments, had been a standard vehicle for describing the New World since the period of discovery" (Ross 108).

56. Several of the third-volume HTM narratives, though, are addressed to figures of political power. The third volume testifies to a growing codification and self-consciousness of the shipwreck account as a specific kind of narrative,

and a concomitant attempt to inscribe shipwreck, textually, within the boundaries of the state.

57. For the complete texts of the three versions of the *S. M. da Barca*, see Lanciani, *Santa Maria da Barca*.

58. Another version of the narrative of the S. Tomé, one Boxer does not mention, can be found in Ataíde.

59. For a study of the shipwreck episodes in Mendes Pinto, see Margarido, "Os relatos de naufrágios." Lobo's text (in its French version) was translated into English as *A Voyage to Abyssinia* by Samuel Johnson and published in 1735 in London, coincident with the appearance of the first volume of the HTM.

60. "No cabo de três dias que a tormenta durou, começando o tempo a abonançar, ordenámos um mastro para proa, que tirámos dos pedaços da ponte que o mar abateu, o qual seria duas ou três braças em comprido, e de três remos do batel, que escaparam, fizemos verga, e de uma velazinha de contra (que esta só escapou) fizemos um modo de traquete, e de alguns pedaços de cordas enxeridos uns nos outros fizemos enxárcia. Estando tudo isto aparelhado, por a nau ser grande e a vela muito pequena, parecia escárnio querermos navegar com ela" (Águas 2:34).

3. MANIFEST PERDITION I

1. "vendo o capitão que . . . ficávamos atrás um grande espaço, aguardou que chegássemos a ele, e então nos disse que bem víamos a desventura a que nossos pecados nos traziam, e que todos aqueles homens se queixavam dele ir esperando por nós . . . portanto nos determinássemos no que havíamos de fazer, que se podíamos não ficássemos atrás; e se também as forças de António Sobrinho não abrangiam, e eu estava posto em ficar com ele, assim lho dissesse, porque não gastasse mais o tempo em coisas com que a nós não podia remediar e aos outros punha em manifesta perdição" (274).

2. Camerarius summarizes the story of Manuel de Sousa Sepúlveda in chapter 12 ("Of the doubtfull, uncertaine, inconstant, and miserable condition of Mans life") of "The First Booke of Historicall Meditations." He begins: "I could here alledge a number of examples, of such as from the top of great riches and dignities, haue suddenly fallen to the bottom of extreme afflictions and miseries: but it shall suffice for the present to specifie one, memorable among many other *[sic]*. It is a storie altogether lamentable, and a calamitie full of astonishment, which happened in the parts of the *Cape de bona Speranza*, to *Manuel de Sousa*, surnamed *Sepulueda*, Gouernor of the Citadell of Diu for the King of Portugall" (38). A recent incarnation of the story is Moura's novel

Naufrágio de Sepúlveda. On the literary legacy of the *S. João,* see note 1 of the Prologue. Also see Leal, "O naufrágio de Sepúlveda."

3. I realize that the term *Kaffir* is a derogatory one and may offend modern sensibilities. It must be acknowledged, though, as the only historically accurate translation of *cafre.*

4. "Cousa é esta que se conta neste naufrágio para os homens muito temerem os castigos do Senhor e serem bons cristãos, trazendo o temor de Deus diante dos olhos para não quebrar seus mandamentos. Porque Manuel de Sousa era um fidalgo mui nobre e bom cavaleiro, e na Índia gastou em seu tempo mais de cinquenta mil cruzados em dar de comer a muita gente e em boas obras, que fez a muitos homens; por derradeiro foi acabar sua vida, e de sua mulher e filhos, em tanta lástima e necessidade, entre os cafres, faltando-lhe o comer, e beber e vestir. E passou tantos trabalhos antes de sua morte, que não podem ser cridos senão de quem lhos ajudou a passar, que entre os mais foi um Álvaro Fernandes, guardião do galeão, que me contou isto muito particularmente, que por acerto achei aqui em Moçambique o ano de mil e quinhentos e cinquenta e quatro. E por me parecer história que daria aviso e bom exemplo a todos, escrevi os trabalhos e morte deste fidalgo e de toda a sua companhia para que os homens que andam pelo mar se encomendem a Deus e a Nossa Senhora, que rogue por todos. Ámen" (185).

5. Lanciani notes the importance of the departure in shipwreck narrative, remarking that it is "the first link, necessary and sufficient as the beginning of the narration, in a chain of constant unities that is configured as a model of the shipwreck narrative" (*Sucessos* 90–91). Although Lanciani is correct in positing that the departure functions structurally in a constitutive manner, its overall effect is to establish a space of absence that participates in the dissolution of the cohesiveness of experience. For related thoughts on shipwreck "beginnings," see Meira.

6. "Desta praia, onde se perderam em 31 graus aos sete de Julho de cinquenta e dois, começaram a caminhar com esta ordem que se segue, a saber: Manuel de Sousa com sua mulher e filhos, com oitenta portugueses e cem escravos; e André Vaz, o piloto, na sua companhia, com uma bandeira com um crucifixo erguido, caminhava na vanguarda, e D. Leonor sua mulher levavam-na escravos em um andor. Logo atrás vinha o mestre do galeão com a gente do mar e com as escravas. Na retaguarda caminhava Pantaleão de Sá com o resto dos portugueses e escravos, que seriam até duzentas pessoas: e todas juntas seriam quinhentas, das quais eram cento e oitenta portugueses. Desta maneira caminharam um mês com muitos trabalhos, fomes e sedes" (198).

7. For example, the abandonment of Sepúlveda's illegitimate son when he becomes too weak and sick to continue on.

8. Sepúlveda's company meets two bands of natives *(cafres)* in their survival march: the first one is friendly, headed by the chief Oinhaca who is renamed "Garcia de Sá" by the Portuguese as an honor to the man of the same name; the second one is hostile and is the one I am referring to here.

9. "(E) já então D. Leonor era uma das que caminhavam a pé, e sendo uma mulher fidalga, delicada e moça, vinha por aqueles ásperos caminhos tão trabalhosos como qualquer robusto homem do campo, e muitas vezes consolava as da sua companhia e ajudava a trazer seus filhos. . . . Parece verdadeiramente que a graça de Nosso Senhor supria aqui, porque sem ela não pudera uma mulher tão fraca, e tão pouco costumada a trabalhos, andar tão compridos e ásperos caminhos, e sempre com tantas fomes e sedes, que já então passavam de trezentas léguas as que tinham andado, por causa dos grandes rodeios" (205).

10. See the studies by Carvalho ("Viagens"), Hutchinson, and Tonnies on women in the HTM. They conclude that, except in Leonor's case, the HTM construes women in negative terms. Sepúlveda's loss of command, and Leonor's abandonment of her litter to travel by foot constitute further evidence of the "suspension of hierarchical relations" that Glantz finds to be characteristic of shipwreck (417). Glantz identifies these as suspensions of "that which is civilized" *(lo civilizado),* and elaborates by observing that "the state of shipwreck . . . *is a category of civilization*: boats and clothing are needed, in the majority of cases, in addition to a sophisticated social organization, in order to shipwreck" ("el estado de naufragio . . . *es una categoría de la civilización*: se requiere de embarcaciones y vestimenta, la mayor parte de las veces, además de una organización social sofisticada, para poder naufragar" [417; emphasis in original]). In the case of the *S. João,* it is best to think of the erosion of hierarchies as political and cultural as opposed to "civilized." "Civilized" implies that its opposite (e.g., "primitive," "barbaric," or "uncivilized") is by definition negative in that it is achieved or entered into by suffering loss or by the suspension of certain traits or structures. In the *S. João,* the natives prove that their own civilization is formidable indeed, just as powerful as Portuguese civilization is in the *pátria* (homeland) or in other parts of the empire.

11. See book 1 of Aristotle's *The Politics.*

12. "No primeiro e segundo dia depois da perdição . . . andavam todos cingidos com duas, três cordas para se atarem às jangadas, e depois de darem muitas voltas com as cordas pela cintura para andarem mais lestes, davam com elas outras tantas pelos pescoços. Era tão triste o espectáculo, que pareciam todos assim com os baraços nos pescoços, condendados à morte. Neste mesmo dia abriu a nau pelo costado, e a modo de parto lançou de si o batel com um terço menos" (Águas 2:63).

13. Similarly, Andrew Marvell writes, "'Twas in a Shipwrack, when the Seas /

Rul'd, and the Winds did what they please, / That my poor Lover floting lay, / And, e're brought forth, was cast away: / Till at the last the master-Wave / Upon the Rock his Mother drave; / And there she split against the Stone, / In a *Cesarian Section*" (qtd. in Warnke 56).

14. "viam aos seus olhos os elementos conjurados contra eles, prometendo-lhes as ondas, tão furiosas, pela separação de suas almas, serem sepulturas de suas carnes; e sem dúvida que não havia aí nenhum, por mais esforçado que fosse e por mais que blasonasse, que não se desejasse neste tempo ser um dos mais ínfimos bichos da terra; o que parece pede a cada um sua natureza desejar tornar à sua mãe antiga, a terra, de que foi nosso primeiro pai, Adão, formado. Mas são os homens no mar mui semelhantes às mulheres no tempo de seus par-tos, em suas mui estranhas e grandíssimas dores, que juram se daquela escapam não terem mais cópula nem ajuntamento nunca com varão" (Águas 1:197–98).

15. Leonor's womb, and the ship's, have become symbols and agents of death. Perhaps this is one reason why the *S. João* author frequently refers to the "sterility" of uncharted Sofala. In Peri Rossi's poem, according to Arkinstall, "the landscape constitutes an *hortus anatomicus,* the focus of which invariably returns to the source of reproduction: the female sexual organs and the womb, a fertile ground which must be carefully husbanded and tilled in order to pro-duce" (435–36). Despite the abundant presence of water surrounding it, ship-wreck nonetheless dries up life and the possibilities of its real and symbolic rejuvenation.

16. The dismasting of a ship is frequently the decisive moment of breaking in the *Cantigas de Santa Maria,* except that here imperialism is not at stake but the symbolic body of a male god.

17. "disse . . . a André Vaz, o piloto: 'Bem vedes como estamos, e que já não podemos passar daqui, e que havemos de acabar por nossos pecados. Ide-vos muito embora, fazei por vos salvar, e encomendai-nos a Deus. E se fordes à Índia, e a Portugal em algum tempo, dizei como nos deixastes a Manuel de Sousa e a mim com meus filhos" (210).

18. "Three of these (female) slaves survived and reached Goa, where they told how they saw D. Leonor die" ("das quais se salvaram três, que vieram a Goa, que contaram como viram morrer D. Leonor" [210]).

19. For a study and anthology of some of these narratives, see Baepler. Baepler's introduction, which characterizes the captivity tales and locates them in their historical context, offers many points of comparison to the Portuguese shipwreck narratives.

20. Haberly provides in his study of the *cautiva* (female captive) a lucid ar-gument about this figure in the North American and Argentinian literary tradi-

tion, noting that in the North American colonial period "these narratives fell easily into a satisfying metaphorical framework: captivity by the forces of evil; suffering and temptation; and final redemption and salvation" (7). The Portuguese narratives exemplify some of these qualities. The most important difference between the narratives Haberly studies and the Portuguese ones is that in the latter there is no systematic redemption and salvation.

21. "Aqui dizem que D. Leonor se não deixava despir, e que às punhadas e às bofetadas se defendia, porque era tal, que queria antes que a matassem os cafres que ver-se nua diante da gente. E não há dúvida que logo ali acabara sua vida, se não fora Manuel de Sousa, que lhe rogou se deixasse despir, que lhe lembrava que nasceram nus, e pois Deus daquilo era servido, que o fosse ela. . . . E vendo-se D. Leonor despida, lançou-se logo no chão e cobriu-se toda com os seus cabelos, que eram muito compridos, fazendo uma cova na areia, onde se meteu até à cintura, sem mais se erguer dali. Manuel de Sousa foi então a uma velha sua aia, que lhe ficara ainda uma mantilha rota, e lha pediu para cobrir D. Leonor, e lha deu; mas contudo nunca mais se quis erguer daquele lugar, onde se deixou cair quando se viu nua. . . . E Manuel de Sousa, ainda que estava maltratado do miolo, não lhe esquecia a necessidade que sua mulher e filhos passavam de comer. E sendo ainda manco de uma ferida que os cafres lhe deram em uma perna, assim maltratado se foi ao mato buscar frutas para lhe dar de comer. Quando tornou, achou D. Leonor muito fraca . . . e achou um dos meninos mortos, e por sua mão o enterrou na areia. Ao outro dia tornou Manuel de Sousa ao mato a buscar alguma fruta, e quando tornou achou D. Leonor falecida e o outro menino. . . . Dizem que ele não fez mais, quando a viu falecida, que apartar as escravas dali e assentar-se perto dela, com o rosto posto sobre uma mão, por espaço de meia hora, sem chorar nem dizer coisa alguma. . . . E acabando este espaço, se ergueu e começou a fazer uma cova na areia com ajuda das escravas, e sempre sem se falar palavra a enterrou, e o filho com ela. E acabado isto, tornou a tomar o caminho que fazia quando ia a buscar as frutas, sem dizer nada às escravas, e se meteu pelo mato, e nunca mais o viram" (209–11).

22. "Vós entregais as armas, agora me dou por perdida com toda esta gente" (207).

23. "Amigos e senhores: bem vedes o estado a que por nossos pecados somos chegados, e eu creio verdadeiramente que os meus só bastavam para por eles sermos postos em tamanhas necessidades, como vedes que temos. Mas é Nosso Senhor tão piedoso, que ainda nos faz tamanha mercê que nos não fôssemos ao fundo naquela nau, trazendo tanta quantidade de água debaixo das cobertas. Prazerá a ele que pois foi servido de nos salvar daquele perigo, que o será de nos

levar a terra de cristãos, e os que nesta demanda acabarem com tantos trabalhos, haverá por bem que sejam para salvação de suas almas. Estes dias que aqui estivemos, bem vedes, senhores, que foram necessários para nos convalescerem os doentes que trazíamos; já agora, Nosso Senhor seja louvado, estão para caminhar, e portanto vos ajuntei aqui para assentarmos que caminho havemos de tomar para remédio de nossa salvação, que a determinação que trazíamos de fazer alguma embarcação se nos atalhou, como vistes, por não podermos salvar da nau coisa nenhuma para a podermos fazer. E pois, senhores e irmãos, vos vai a vida como a mim, não será razão fazer nem determinar coisa sem conselho de todos. Uma mercê vos quero pedir, a qual é que me não desampareis nem deixeis, dado caso que eu não possa andar tanto como os que mais andarem, por causa de minha mulher e filhos. E assim todos juntos quererá Nosso Senhor pela sua misericórdia ajudar-nos" (197).

24. "por onde passaram tão grande esterilidade qual se não pode crer nem escrever" (198).

25. "[D]e modo que a rastos, de costas e de bruços, segundo o perigo e disposição do lugar davam de si, prouve a Nosso Senhor pôr-nos salvos na borda do rio" (248).

26. The S. Bento's most famous passenger was Luís de Camões, who disembarked and remained in India before the vessel set return sail on its doomed voyage. Of the 473 passengers on board, all but sixty-two died before reaching Mozambique. Perestrelo returned to Portugal in 1555 (Lach, *The Literary Arts* 132).

27. "E assim passavam uns pelos outros sem neles se enxergar sinal algum de sentimento, como que todos foram alimárias irracionais que por ali andavam pascendo, trazendo somente o intento e olhos pasmados pelo campo a ver se poderiam descobrir erva, osso ou bicho (a que não valia ser peçonhento) de que pudessem lançar mão" (272–73).

28. "como homens que esperávamos antes de poucas horas dar conta a Nosso Senhor de nossas bem ou mal gastadas vidas, cada um começou de a ter com sua consciência, confessando-se sumariamente a alguns clérigos que aí iam" (228).

29. "Tanto que escureceu a noite, agasalhando-nos pelos pés das árvores que ali estavam, cada um se recolheu aos pensamentos da sua fortuna, ocupando-os no sentimento das coisas que lhe mais doíam. E para que ainda este pequeno refrigério não tivéssemos com quietação, choveu aquela noita tanta água que, não podendo nossos mal enroupados corpos sofrer o demasiado frio que com ela fazia, nos levantávamos, e assim, às escuras, andávamos choutando de umas partes para outras, tomando este trabalho por remédio dos outros que o frio e

pouco sono e o medo de nossas próprias imaginações causavam, as quais coisas todas nos faziam desejar grandemente a torna da manhã" (234).

30. "E verdadeiramente que era uma confusa ordem com que a desventura tinha tudo aquilo ordenado, e que bastava a memória daquele passo para não ser a pobreza havida por tamanho mal, que por lhe fugir deixemos a Deus e o próximo, pátria, pais, irmãos, amigos, mulheres e filhos, e troquemos tantos gostos e quietações pelos sobejos que cá ficam; e enquanto vivemos nos fazem atravessar mares, fogos, guerras e todos os outros perigos e trabalhos, que nos tanto custam. Mas por não contrariar de todo as justas escusas que por si podem alegar os atormentados das necessidades, cortarei o fio . . . porque já me levava a memória e medo do que ali foi representado, recolhendo-me a meu propósito, que é escrever somente a verdade do que toca aos acontecimentos desta história" (235).

31. Susan Antebi, in an excellent seminar paper, first proposed reading Perestrelo and his double breakages in the terms presented here.

32. "determinámos esperar pelos cafres . . . para que nos ensinassem algum caminho que fosse ter a povoado" (241).

33. "mas tanto que os cafres isto entenderam, puseram-se diante com as aza-gaias postas em tiro, dizendo-nos que não fôssemos senão por onde nos eles guiassem" (267).

34. "Ao outro dia amanheceu obra de uma légua da terra . . . [t]anto que esclareceu o dia e nos vimos perto das íngremes serras e bravas penedias daquela tão estranha e bárbara terra, não houve quem, posto que o perigo presente por uma parte fizesse folgar com sua vizinhança, por outra a não acometesse com grande receio, tendo por mui fresco na memória quão cobertos deviam ainda estar os seus espaçosos e desaproveitados matos de ossadas portuguesas dos que vinham o ano de 52 no galeão S. João com Manuel de Sousa Sepúlveda" (229).

35. "[U]m marinheiro . . . começou de se benzer e chamar pelo nome de JESUS muito alto; e perguntando-lhe algumas pessoas que era aquilo, lhe mostrou pela banda do estibordo uma onda que de muito longe vinha levanta-da por cima das outras todas em demasiada altura, dizendo que diante dela via vir uma grande folia de vultos negros, que não podiam ser senão diabos. Enquanto com o alvoroço disto a gente começou a recrescer aos bordos para ver coisa tão espantosa, chegou este mar que, por a nau estar morta, sem lhe podermos fugir, nos alcançou pela quadra de estibordo, e foi o ímpeto e peso dela tamanho que quase nos soçobrou daquele primeiro golpe" (224).

36. "[E]sta noite, depois que fomos recolhidos, como a outra atrás passada e as mais que neste lugar estivemos, quando era já bem cerrada a noite, ouvíamos claramente brados altos no lugar onde se a nau quebrara, que por muitas vezes

gritavam, dizendo 'A bombordo, a estibordo, arriba', e outras muitas palavras confusas, que não entendíamos, assim e da maneira que nós fazíamos quando, já alagados, vínhamos na força da tormenta que nos ali fez encalhar. O que isto fosse, nunca se pôde saber de certo, somente suspeitámos que ou a nós se representava aquilo nos ouvidos, pelos trazermos atroados dos brados que continuamente naquele tempo ouvíamos, ou eram alguns espíritos malignos que festejavam o que de alguns ali poderiam alcançar (coisa que Nosso Senhor, por sua piedade, não permitiria). Mas qualquer destas que fosse, o certo é que foi, ou ao menos a todos pareceu sê-lo: porque, posto que ao princípio cada um cuidasse que a ele só se representava aquele espantoso som, e pela dificuldade que nisso havia não cresse ser verdade, a continuação do tempo fez perguntar uns aos outros se ouviam o mesmo; e afirmando todos que sim, assentámos, segundo as horas, escuro e tempestade das noites, ser alguma coisa das que dito tenho" (237–38).

37. For a study of the marvelous in this era, see Greenblatt, *Marvelous Possessions*.

38. Similarly, Guimarães and Ribeiro note a "permanent paradox" of shipwreck narratives in that they seek to narrate what cannot be narrated, arguing that their underlying principle is an experience "inconvertible" into words or images (87).

39. "todos nos enganávamos em cuidar que o sertão havia de ser mais povoado que a fralda do mar, pelo pouco comércio que aquela gente tem com ela" (241).

40. "levando a fantasia ocupada nesta angústia e os olhos arrasados de água, não podíamos dar passo, que muitas vezes não tornássemos atrás para ver a ossada daquela tão formosa e mal-afortunada nau, porque, posto que já nela não houvesse pau pregado e tudo fosse desfeito naquelas rochas, todavia, enquanto a víamos, nos parecia que tínhamos ali umas relíquias e certa parte desta nossa desejada terra, de cujo abrigo e companhia (por ser aquela a derradeira coisa que dela esperávamos) nos não podíamos apartar sem muito sentimento" (242).

41. Thanks to Susan Antebi for suggesting this point.

42. See Madeira for an analysis of memory in the HTM.

43. "um pranto que atroava as concavidades daquela ribeira" (262).

44. "E como os que ainda ficavam vivos trouxessem os espíritos e corpos tão cansados e debilitados, que o mais a que suas forças e caridades então abrangiam era tomar estes, qeu assim faleciam, e fazer-lhes em estacas uma pequena cova onde os deixavam mal cobertos, se veio daqui a principiar outra desventura não menos que a da fome. E foi que, por este lugar em que el-Rei e nós vivíamos, estar situado em uma mata antiga e grande, onde havia muitos tigres,

leões e todo o outro género de alimárias nocivas, estes, [encarniçaram-se] de princípio em comer os que assim ficavam mal soterrados" (300–301).

45. The beach, then, finds the European body cast out of the symbolic confines of its home and authenticating culture, a body on which a violence may be visited, even after death. The beach is thus a space of estrangement, of dissolution of the body as an empowering metaphor through which the ideology of expansion may be partially achieved and consecrated.

46. "Mas como a fortuna nunca comece por pouco, a todas estas obras suas acrescentou outra, que conquanto já nele não pudesse ser mais negra, não careceu contudo de muito sentimento, por serem dela executores uns homens que tão obrigados lhe estavam por benefícios recebidos. E foi que, como a maior parte que ali íamos fosse gente do mar, de cujos primores até agora poucos autores escreveram, estes, começando de dia em dia a perder o medo e a vergonha, fazendo todos um corpo, cuja cabeça (posto que não nestes maus ensinos) era o contramestre, vieram a tanta desenvoltura, que totalmente não tinham conta com Fernão d'Álvares: antes, todas as vezes que os ele repreendia de suas desordens (que não eram poucas), lhe diziam que não ousasse de os emendar, porque não era já seu capitão, nem lhe deviam obediência. . . . [p]elo que, vendo o mestre da nau, que ia deste reino e lhe levara ódio particular . . . se determinou em cometer sua obra diabólica e de todo inumana" (258).

4. MANIFEST PERDITION II

1. Jackson writes of a "voice" given to water in the case of Adamastor and explores "the confluence of the geographical voyage with the mythical and oneiric subcurrents of the oceans, full of dangers and passions" (*Builders* 23).

2. Centeno argues that the Portuguese can conquer the elements only through the mediation of Venus (23).

3. See esp. Zurara's *Guiné*. Of all the maritime skills boasted by Portuguese sailors, swimming is not one of them.

4. Also of note are Cohen's remarks on the ambivalence of water in the work of the noted Jesuit António Vieira: "The manner in which Vieira evokes the importance of water in Amazonian life suggests the polemical nature of his exegesis. Vieira praises these river dwellers for the same skills he once denigrated in the seafaring Dutch, whom the Portuguese had recently expelled from Bahia. . . . The amphibiousness of the invaders, Vieira argued, manifested the blasphemy that prevented the Dutch from seeing the banner of St. Anthony" (166–67).

5. "When he saw these misfortunes, a lad, captive of a passenger, Manoel Rodrigues, began to make great rejoicings . . . jumping very happily into the

pool in the middle of the ship. He swam and dived there . . . and he jested at the others. . . . Whence we see that brutishness sometimes produces the same effects in barbarians as learning and philosophy in the civilized" (Ley 271) ("À vista destas calamidades, um moço cativo de Manuel Rodrigues, passageiro, começou a fazer muita festa . . . saltou com muito contentamento na água dentro no tanque que a nau em si recolheu, onde nadando dava muitos mergulhos, zombando dos mais. . . . Donde se vê que os mesmos efeitos obram às vezes nos bárbaros a bruteza que nos bem instruídos a lição e filosofia" [Águas 2:62–63]).

6. "iam sempre com água pela cinta, quando menos, sem nunca poderem tomar sono, porque se algum adormecia vinha a onda e dando-lhe no rosto o fazia estar sempre esperto" (Águas 2:80).

7. "Começou a romper a manhã, e já muitos diziam que viam terra, e alguns afirmavam ser terra firme, mas acabando de aclarar o dia se desenganaram de todo, porque o que parecia terra e árvores eram os quartéis da nau em pedaços, pipas e caixões, que as águas levaram para aquela parte onde apareciam e onde por ser mais baixo encalharam" (Águas 2:57).

8. "destroço e ruína de tão fermosa máquina como era a da nau" (Águas 2:62).

9. "Aqui se viu o mais horrendo espectáculo de todos os do naufrágio, porque assim os das jangadas como os que estavam nos penedos esperando ter algum refúgio no batel, se saíram deles e se vinham nus com água pelos peitos, estando toda a noite em um perpétuo grito, por razão da frieza da água e incompatíveis dores; não se ouviam outras vozes mais que ais, gemidos e grandes lástimas; bradavam pelos do batel que lhes valessem" (Águas 2:65).

10. See chapter 29 of Lucena for a particularly vivid account of the fascination with Xavier's corpse. In a discussion of the HTM, Jackson notes: "This tragic vision of empire suggests another relationship between the sea and the body of the empire: to the Utopia of the re-encounter of Western being with its lost origins and the miracle of the uncorrupted body (of St. Francis Xavier) can be contrasted the loss of life and the official and moral corruption" (*Builders* 25). Also see Jackson's remarks on Xavier in "Sinkings" (157–58). For further studies on Jesuit texts in overseas expansion, see M. Barchiesi ("Il naufragio"), R. Barchiesi ("Andare in Oriente," "La *Lusiade Leonina*"), and Wicki.

11. "a mais gente veio à terra . . . como a Nosso Senhor aprouve, e muita dela ferida dos pregos e madeira" (195).

12. "com . . . mui grandes mares . . . estando o gajeiro da gávea em pé em cima para descer, bem descuidado, deu a nau um balanço grande, com que meteu e lançou o pobre grumete por cima da gávea, que veio pelo ar cair e dar na ponta de uma entena que estava por banda do bombordo em popa; e caiu ao

mar, dando com as pernas e partes do corpo em os pés de um homem que a
bordo estava pegado, o qual consigo houvera de levar ao mar, deixando-o aleija-
do da grande pancada que lhe deu de um deles, e desfazendo a cabeça em
pedaços, com os miolos fora dela, nas vergas, que todas ficaram tintas do seu
sangue. . . . Logo daí a três dias nos aconteceu . . . outro desastre mui semel-
hante a este no gajeiro da proa. . . . caiu da gávea ao mar, tocando, ao cair, em
uma unha das âncoras . . . lhe levou a âncora toda a pele da cabeça, que lhe
ficou propriamente com o capelo pegado da banda do toutiço por detrás"
(Águas 1:176).

13. See esp. 140–47.

14. Lucan's *Pharsalia* stands as the "opposition to the imperial establish-
ment that made the *Aeneid* its official poem and that might silence other, dis-
senting versions of Roman history" (Quint 133); it initiated an "anti-Virgilian
tradition of epic whose major poems . . . embrace the cause of the politically defeated" (ibid.).

15. "[T]he body . . . 'in' parts . . . is constituted by a multiplicity of individu-
ated organs" (xi).

16. One of the passengers on board the Conceição was the famous Italian
merchant Francesco Carletti, who wrote his own account in *My Voyage around
the World*. For studies on Carletti and his account of the Portuguese vessel, see
Barchiesi ("Francesco Carletti"), Disney, and Peloso. On the narrative structure
of the *Conceição,* read Matos ("Para o estudo").

17. The pursuit of *carreira da Índia* wealth falls within the perception of the
"*unnaturalness* of the desire for gold" in the sixteenth century (Greenblatt,
Marvelous Possessions 64).

18. "[C]rescendo . . . o perigo, se deitou ao mar tudo o que havia na tolda
dos bombardeiros e nos paióis das drogas, com que ficou coberto de infinitas
riquezas, lançadas as mais delas por seus próprios donos, dos quais eram naquele tempo tão aborrecidas e desprezadas como em outro foram amadas e esti-
madas" (Águas 2:125).

19. "A este tempo andava o mar todo coalhado de caixas, lanças, pipas e
outras diversidades de coisas que a desventurada hora do naufrágio fez aparecer"
(*S. Bento* 232).

20. "em poucas horas se pudera ver um lustroso e soberbo alojamento, feito
de alcatifas riquíssimas e de outras muitas peças de ouro e seda, gastadas em
bem diferente uso do para que foram feitas e dos propósitos com que seus donos
as tinham ganhadas com tão largos trabalhos com que semelhantes coisas se
adquirem" (*S. Bento* 236).

21. "E tanto que Deus nos mandou madeira e mantimento, determinámos

com alguns marinheiros que ali ficaram de fazer alguma embarcação em que coubéssemos sessenta ou setenta pessoas. E logo determinaram de ir à nau em uma jangada, que fizeram de uma antena, a tirar madeira. . . . E enquanto se fez a jangada se desfez a nau, pelo que nunca mais apareceu tábua nem pau. . . . E ainda que o marinheiro que a ordenava nunca tomara machado na mão, parecia que Deus visivelmente andava entre nós ajudando-nos e dando-nos entendimento para o sabermos fazer" (326–27).

22. "ele deu escrito seu que o cumpriria, que foi escrito com sangue de um companheiro dos doentes" (Águas 2:78).

23. This principle of imminent edibility determines the fate of documents in the *S. Lourenço*: some barrels are inspected to see if they contain food, but only papers *(cartas)* are found, and are consequently thrown into the sea (Pereira 10:174).

24. "que lhes trazia cartas de Fernão Rodrigues Caldeira e de outro português, e ordem para os tirar dali, então lhes deu as cartas: uma vinha para Diogo Rodrigues Caldeira, irmão de Fernão Rodrigues, e outra para todos" (Águas 2:72).

25. "foi isto causa de tanta alegria em todos que lhes parecia que viam algum português" (Águas 2:72).

26. Apropos of a moment in the *S. Paulo,* Boxer muses that "[i]t is extraordinary how often the Portuguese castaways in these shipwrecks when they had either lost nearly everything or abandoned so much in order to 'travel light', still contrived to produce ink and paper with which to draw up notarial documents" (*Further Selections* 90 n. 1).

27. "Depois de recolhida a gente dela [Garça], fez Francisco Barreto um escrito em que dizia estas palavras: "A nau Garça se perdeu tanto avante como o cabo das Correntes, em altura de 25 graus da banda do sul, e foi-se ao fundo por fazer muita água. Eu, com os fidalgos e mais gente que levava na minha nau, lhe salvei a sua toda; e imos fazendo nossa viagem para Portugal com o mesmo trabalho. Pedimos, pelo amor de Deus, a todos os fiéis cristãos que disto tiverem notícia, indo ter este batel aonde houver portugueses, que nos encomendem a Nosso Senhor em suas orações, nos dê boa viagem e nos leve a salvamento a Portugal." Este escrito se meteu em um canudo e o taparam e brearam muito bem, e fizeram uma cruzeta alta no batel, aonde o ataram porque lhe não chegasse a água, e deixaram o batel que o levassem as águas aonde quisessem. Foi Deus servido que fosse ter dentro a Sofala, onde estava Bastião de Sá por capitão, como depois se soube, quando Francisco Barreto tornou a invernar a segunda vez a Moçambique" (369).

28. See especially chapter 1.

29. Shipwreck not only breaks apart the "secret knowledge" of ordered society, but allows that knowledge to break free of limitations as they are (socially) imposed by home-country order. Thus, in the shipwreck narrative, knowledge can be reconstructed and democratized, as in the case of the sailors who practice shipbuilding or the apothecary, Henrique Dias, who becomes a doctor in the wake of shipwreck: "I cured all these people and was a practicing physician even though, as an apothecary, I had no training in this profession" ("curei toda esta gente e usei de médico, sem nesta ciência ter profissão nenhuma, pois era boticário" [*S. Paulo*, Águas 1:177]).

30. The violation of the boundary of the sea underlies the conflict of *Os Lusíadas* in which the deity of the sea is angered that his unsailed waters are being cut by the prows of Portuguese ships.

31. Castilian writer Antonio de Guevara takes on the topic in his *Arte de marear* (1539), a treatise on navigation that mockingly lists fifty-eight "privileges" reserved for those who take to life at sea. Guevara provides a wealth of detail about the uncomfortable conditions of life on a ship, implicitly condemning anyone who would willingly embrace them. He identifies *codicia* (avarice) not simply as a moral weakness, but as one of the very reasons the art of navigation was invented, observing that "in this it is seen how bestial man is of all the beasts, since animals flee for no other reason than to escape death, and only man sets sail in such great danger to life" ("[e]n esto se ve cuán más bestial es el hombre que todas las bestias, pues todos los animales huyen no por más de por huir la muerte, y sólo el hombre navega en muy gran perjuicio de la vida" [325]). It is avarice, then, the driving force of the India voyage, that fundamentally—and definitionally—joins navigation and the breaking of natural order. Complements to Guevara's text in their sardonic vision of maritime life are Erasmus's colloquy "The Shipwreck" (1523) and Eugenio de Salazar's *Carta,* or "Landlubber's Lament" (1573).

32. "la tierra crió Dios para los hombres y la mar para los peces" (124).

33. "Enfim tudo era contra eles, até o leme da nau deixou de governar, por cuja causa ela ficou atravessada, sem velas, por serem todas rotas. . . . Toda esta noite passaram com grandes trabalhos e desconsolações, porque tudo quanto viam lhes representava a morte, porque, por baixo, viram a nau cheia de água, por cima, o céu conjurado contra todos, porque até ele se lhe encobriu com a maior cerração e escuridade que si viu. O ar assobiava de todas as partes, que parecia lhes estava bradando, morte, morte; e não bastando a água que por baixo lhes entrava, e de cima que o céu lançava sobre eles, parecia que os queria alagar com outro dilúvio. Dentro na nau tudo o que se ouvia eram suspiros, gemidos, gritos, prantos e misericórdias que se pediam a Deus, que parecia que

por alguns pecados de alguns que iam naquela nau estava irado contra eles"
(Águas 2:96).

34. "e foi tanta a necessidade da fome que padecíamos que alguns dos nossos companheiros se foram a Jorge de Albuquerque e lhe disseram que bem via
os que morriam e acabavam de pura fome, e os que estavam vivos não tinham
cousa de que se sustentar; e que pois assim era, lhes desse licença para comerem
os que morriam, pois eles vivos não tinham outra cousa de que se manter.
Abriu-se a alma a Jorge de Albuquerque de lástima e compaixão, e arrasaram-
lhes os olhos de água quando ouviu este espantoso requerimento, por ver a que
estado os tinha chegado a sua necessidade, e lhes disse com muita dor que aquilo que lhe diziam era tão fora de razão que erro e cegueira muito grande seria
consentir em tão bruto desejo. . . . E . . . o perverso inimigo . . . começou a usar
um novo e não cuidado ardil contra nós. . . . vendo que a braveza do mar e fúria
da tormenta nos não pudera acabar, encaixou nos corações de alguns dos nossos
uma persuasão infernal de se não poderem salvar nem escapar daquele perigo e
que todos havíamos de morrer forçadamente. Vencidos de tão mau conselho do
falso inimigo, consultaram alguns deles entre si, pois não podiam escapar por
nenhum caso . . . para escusarem a pena que padeciam com ela, que arran-
cassem uma tábua do fundo da nau para com mais brevidade se irem ao fundo,
e com isso ficarem sem vida e sem trabalhos, que com a ter padeciam" (Águas
2:42–43).

35. Interpreting passages from Ovid and Seneca, Calvo-Stevenson remarks:
"navigation is construed as a 'fallenness' from a previous state of community
with nature. It is conceived as an evil activity that entails a sense of lack, the loss
of a previous state of plenitude that represented a 'natural,' unmediated existence. Navigation is the sign of this lack. . . . In this mythical tale of origins,
ships and sailing represent a transgression of the natural limits of humankind"
(32–33).

36. "não só arriscava o corpo, mas . . . tambem arriscava a alma por ficar em
terra de infieis, aonde lhe podiam entrar os seus máos costumes, e cerimonias"
(S. João Baptista, Pereira 9:32).

5. AN ILLUSTRIOUS SCHOOL OF CAUTION

1. For Portugal under D. João V, see Russell-Wood, "Portugal and the
World."

2. "se escrevesse a historia ecclesiastica d'estes reinos, e depois tudo o que
pertencesse á historia d'elles e de suas conquistas" (qtd. in Ribeiro 169). See
Ribeiro 169–200 for a list of academies during the time of D. João V.

3. "se propunha restituir á noticia do mundo as acções e feitos dos portuguezes" (qtd. in Ribeiro 169).

4. "SENHOR: Como V. Magestade, por sua Real grandeza, se fez Augusto Protector da Historia, erigindo a sua preclara Academia; parece, que permittio aos afortunados Historiadores deste Seculo a gloria de recorrer ao seo Real azilo; indulto de que agora me valho, para pôr aos Reaes pès de V. Magestade nestes tomos, estes fragmentos Historicos, que jà perdem o horror de lastimosos, na fortuna de dedicados; conseguindo eu para aquelles Vassallos desta Coroa (que agora o saõ de V. Magestade com melhor estrella) nos seos naufragios o mais felis porto, senaõ para as suas vidas, para as suas memorias. O Ceo dilate a vida de V. Magestade para felicidade desta Monarquia" (§ª–[§iiᵇ]).

5. Tabucchi reads Gomes de Brito's allusion to the "intrinsic tragic sense" contained in the title as a strategy of self-promotion; by appealing to the narratives' *pathos*, Gomes de Brito desires to incite an interest so that he can become a "historiador do reino" (historian of the realm) (27). The volumes were printed by the Congregação do Oratório (Congregation of the Oratorians), a religious order that enjoyed the special favor of D. João V (Marques 413).

6. "[e]m que se escrevem chronologicamente os Naufragios que tiveraõ as Naos de Portugal, depois que se poz em exercicio a Navegaçaõ da India."

7. Tabucchi argues that all titles are a form of self-interpretation, particularly those of anthologies because they synthesize the meaning of the texts united under them (24).

8. "offered to his august Majesty, the most high and most powerful king D. João V" ("Offerecido á Augusta Magestade do Muito Alto e Muito Poderoso Rey D. JOAÕ V").

9. The licenses are reprinted in Tabucchi.

10. See Carruthers 82–84, 164–65 for further elaboration.

11. "Offereço ao desejo dos curiosos, exponho à mordacidade dos criticos este volume, que comprehende os primeiros quatro mezes do Anno Historico, e os primeiros cento e vinte dias do Diario Portuguez. . . . Aqui achará o curioso leitor muitas, e diversas noticias, em que pòde exercitar o genio, e instruir, naõ inutilmente, a sua aplicaçaõ. . . . Os successos Tragicos, os Bellicos, os Politicos, que se referem do tempo passado, tambem saõ regra, por onde se devem medir, e regular os do tempo presente, e futuros. Os signaes do Ceo, as péstes, os incendios, os naufragios, saõ outras tantas admoestaçoens para a nossa emenda, e para o temor de semelhantes castigos" (ix).

12. "este livro depois de impresso servirà sem duvida de melhor Roteiro a todos os navegantes dos màres da India" ([§§iiiª]).

13. "Dos tragicos successos, que se lem nas Relaçoens destes infortunios, tem muito de que se gloriar a heroicidade daquelles espiritos magnanimos" ([§iiiᵇ]).

14. "este Livro . . . no theatro da Historia representa hum papel verdadeiramente tragico" ([§iv^a]).

15. "invictos Varoens dos quaes esta presente historia nos faz especial mençaõ" ([§iii^b]–[§iv^a]).

16. "as tempestades, que causáraõ os horrorosos naufragios . . . se bem reflectirmos, ainda excedem no horror dos successos a todas aquellas taõ memoraveis tempestades que descrevem [sic] Virgilio" ([§§ii^b]).

17. The third, "apocryphal" volume boasts no licenses for the book as a whole, although *licenças* appear at the head of some of the narratives.

18. "ensayos de sua ira, (que) saõ tambem prendas do seo amor" ([§iv^a]).

19. "Este Segundo Tomo da *Historia Tragico-Maritima* . . . a que curiosamẽte dà o ser Bernardo Gomes de Brito, e pretende se faça a todos manifesto por meyo da estampa, se faz taõ acredor desta publicidade, quaõ merecedor he de que seja espelho em que cada hum dos que neste proceloso mar deste mundo vivem, todos os dias se contemplem" ([§iii^b]).

20. "Estes (autores) nos deixàraõ impressos os naufragios Portuguezes nas folhas deste livro, como os antigos naufragantes nas amargosas do Zambujeiro, aonde, em testemunho do beneficio, penduravaõ os despojos do seo naufragio, como refere Virgilo.

> *Fortè sacer Fauni foliis Oleaster amaris*
> *Hic steterat, nautis olim venerabile signum,*
> *Servati ex undis ubi figere dona solebant*
> *Laurenti divo, & votas suspendere vestes.*

Que outra couza lemos nas amargosas folhas deste livro, symbolisado Zambujeiro, senaõ os despojos de hum naufragio" ([§ii^b]). The English translation of Virgil's passage cited in the text is from the Loeb Classical Library edition of the *Aeneid* (XII, ll. 766–69).

21. "Sendo taõ lastimòsos, e infelices os successos, de que se compoem [o livro], com tudo [sic] a variedade dos mesmos successos, e o desejo, que o animo concebe logo ao principio de qualquer delles, de ver o fiem m, [sic, for *fim*] que ultimamente veyo a parar, fazem a liçaõ deste livro taõ suave, e taõ agradavel, que naõ permitte a menor interrupçaõ: pelo menos o breve tempo, em que eu o li, ainda me pareceo mais breve pela suavidade da lição" ([§§^a]–[§§^b]).

BIBLIOGRAPHY

ABBREVIATIONS

HTM	*História Trágico-Marítima*
Tragic History	C. R. Boxer, *The Tragic History of the Sea* (first part of the University of Minnesota Press edition)
Further Selections	C. R. Boxer, *Further Selections from the Tragic History of the Sea* (second part of the University of Minnesota Press edition of *The Tragic History of the Sea*)

EDITIONS OF THE HISTÓRIA TRÁGICO-MARÍTIMA

Editio princeps

HISTORIA | TRAGICO-MARITIMA | *Em que se escrevem chronologicamente os Nau-* | *fragios que tiveraõ as Naos de Portugal, de-* | *pois que se poz em exercicio a Navegaçaõ* | *da India.* | TOMO PRIMEIRO. | *OFFERECIDO* | A' Augusta Magestade do Muito Alto e Muito | Poderoso Rey | D. JOAÕ V. | Nosso Senhor. | POR BERNARDO GOMES DE BRITO. | [Woodcut of royal arms.] | LISBOA OCCIDENTAL. | Na Officina da Congregaçaõ do Oratorio. | M. DCC. XXXV. | *Com todas as licenças necessarias.* This and the following volume in the Stanton Collection, University of Toronto.

HISTORIA | TRAGICO-MARITIMA | *Em que se escrevem chronologicamente os Nau-* | *fragios que tiveraõ as Naos de Portugal,* | *depois que se poz em exerci-* | *cio a Na-* | *vegaçaõ da India.* | TOMO SEGUNDO | *OFFERECIDO* | A' Augusta Magestade do muito Alto, e muito | Poderoso Rey | D. JOAÕ V. | Nosso Senhor. | POR BERNARDO GOMES DE BRITO. | [Woodcut of royal arms.] | LISBOA OCCIDENTAL, | Na Officina da Congregaçaõ do Oratorio. | M. DCC. XXXVI. | *Com todas as licenças necessarias.*

[História Trágico-Marítima.] Some exemplars bear the title *Collecção de naufragios, servindo de continuação á Historia Tragico-Maritima.* This exemplar is housed at Harvard University; it lacks a title page and table of contents.

Other Editions (Includes Partial Editions)

Álvares, Manuel. *Naufrágio da Nau "S. Paulo" em um ilheu próximo de Samatra, no ano de 1561. Narração inédita, escrita em Goa em 1562 pelo Padre Manuel Álvares, S.J.* Ed. Frazão de Vasconelos. Lisbon, 1948.

Amaral, Melchior Estácio do. *Tratado das batalhas e sucessos do galeam Santiago com os Olandezes na Ilha de Santa Elena, e da nao Chagas com os Inglezes entre as ilhas dos Açores: ambas capitanias da carreyra da India, & da causa, & desastres, porque em vinte annos de perdêraõ trinta, & oyto naos della.* Lisbon: António Alves, 1604 (1735?). (counterfeit edition)

Brito, Bernardo Gomes de. *História Trágico-Marítima.* [Ed. Neves Águas.] 2 vols. Mira-Sintra: Europa-América, n.d.

———. *História Trágico-Marítima.* Ed. Neves Águas. 2 vols. Lisbon: Afrodite, 1971–72.

———. *História Trágico-Marítima compilada por Bernardo Gomes de Brito com outras notícias de naufrágios.* [Ed. Gabriel Pereira.] Biblioteca de Clássicos Portugueses 40–49, 57–58. 12 vols. Lisbon: Escriptorio, 1904–9.

———. *História Trágico-Marítima.* Ed. Damião Peres. 5 vols. Porto: F. Machado, 1936–37.

———. *História Trágico-Marítima.* Ed. António Sérgio. 3 vols. Lisbon: Sul, 1955–56.

Lanciani, Giulia. *Naufragi e peregrinazioni americane di Gaspar Afonso.* Lettera-
ture e Culture dell'America Latina 10. Milan: Cisalpino-Goliardica, 1984.

———. *Santa Maria da Barca: três testemunhos para um naufrágio.* Lisbon:
Imprensa Nacional-Casa da Moeda, 1983.

———. *Sucessos e naufrágios das naus portuguesas.* Lisbon: Caminho, 1997.

Lapa, Rodrigues. *Quadros da* História Trágico-Marítima. 5th ed. Mafra: Seara
Nova, 1972.

Luiz, Afonso (Piloto), and Bento Teyxeyra. *Naufragio & prosopopea.* Ed.
Fernando de Oliveira Mota. Recife: Universidade Federal de Pernambuco,
1969.

Martins, J. Cândido. *Naufrágio de Sepúlveda: texto e intertexto.* Lisbon:
Replicação, 1997.

Passos, Carlos de. "Navegação portuguesa dos séculos XVI e XVII: naufrágios
inéditos: novos subsídios para a História trágico-marítima de Portugal."
Biblos 4 (1928): 224–50.

Peres, Damião. *Viagens e naufrágios célebres dos séculos XVI, XVII, e XVIII.*
Crónicas e Memórias. 4 vols. Porto: F. Machado, 1937–38.

Sérgio, António. *Naufrágios e combates no mar.* 2 vols. Lisbon: Sul, 1958–59.

Simões, Manuel. *A literatura de viagens nos séculos XVI e XVII.* Textos Literários
40. Lisbon: Comunicação, 1985.

Theal, George McCall, ed. and trans. *Records of South-Eastern Africa Collected
in Various Libraries and Archive Departments in Europe.* 9 vols. London:
The Government of the Cape Colony, 1898–1903.

TRANSLATIONS OF HTM NARRATIVES

Blackmore, Josiah, trans. *Account of the very remarkable loss of the Great Galleon
S. João, which narrates the great hardships and pitiful trials visited on Captain
Manuel de Sousa Sepúlveda, and the lamentable end that he, his wife, and
children met, along with all the others, in the land of Natal where they wrecked
on June 24, 1552. The Tragic History of the Sea.* Ed. and trans. C. R. Boxer.
Minneapolis: University of Minnesota Press, 2001. 1–26.

Blanco Suárez, P., trans. *Historia Trágico-Marítima.* Colección Austral. Buenos
Aires: Espasa-Calpe Argentina, 1948. *(S. João, S. Bento, Conceição, S. Maria
da Barca.)*

Boxer, C. R., ed. and trans. *The Tragic History of the Sea.* Minneapolis: University of Minnesota Press, 2001.

Deperthes, Jean Louis Hubert Simon, comp. *Histoire des naufrages, ou recueil
des relations les plus intéressantes des naufrages, hivernemens, délaissemens,
incendies, famines, & autres evénemens funestes sur mer; qui ont été publiées*

depuis le quinzieme siecle jusqu'a présent. 3 vols. Paris: Cuchet, [1795].
(Summary of *S. João.*)

————. *Histoire des naufrages, ou recueil des relations les plus intéressantes des
naufrages, hivernemens, délaissemens, incendies, et autres evénemens funestes
arrivés sur mer.* Ed. J. B. B. Eyriès. New ed. Refondue, corrigée et augmen-
tée de plusieurs morceaux tels que les *Aventures de Drury à Madagascar;
celles de Quirini, navigateur vénitien; les naufrages du Grosvenor, du brig
américain le Commerce, du vaisseau l'Alceste, de la frégate la Méduse, etc.,
etc.* 3 vols. Paris: Ledoux et Tenré, 1818. (Summary of *S. João, Santiago.*)

Huntress, Keith, ed. *Narratives of Shipwrecks and Disasters, 1586–1860.* Ames:
Iowa State University Press, 1974. (Partial trans. of *Santiago.*)

Lanciani, Giulia, trans. *Tempeste e naufragi sulla via delle Indie.* Biblioteca
di Cultura 440. Rome: Bulzoni, 1991. (*S. João, S. Bento, Santiago/Chagas,
N. S. da Candelária.*)

Le Gentil, Georges, trans. *Histoires tragico-maritimes: trois récits portugais du
XVIᵉ siècle.* Paris: Chandeigne, 1992. (*Conceição, S. João, S. Paulo.*)

Ley, Charles David, trans. *Portuguese Voyages 1498–1663.* Everyman's Library
986. London: J. M. Dent & Sons; New York: E. P. Dutton, 1947. (*S. João,*
partial trans. of *Santiago.*)

Theal, George McCall, ed. and trans. *Records of South-Eastern Africa Collected
in Various Libraries and Archive Departments in Europe.* 9 vols. London:
The Government of the Cape Colony, 1898–1903. (*S. João,* partial trans.
of *S. Bento,* partial trans. of *Santiago, S. Tomé, S. Alberto, S. João Baptista,
Nossa Senhora de Belém, Sacramento/Nossa Senhora de Atalaya.*)

OTHER PRIMARY SOURCES

Adorno, Rolena, and Patrick Charles Pautz. *Álvar Núñez Cabeza de Vaca: His
Account, His Life, and the Expedition of Pánfilo de Narváez.* 3 vols. Lincoln:
University of Nebraska Press, 1999.

Afonso X, o Sábio. *Cantigas de Santa Maria.* Ed. Walter Mettmann. 4 vols.
Coimbra: Universidade de Coimbra, 1959–72.

Alfonso X. *El 'Códice rico' de las cantigas de Alfonso x el Sabio: ms. T.I.1 de la
Biblioteca de El Escorial.* Madrid: Edilan, 1979.

Aristotle. *The Politics.* Ed. and trans. Ernest Barber. London: Oxford University Press, 1958.

Assunção, José da. *Censura do M.R.P.M. Fr. José da Assumpção, Qualificador
do Santo Officio & c.* In vol. 2 of *História Trágico-Marítima,* 1736.
[§iiiᵇ]–[§ivᵇ].

[Ataíde, António de.] *A derradeira aventura de Paulo de Lima.* As Grandes

Aventuras e os Grandes Aventureiros 2. Ed. Luís Silveira. Lisbon: Bertrand, 1942.

Baepler, Paul, ed. *White Slaves, African Masters: An Anthology of American Barbary Captivity Narratives.* Chicago: University of Chicago Press, 1999.

Barros, João de. *Ásia: dos feitos que os portugueses fizeram no descobrimento e conquista dos mares e terras do Oriente.* Ed. Hernani Cidade. 4 vols. Lisbon: Agência Geral das Colónias, 1945–46.

Berceo [Gonzalo de]. *Milagros de Nuestra Señora.* Ed. Antonio G. Solalinde. Madrid: Espasa-Calpe, 1978.

———. *Miracles of Our Lady.* Trans. Richard Terry Mount and Annette Grant Cash. Lexington: University Press of Kentucky, 1997.

Biblia Sacra iuxta Vulgatam Clementinam. Ed. Alberto Colunga and Laurentio Turrado. 4th ed. Madrid: Biblioteca de Autores Cristianos, 1965.

Boisvert, Georges, trans. *Le Naufrage des portugais sur les côtes de Saint-Jean-de-Luz & d'Arcachon (1627).* Ed. Jean-Yves Blot and Patrick Lizé. Paris: Chandeigne, 2000.

Brea, Mercedes, ed. *Lírica profana galego-portuguesa: corpus completo das cantigas medievais, con estudio biográfico, análise retórica e bibliografía específica.* 2 vols. Santiago de Compostela: Centro de Investigacións Lingüísticas e Literarias Ramón Piñeiro, 1996.

Cabeza de Vaca, Álvar Núñez. *Castaways.* Trans. Frances M. López-Morillas. Berkeley: University of California Press, 1993.

———. *Los naufragios.* Ed. Enrique Pupo-Walker. Madrid: Castalia, 1992.

Camerarius, P. *The Living Librarie, or, Meditations and Observations Historical, Natural, Moral, Political, and Poetical.* Trans. John Molle. London: Adam Islip, 1621.

Caminha, Pero Vaz de. *A Carta.* Ed. Jaime Cortesão. Lisbon: Imprensa Nacional-Casa da Moeda, 1994.

Camões, Luís de. *Os Lusíadas.* Ed. Emanuel Paulo Ramos. Porto: Porto Editora, n.d.

———. *Lusiadas de Luis de Camoens . . . comentadas por Manuel de Faria i Sousa . . .* 2 vols. Madrid: Ivan Sánchez, 1639.

———. *La Lusiade de Louis Camoëns; poëme héroique, en dix chants, nouvellement traduit du portugais.* 2 vols. Paris: Nyon, 1776.

———. *The Lusiads.* Trans. Leonard Bacon. New York: Hispanic Society of America, 1950.

Carletti, Francesco. *My Voyage around the World.* Trans. Herbert Weinstock. New York: Pantheon, 1964.

Castanheda, Fernão Lopes de. *História do descobrimento e conquista da Índia pelos portugueses.* 3d ed. Ed. Pedro de Azevedo. 2 vols. Coimbra: Imprensa da Universidade, 1924, 1928.

Cesariny, Mário, comp. *Horta de literatura de cordel.* Lisbon: Assírio e Alvim, 1983.

Colón, Cristóbal. [Columbus]. *Diario del primer viaje. Textos y documentos completos.* Ed. Consuelo Varela. Madrid: Alianza, 1982. 15–138.

Contreras, Francisco de. *Nave trágica de la India de Portugal.* Madrid, 1624. (British Museum 1073.i.31.)

Corte-Real, Jerónimo. *Naufragio e lastimoso sucesso da perdiçam de Manoel de Sousa de Sepulueda, & dona Lianor de Sá sua molher & filhos, vindo da India para este reyno na nao chamada o galião grande S. Ioão que se perdeo no Cabo de Boa Esperança na terra do Natal . . .* Lisbon: Simão Lopez, 1594.

Cortés, Hernán. *Cartas de relación.* Mexico City: Porrúa, 1993.

Couto, Diogo do. *Da Asia de João de Barros e de Diogo do Couto.* 23 vols. New ed. Lisbon: Regia Officina Typografica, 1778.

———. *O soldado prático.* Lisbon: Sá da Costa, 1980.

Davenport, Frances Gardiner, ed. *European Treaties Bearing on the History of the United States and Its Dependencies to 1648.* Gloucester, Mass.: Peter Smith, 1967.

Díaz del Castillo, Bernal. *Historia verdadera de la conquista de la nueva España.* Mexico City: Porrúa, 1968.

Erasmus. "The Shipwreck/*Naufragium.*" In *Collected Works of Erasmus: Colloquies,* trans. Craig R. Thompson. Vol. 39. Toronto: University of Toronto Press, 1997. 351–67.

Ercilla, Alonso de. *La Araucana.* Mexico City: Porrúa, 1979.

Fowler, Barbara Hughes, trans. *Songs of a Friend: Love Lyrics of Medieval Portugal: Selections from Cantigas de Amigo.* Chapel Hill: University of North Carolina Press, 1996.

Francisco, Júlio. *Censura do M.R.P.M. Julio Francisco da Congregaçaõ do Oratorio.* In vol. 1 of *História Trágico-Marítima,* 1735. §§ª–§§iiª.

González de Clavijo, Ruy. *Relación de la embajada de Enrique III al gran Tamorlán.* Buenos Aires: Espasa-Calpe, 1952.

Guevara, Antonio de. *Menosprecio de Corte y Arte de Marear.* Ed. Asunción Rallo Gruss. Madrid: Cátedra, 1984.

Holy Bible. Rev. standard version. Ed. Herbert G. May and Bruce M. Metzger. New York: Oxford University Press, 1973.

Jensen, Frede, ed. and trans. *Medieval Galician-Portuguese Poetry: An Anthology.* Garland Library of Medieval Literature A/87. New York: Garland, 1992.

Johnson, Samuel. *A Voyage to Abyssinia.* Ed. Joel J. Gold. New Haven: Yale University Press, 1985.

Kulp-Hill, Kathleen, trans. *Songs of Holy Mary of Alfonso X, the Wise: A Translation of the* Cantigas de Santa Maria. Medieval and Renaissance Texts and Studies 173. Tempe: Arizona Center for Medieval and Renaissance Studies, 2000.

Linschoten, John Huyghen van. *The Voyage of John Huyghen van Linschoten to the East Indies.* Ed. Arthur Coke Burnell and P. A. Tiele. Vol. 1. London: Hakluyt Society, 1885.

Lobo, Jerónimo. *The* Itinerário *of Jerónimo Lobo.* Trans. Donald M. Lockhart. London: Hakluyt Society, 1984.

Lopes, Fernão. *Cronica del Rei Dom Joham de boa memoria e dos reis de Portugal o decimo.* 2 vols. Lisbon: Imprensa Nacional-Casa da Moeda, 1977.

Lucan. *Pharsalia.* Trans. Jane Wilson Joyce. Ithaca, N.Y.: Cornell University Press, 1993.

Lucena, João de. *História da vida do padre Francisco de Xavier.* Vol. 4. Lisbon: Alfa, 1989. 4 vols.

[Luís, Nicolau.] *Tragedia intitullada os Successos de Sepulveda. Theatro popular ou peças vulgarmente chamadas de cordel, as quaes á custa de não pouco trabalho e paciencia colligiu Rodrigo Felner.* Vol. 3. Lisbon: 1872.

Maldonado, Maria Hermínia, ed. *Relação das náos e armadas da India com os successos dellas que se puderam saber, para noticia e instrucção dos curiozos, e amantes da historia da India (British Library, Códice Add. 20902).* Coimbra: Biblioteca Geral da Universidade de Coimbra, 1985.

Medina, Pedro de. *Regimiento de navegación* (trascripción). 1563. Madrid: Instituto de España, 1964.

Melo, Francisco Manuel de. "Naufrágio da armada portuguesa em França ano 1627, Epanáfora Trágica Segunda . . . escrita a um amigo." In *Naufrágios e combates no mar,* vol. 1, ed. António Sérgio. Lisbon: Sul, 1958. 7–86.

Moura, Vasco Graça. *Naufrágio de Sepúlveda.* Lisbon: Quetzal, 1988.

Neider, Charles, ed. *Great Shipwrecks and Castaways: Firsthand Accounts of Disasters at Sea.* New York: Cooper Square Press, 2000.

Oviedo y Valdés, Gonzalo Fernández de. *Historia general y natural de las Indias, islas, y tierra-firme del mar oceano.* 14 vols. Asunción del Paraguay: Guarania, 1944–45.

Palma-Ferreira, João, ed. *Naufrágios, viagens, fantasias e batalhas.* Lisbon: Imprensa Nacional-Casa da Moeda, 1980.

Peri Rossi, Cristina. *Descripción de un naufragio.* Barcelona: Lumen, 1975.

Pessoa, Fernando. *Obra poética.* Ed. Maria Aliete Galhoz. Rio de Janeiro: Nova Aguilar, 1983.

Pinto, Fernão Mendes. *Peregrinação.* Ed. Fernando Riberio de Mello. 2 vols. Lisbon: Afrodite, 1979.

Sá, Manuel de. *Censura do M.R.P.M. Fr. Manoel de Sà, Religioso da Ordem de N. Senhora do Carmo, Ex-Provincial, e Definidor perpetuo da Provincia Carmelitana de Portugal, Chronista geral da mesma Ordem nestes Reynos e seos Dominios, Qualificador e Revedor do Santo Officio, Examinador das Tres Ordens Militares, Consultor da Bulla da Cruzada, e Academico da Academia Real da Historia Portugueza.* In vol. 1 of *História Trágico-Marítima,* 1735. [§iiiª]–[§ivª].

Salazar, Eugenio de. *Life at Sea in the Sixteenth Century: The Landlubber's Lament of Eugenio de Salazar.* Trans. Carla Rahn Phillips. The James Ford Bell Lectures 24 [Minneapolis]: The Associates of the James Ford Bell Library, University of Minnesota, 1987.

S[anta] Maria, Francisco de, comp. *Anno historico, diario portuguez, noticia abreviada de pessoas grandes, e cousas notaveis de Portugal.* 3 vols. Lisbon: Domingos Gonsalves, 1744.

S[anta] Teresa, Francisco Xavier de. *Aprovaçaõ do M.R.P.M. Fr. Francisco Xavier de Santa Tereza da Ordem de S. Francisco, Academico da Academia Real.* In vol. 2 of *História Trágico-Marítima,* 1736. §§ª–[§§iiiᵇ].

Troyano, José. *Censura do M.R.P.M. José Troyano da Congregaçaõ do Oratorio Qualificador do Santo Officio & c.* In vol. 2 of *História Trágico-Marítima,* 1736. §iiª–[§iiiª].

Vicente, Gil. *Auto da Índia.* In *Obras completas,* ed. Marques Braga. Vol. 5. Lisbon: Sá da Costa, 1978. 89–116.

———. *Three Discovery Plays: Auto da Barca do Inferno, Exortação da Guerra, Auto da Índia.* Ed. and trans. Anthony Lappin. Warminster, England: Aris & Phillips, 1997.

Virgil. *Aeneid 7–12/The Minor Poems.* Trans. H. R. Fairclough. Loeb Classical Library 64. Cambridge: Harvard University Press, 1934.

———. *Eclogues/Georgics/Aeneid 1–6.* Trans. H. R. Fairclough. Loeb Classical Library 63. Cambridge: Harvard University Press, 1935.

Zenith, Richard, ed. and trans. *Fernando Pessoa & Co.: Selected Poems.* New York: Grove Press, 1998.

———. *113 Galician-Portuguese Troubadour Poems.* Manchester, England: Carcanet Press, 1995.

Zurara, Gomes Eanes de. *Crónica da tomada de Ceuta por El Rei D. João I.* Ed. Francisco Maria Esteves Pereira. Coimbra: Imprensa da Universidade, 1915.

———. *Crónica dos feitos notáveis que se passaram na conquista da Guiné por mandado do infante D. Henrique.* Ed. Torquato de Sousa Soares. Vol. 1. Lisbon: Academia Portuguesa da História, 1978.

SECONDARY SOURCES

Abad, Manuel. "La contextura estética de 'La Nave Trágica'. Poema épico de Francisco de Contreras." In *Actas del IX congreso de la Asociación Internacional de Hispanistas. 18–30 agosto 1986, Berlín,* ed. Sebastian Neumeister. Vol. I. Frankfurt: Vervuert, 1989. 281–89.

Alden, Dauril. *The Making of an Enterprise: The Society of Jesus in Portugal, Its Empire, and Beyond, 1540–1750.* Stanford, Calif.: Stanford University Press, 1996.

Ames, Glenn J. *Renascent Empire?: The House of Braganza and the Quest for Stability in Portuguese Monsoon Asia, c. 1640–1683.* Amsterdam: Amsterdam University Press, 2000.

Antebi, Susan. "On Historiography and Narrative Impossibility: An Approach to the *História Trágico-Marítima.*" Unpublished essay. 1997.

Araújo, Maria Benedita. "Os relatos de naufrágios." In *Condicionantes culturais da literatura de viagens: estudos e bibliografias,* ed. Fernando Cristóvão. Lisbon: Cosmos/Centro de Literaturas de Expressão Portuguesa da Universidade de Lisboa, 1999. 391–421.

Ares Montes, José. "I resti di un naufragio." *Quaderni portoghesi* 5 (1979): 45–67.

Arkinstall, Christine. "Refiguring the Blazon: The Politics of Empire-Building in Cristina Peri Rossi's *Descripción de un naufragio.*" *Revista Hispánica Moderna* 51 (1998): 423–40.

Bachelard, Gaston. *Water and Dreams: An Essay on the Imagination of Matter.* The Bachelard Translations. Trans. Edith R. Farrell. Dallas: Pegasus Foundation/Dallas Institute of Humanities and Culture, 1983.

Banks, Jared. "Adamastorying Mozambique: *Ualalapi* and *Os Lusíadas.*" *Luso-Brazilian Review* 37 (2000): 1–16.

Barchiesi, Maria Helena de Portugal Pereira. "Il naufragio della 'Nau Conceição' (1555). Relazioni e redazioni." *Quaderni portoghesi* 5 (1979): 165–82.

Barchiesi, Roberto. "Andare in Oriente. Lettere di missionari gesuiti del XVI secolo." In *Per via: miscellanea di studi in onore di Giuseppe Tavani.* Ed. Ettore Finazzi Agrò. Rome: Bulzoni, 1997. 73–99.

———. "Francesco Carletti: Nota all' *História Trágico-Marítima.*" *Estudos italianos em Portugal* 14–15 (1955–56): 169–77.

———. "La *Lusiade Leonina* di Ignazio Arcamone S.J." In Ceccucci 217–23.

———. "'Os sucessos de Sepúlveda'. Tragedia portoghese del XVIII secolo." *Annali dell'Istituto Universitario Orientale–Sezione Romanza* 17 (1975): 229–39.

————. "Un tema portoghese: il naufragio di Sepúlveda e la sua diffusione." *Annali dell'Istituto Universitario Orientale, Sezione Romanza* 18 (1976): 193–231.

————. "Terminologia da História Trágico-Marítima: O naufrágio." In *Actas. III Colóquio Internacional de Estudos Luso-Brasileiros, Lisboa, 1957*. Vol. 1. Lisbon: n.p., 1959. 207–13.

Barreto, Luís Filipe. "Gomes Eanes de Zurara e o nascimento do discurso historiográfico de transição." *Descobrimentos e renascimento: formas de ser e pensar nos séculos XV e XVI*. Lisbon: Imprensa Nacional-Casa da Moeda, 1983. 63–125.

Belardinelli, Renata Cusmai. "Il naufragio di Francesco Manuel de Melo e l' 'ipsi vidi' dell' 'Epanáfora Trágica'." *Quaderni portoghesi* 5 (1979): 143–63.

Blanchot, Maurice. *The Writing of the Disaster*. Trans. Ann Smock. New ed. Lincoln: University of Nebraska Press, 1995.

Blumenberg, Hans. *Shipwreck with Spectator: Paradigm of a Metaphor for Existence*. Trans. Steven Rendall. Cambridge: MIT Press, 1997.

Bluteau, Rafael. *Diccionario da lingua portugueza composto pelo Padre D. Rafael Bluteau, reformado, e accrescentado por Antonio de Moraes Silva natural do Rio de Janeiro*. Vol. 2. Lisbon: Simão Thaddeo Ferreira, 1789. 2 vols.

Boxer, C. R. *From Lisbon to Goa, 1500–1750: Studies in Portuguese Maritime Enterprise*. London: Variorum, 1984.

————. "An Introduction to the *História Trágico-Marítima*." In *Miscelânea de estudos em honra do Prof. Hernâni Cidade*. Lisbon: Faculdade de Letras da Universidade de Lisboa, 1957. 48–99. (Rpt. in *From Lisbon to Goa*.)

————. "An Introduction to the 'História Trágico-Marítima' (1957): Some Corrections and Clarifications." *Quaderni portoghesi* 5 (1979): 99–112. (Rpt. in *From Lisbon to Goa*.)

————. "Jorge de Albuquerque Coelho: Duas cartas inéditas e uma rectificação da 'História Trágico-Marítima'." *Anais* (Academia Portuguesa da História) 2d ser. 15 (1965): 134–47.

————. *The Portuguese Seaborne Empire 1415–1825*. New York: Alfred A. Knopf, 1969.

————. *Race Relations in the Portuguese Colonial Empire, 1415–1825*. Oxford: Clarendon Press, 1963.

————. "Some Second Thoughts on 'The Tragic History of the Sea, 1550–1650.'" *Annual Talk. The Hakluyt Society* (1978): 1–9.

Braudel, Fernand. "History and the Social Sciences." In *Economy and Society in Early Modern Europe: Essays from* Annales, ed. Peter Burke. London: Routledge & Kegan Paul, 1972. 11–42.

Burch, Julia Frances. "Sink or Swim: Shipwreck Narratives, Survival Tales, and Postcultural Subjectivity." Diss., University of Michigan, 1994.

Burke, James F. *Vision, the Gaze, and the Function of the Senses in* Celestina. University Park: Pennsylvania State University Press, 2000.

Calvo-Stevenson, Hortensia. "Sinking Being: Shipwrecks and Colonial Spanish American Writing." Diss., Yale University, 1990.

Carruthers, Mary. *The Craft of Thought: Meditation, Rhetoric, and the Making of Images, 400–1200.* Cambridge, England: Cambridge University Press, 1998.

Carvalho, Alberto. "Acerca dos 'relatos de naufrágio': significações narrativas e semânticas." In Seixo and Carvalho 13–65.

Carvalho, Isabel Boavida. "Viagens e naufrágios no feminino: da mulher invocada à mulher (quase) invisível." In Souza, Joaquim, Canço, Pires, and Castro. 235–44.

Castelo-Branco, Fernando. "Significado cultural das academias de Lisboa no século XVIII." In *Portugaliae historica.* Vol. 1. Lisbon: Universidade de Lisboa/Instituto Histórico Infante Dom Henrique, 1973. 175–201.

Ceccucci, Piero, ed. *Le caravelle portoghesi sulle vie delle Indie: le cronache di scoperta fra realtà e letteratura: Atti del Convegno Internazionale, Milano 3–4–5 dicembre 1990.* Rome: Bulzoni, 1993.

Centeno, Y. K. "O cântico da água em *Os Lusíadas.*" In *A viagem de "Os Lusíadas": símbolo e mito,* ed. Y. K. Centeno and Stephen Reckert. Lisbon: Arcádia, 1981. 11–32.

Cohen, Thomas M. *The Fire of Tongues: António Vieira and the Missionary Church in Brazil and Portugal.* Stanford, Calif.: Stanford University Press, 1998.

Cooney, Nicola Trowbridge. "Rereading Camões' Adamastor." Unpublished essay. 1997.

Cortesão, Jaime. "Sobre as viagens da carreira da Índia." In *Naufrágios e combates no mar,* ed. António Sérgio. Vol. 2. Lisbon: Sul, 1959. 279–92.

Covarrubias Orozco, Sebastián de. *Tesoro de la lengua castellana o española.* Ed. Felipe C. R. Maldonado. Madrid: Castalia, 1994.

Cusati, Maria Luisa, ed. *Il Portogallo e i mari: un incontro tra culture: congresso internazionale (Napoli, 15–17 dicembre 1994).* 3 vols. Naples: Liguori, 1997.

Diffie, Bailey W., and George D. Winius. *Foundations of the Portuguese Empire, 1415–1580.* Europe and the World in the Age of Expansion 1. Minneapolis: University of Minnesota Press, 1977.

Disney, Anthony. "Voyaging, Ports-of-call and Exotic Hinterlands in the Travel Narratives of Francesco Carletti and Tranquillo Grasseti." In *A vertigem do*

oriente: modalidades discursivas no encontro de culturas, ed. Ana Paula
Laborinho, Maria Alzira Seixo, and Maria José Meira. Lisbon-Macau:
Cosmos/Instituto Português do Oriente, 1999. 137–54.

Donahue, Jane. "Colonial Shipwreck Narratives: A Theological Study." *Books
at Brown* 23 (1969): 101–34.

Duffy, James. *Shipwreck and Empire: Being an Account of Portuguese Maritime
Disasters in a Century of Decline.* Cambridge: Harvard University Press,
1955.

Falcão, Ana Margarida, Maria Teresa Nascimento, and Maria Luísa Leal, eds.
Literatura de viagem: narrativa, história, mito. Viagem 2. Lisbon: Cosmos,
1997.

Ferreira, Ana Paula. "Intersecting Historical Performances: Gil Vicente's *Auto
da India.*" *Gestos* 17 (April 1994): 99–113.

Foucault, Michel. *The Archaeology of Knowledge and the Discourse on Language.*
Trans. A. M. Sheridan Smith. New York: Pantheon, 1972.

———. "Of Other Spaces." Trans. Jay Miskowiec. *Diacritics* 16 (1986): 22–27.

Freitas, Jordão de. *O naufrágio de Camões e dos Lusíadas.* Lisbon: Castro Irmão,
1915.

Garcia, José Manuel. "O significado do naufrágio do Sepúlveda na cultura portuguesa." In *Ao encontro dos descobrimentos: temas de história da expansão.*
Lisbon: Presença, 1994. 229–33.

Gerbi, Antonello. *Nature in the New World: From Christopher Columbus to
Gonzalo Fernández de Oviedo.* Trans. Jeremy Moyle. Pittsburgh: University
of Pittsburgh Press, 1985.

Glantz, Margo. "El cuerpo inscrito y el texto escrito o la desnudez como
naufragio." In *Notas y comentarios sobre Álvar Núñez Cabeza de Vaca,* ed.
Margo Glantz. Mexico City: Grijalbo, 1993. 403–34.

Godinho, Vitorino Magalhães. *Mito e mercadoria, utopia e a prática de navegar,
séculos XIII–XVIII.* Lisbon: Difel, 1990.

Goedde, Lawrence Otto. *Tempest and Shipwreck in Dutch and Flemish Art:
Convention, Rhetoric, and Interpretation.* University Park: Pennsylvania
State University Press, 1989.

González Echevarría, Roberto. *Myth and Archive: A Theory of Latin American
Narrative.* Durham, N.C.: Duke University Press, 1998.

Greenblatt, Stephen. *Marvelous Possessions: The Wonder of the New World.*
Chicago: University of Chicago Press, 1991.

Greene, Roland. *Unrequited Conquests: Love and Empire in the Colonial
Americas.* Chicago: University of Chicago Press, 1999.

Guimarães, Ana Paula, and Carlos Augusto Ribeiro. "Do vivo ao pintado:
sobre naufrágios, histórias e imagens; sobre cousas contra as quais não vale

força do corpo nem esforço de ânimo; sobre naus rotas, fúria de mar, novas invenções de mortes e sobejidão das cousas." In Cusati 1:87–100.

Guinote, Paulo, Eduardo Frutuoso, and António Lopes. *Naufrágios e outras perdas da "carreira da Índia": séculos XVI e XVII*. Lisbon: Grupo de Trabalho do Ministério da Educação para as Comemorações dos Descobrimentos Portugueses, 1998.

Haberly, David T. "Captives and Infidels: The Figure of the *Cautiva* in Argentine Literature." *American Hispanist* 4 (1978): 7–16.

Hart, Henry H. *Luis de Camoëns and the Epic of the Lusiads*. Norman: University of Oklahoma Press, 1962.

Hart, Jonathan. "Review Article: Rediscovering Alternative Critique of Europe in the New World." *Bulletin of Hispanic Studies* 76.4 (1999): 533–41.

Hillman, David, and Carla Mazzio, eds. *The Body in Parts: Fantasies of Corporeality in Early Modern Europe*. New York: Routledge, 1997.

Huntress, Keith. *A Checklist of Narratives of Shipwrecks and Disasters at Sea to 1860, with Summaries, Notes, and Comments*. Ames: Iowa State University Press, 1979.

Hutchinson, Amélia P. "*Dea* ou *deabus*? O declínio das relações masculino-feminino como reflexo do declínio do império." In Souza, Joaquim, Canço, Pires, and Castro. 181–86.

Jackson, K. David. *Builders of the Oceans*. Notebooks on the Portuguese Pavilion, EXPO '98. Lisbon: Assírio & Alvim, 1997.

———. "Sinkings, Sailors, Soldiers, Spice: O corpo encoberto do português na Índia." *Revista de história* (São Paulo) 127–28 (August/December 1992–January/July 1993): 141–62.

———. "Utopia and Identity in the Voyages: Camões between India and Portugal." *Arquivos do Centro Cultural Calouste Gulbenkian* 37 (1998): 185–94.

Jorge, Carlos Figueiredo. "Ética e acção nas narrativas de viagens. Unidades e ordem discursiva no 'Tratado das batalhas do galeão *Santiago* e da nau *Chagas*.'" In Seixo and Carvalho 93–108.

Kadir, Djelal. *Columbus and the Ends of the Earth: Europe's Prophetic Rhetoric as Conquering Ideology*. Berkeley: University of California Press, 1992.

Knauff, Barbara. "The Curious Traveler in Foigny's *La Terre australe connue* (1676)." *Papers on French Seventeenth Century Literature* 26 (1999): 273–82.

Kohut, Karl. "Fernández de Oviedo: historiografía e ideología." *Boletín de la Real Academia Española* 73 (1993): 367–82.

Kolve, V. A. *Chaucer and the Imagery of Narrative: The First Five Canterbury Tales*. Stanford, Calif.: Stanford University Press, 1984.

Kreutzer, Winifried. "Algumas observações sobre a 'Relação do naufrágio da nau S. Tomé na Terra dos Fumos, no ano de 1589 . . .' da *História Trágico-Marítima*." In *Lengua y literatura en la época de los descubrimientos. Actas del coloquio internacional Würzburg 1992*, ed. Theodor Berchem and Hugo Laitenberger. Junta de Castilla y León/Consejería de Cultura y Turismo, 1994. 191–203.

Kristeva, Julia. *Powers of Horror: An Essay on Abjection.* Trans. Leon S. Roudiez. New York: Columbia University Press, 1982.

Lach, Donald F. *The Century of Discovery.* Chicago: University of Chicago Press, 1965. Vol. 1, book 1 of *Asia in the Making of Europe.*

———. *The Literary Arts.* Chicago: University of Chicago Press, 1977. Vol. 2, book 2 of *Asia in the Making of Europe.*

Lanciani, Giulia. "Uma história trágico-marítima." In *Lisboa e os descobrimentos 1415–1580: a invenção do mundo pelos navegadores portugueses,* ed. Carlos Araújo. Lisbon: Terramar, 1990. 85–112.

———. *Sucessos e naufrágios das naus portuguesas.* Lisbon: Caminho, 1997.

Landow, George P. *Images of Crisis: Literary Iconology, 1750 to the Present.* Boston: Routledge & Kegan Paul, 1982.

Leal, Maria Luísa. "O naufrágio de Sepúlveda: variantes e invariantes de uma matéria narrativa." In Falcão, Nascimento, and Leal 629–39.

Lepecki, Maria Lúcia. "Da documentação e da criação." In *História Trágico-Marítima,* ed. Neves Águas. Vol. 2. Lisbon: Afrodite, 1972. cxi–cxvi.

Lincoln, Margarette. "Shipwreck Narratives of the Eighteenth and Early Nineteenth Century: Indicators of Culture and Identity." *British Journal for Eighteenth-Century Studies* 20.2 (1997): 155–72.

Lipking, Lawrence. "The Genius of the Shore: Lycidas, Adamastor, and the Poetics of Nationalism." *PMLA* 111.2 (1996): 205–21.

O livro História Trágico-Marítima. Colecção Patrícia. Lisbon: Diário de Notícias, 1927.

Lourenço, Eduardo. "Portugal, 'Nação-Navio'." In Cusati 1:xlv–lii.

Lusitano, Cândido. *Diccionario poetico, para o uso dos que principiaõ a exercitarse na Poesia Portugueza.* Vol. 2. Lisbon: Francisco Luiz Ameno, 1765. 2 vols.

Machado, Diogo Barbosa. *Bibliotheca Lusitana, historica, critica, e cronologica. Na qual se comprehende a noticia dos authores portuguezes, e das obras, que compuseraõ desde o tempo da promulgaçaõ do ley da graça até o tempo prezente.* 1741–59. Vol. 1. Coimbra: Atlântida, 1965. 4 vols.

Madeira, Maria Angélica B. G. "Les dimensions de la mémoire dans les récits de naufrages." In *Passions du passé: recyclages de la mémoire et usages de l'oubli,* ed. Marie-Pascale Hugo, Éric Méchoulan, and Walter Moser. Paris and Montreal: L'Harmattan, 2000. 263–77.

Maravall, José Antonio. *Culture of the Baroque: Analysis of a Historical Structure.* Trans. Terry Cochran. Theory and History of Literature 25. Minneapolis: University of Minnesota Press, 1986.

Margarido, Alfredo. "Os relatos de naufrágios na *Peregrinação* de Fernão Mendes Pinto." In *Estudos portugueses: homenagem a Luciana Stegagno Picchio.* Lisbon: Difel, 1991. 987–1023.

————. "Une incursion sociologique dans le domaine de la critique textuelle à propos de l'*História Trágico-Marítima.*" In *Critique textuelle portugaise: actes du colloque, Paris, 20–24 octobre 1981.* Paris: Fondation Calouste Gulbenkian/Centre Culturel Portugais, 1986. 243–57.

Marques, A. H. de Oliveira. *History of Portugal.* Vol. 1. New York: Columbia University Press, 1972. 2 vols.

Márquez Villanueva, Francisco. "The Alfonsine Cultural Concept." In *Alfonso X of Castile, The Learned King (1221–1284): An International Symposium, Harvard University, 17 November 1984,* ed. Francisco Márquez-Villanueva and Carlos Alberto Vega. Cambridge: Department of Romance Languages and Literatures, Harvard University, 1990. 76–109.

————. *El concepto cultural alfonsí.* Madrid: Mapfre, 1994.

Martins, Adriana Alves de Paula. "As funções do narrador nos relatos de naufrágios: a força lúdica da função comunicativa e a função ideológica." *Máthesis* 5 (1996): 335–48.

Martins, Mário. *Teatro quinhentista nas naus da Índia.* Lisbon: Brotéria, 1973.

Martocq, Bernard. "Note bibliographique sur l'*História Trágico-Marítima.*" *Cahiers d'études romanes* 1 (1998): 19–29.

Matos, Artur Teodoro de, and Luís Filipe F. Reis Thomaz, eds. *A carreira da Índia e as rotas dos estreitos: actas (Angra do Heroísmo, 7 a 11 de Junho de 1996).* Angra do Heroísmo: Comissão Nacional para as Comemorações dos Descobrimentos Portugueses, 1998.

Matos, Helena Maria de. "Para o estudo da relação do *Naufrágio da nau 'Conceição' nos Baixios de Pêro dos Banhos no ano de 1555.*" In Seixo and Carvalho 137–45.

McAlister, Lyle N. *Spain and Portugal in the New World, 1492–1700.* Europe and the World in the Age of Expansion 3. Minneapolis: University of Minnesota Press, 1984.

Meira, Maria José Paredes. "Uma leitura da *Relação do naufrágio da nau 'Santa Maria da Barca', no ano de 1559.*" In Seixo and Carvalho 147–60.

Merrim, Stephanie. "The First Fifty Years of Hispanic New World Historiography: The Caribbean, Mexico, and Central America." In *Discovery to Modernism,* ed. Roberto González Echevarría and Enrique Pupo-Walker.

Cambridge, England: Cambridge University Press, 1996. 58–100. Vol. 1 of *The Cambridge History of Latin Amercian Literature.* 3 vols.

Milanesi, Claudio. "Les récits de naufrage: un essai de structuralisme thématique." *Cahiers d'études romanes* 1 (1998): 1–18.

Miraglia, Gianluca. "Uma leitura oitocentista do *Naufrágio de Sepúlveda.*" *Colóquio literatura dos descobrimentos: comunicações. Colóquio realizado em 22 e 23 de Novembro de 1995 na Universidade Autónoma de Lisboa.* Lisbon: Universidade Autónoma de Lisboa, 1997. 103–9.

Moser, Fernando de Mello. "Dois dramas novilatinos sobre o *Naufrágio de Sepúlveda.*" In *Discurso inacabado: ensaios de cultura portuguesa.* Lisbon: Calouste Gulbenkian, 1994. 321–33.

Moser, Gerald M. "Camões' Shipwreck." *Hispania* 57 (May 1974): 213–19.

Moura, Carlos Francisco. "Teatro a bordo de naus portuguesas nos séculos XVI, XVII, e XVIII." *Tulane Studies in Romance Languages and Literature* 10 (1981): 65–71.

Moura, Vasco Graça. "O texto e o naufrágio." In *Camões e a divina proporção.* Lisbon: n.p., 1985. 65–100.

Ortigão, Ramalho. *As praias de Portugal: guia do banhista e do viajante.* Porto: Magalhães & Moniz, 1876.

Pagliaro, Annamaria. "Leonor de Sá, *doloris heroina,* in una orazione del XVII secolo." In Cusati 3:467–77.

Pastor, Beatriz. "Silence and Writing: The History of the Conquest." Trans. Jason Wood. In *1492–1992: Re/Discovering Colonial Writing,* ed. René Jara and Nicholas Spadaccini. Hispanic Issues 4. Minneapolis: University of Minnesota Press, 1989. 121–63.

Pastor Bodmer, Beatriz. *The Armature of Conquest: Spanish Accounts of the Discovery of America, 1492–1589.* Trans. Lydia Longstreth Hunt. Stanford, Calif.: Stanford University Press, 1992.

Peloso, Silvano. "Le avventure tragico-marittime di un onesto negriero in giro per il mondo: i Portoghesi nei 'Ragionamenti' di Francesco Carletti." *Quaderni portoghesi* 5 (1979): 69–87.

Pérez-Mallaína, Pablo E. *Spain's Men of the Sea: Daily Life on the Indies Fleets in the Sixteenth Century.* Trans. Carla Rahn Phillips. Baltimore: Johns Hopkins University Press, 1998.

Pérez-Mallaína Bueno, Pablo Emilio. *El hombre frente al mar: naufragios en la carrera de Indias durante los siglos XVI y XVII.* Seville: Universidad de Sevilla, 1996.

Pinho, António. "Comentários & correcções ao intitulamento da primeira relação da 'História Trágico-Marítima.'" *Biblos* 14 (1938): 356–73.

Pögl, Johann. "Nachklänge der História trágico-marítima in der Comedia des Siglo de Oro." *Aufsätze zur Portugiesischen Kulturgeschichte* 19 (1984–87): 71–85.

Pranzetti, Luisa. "El naufragio como metáfora." In *Notas y comentarios sobre Álvar Núñez Cabeza de Vaca,* ed. Margo Glantz. Mexico City: Grijalbo, 1993. 57–73.

Quint, David. *Epic and Empire: Politics and Generic Form from Virgil to Milton.* Princeton, N.J.: Princeton University Press, 1993.

Rabasa, José. *Inventing A-m-e-r-i-c-a: Spanish Historiography and the Formation of Eurocentrism.* Norman: University of Oklahoma Press, 1993.

———. *Writing Violence on the Northern Frontier: The Historiography of Sixteenth-Century New Mexico and Florida and the Legacy of Conquest.* Durham, N.C.: Duke University Press, 2000.

Rebelo, Luís de Sousa. "Providencialismo e profecia nas crónicas portuguesas da expansão." *Bulletin of Hispanic Studies* 71 (1994): 67–86.

Ribeiro, José Silvestre. *Historia dos estabelecimentos scientificos, litterarios, e artisticos de Portugal nos successivos reinados da monarchia.* Vol. 1. Lisbon: Academia Real das Sciencias, 1871. 18 vols.

Rogers, Francis M. *The Quest for Eastern Christians: Travels and Rumor in the Age of Discovery.* Minneapolis: University of Minnesota Press, 1962.

[———, ed.] *Europe Informed: An Exhibition of Early Books Which Acquainted Europe with the East.* Cambridge, Mass., and New York: Sixth International Colloquium on Luso-Brazilian Studies, 1966.

Ross, Kathleen. "Historians of the Conquest and Colonization of the New World: 1550–1620." In *Discovery to Modernism,* ed. Roberto González Echevarría and Enrique Pupo-Walker. Cambridge, England: Cambridge University Press, 1996. 101–42. Vol. 1 of *The Cambridge History of Latin American Literature.* 3 vols.

Russell, Peter. *Prince Henry "the Navigator": A Life.* New Haven: Yale University Press, 2000.

Russell-Wood, A. J. R. *Portugal and the Sea: A World Embraced.* Notebooks on the Portuguese Pavilion, EXPO '98. Lisbon: Assírio & Alvim, 1997.

———. "Portugal and the World in the Age of Dom João V." In *The Age of the Baroque in Portugal,* ed. Jay A. Levenson. Washington, D.C.: National Gallery of Art; New Haven: Yale University Press, 1993. 15–29.

———. *The Portuguese Empire, 1415–1808: A World on the Move.* Baltimore: Johns Hopkins University Press, 1998.

Sampaio, Albino Forjaz de. *História da literatura portuguesa ilustrada.* Vol. 3. Paris and Lisbon: Aillaud e Bertrand, 1932. 3 vols. 1929–32.

Saramago, José. "A morte familiar." In *História Trágico-Marítima,* ed. Neves Águas. Vol. 2. Lisbon: Afrodite, 1972. ciii–cix. (Trans. as "La mort familière," Le Gentil 11–20.)

Scarry, Elaine. *The Body in Pain: The Making and Unmaking of the World.* New York: Oxford University Press, 1985.

Seixo, Maria Alzira. "O abismo sob o mar que se ergue (a partir do relato de naufrágio da nau *Santiago,* com recurso aos relatos das naus *São Francisco* e *Conceição,* e com fundamento noutros textos da *História Trágico-Marítima*)." In Seixo and Carvalho 160–88.

———. "Concepção poética do lugar e do tempo na *História Trágico-Marítima.*" In *Poéticas da viagem na literatura.* Lisbon: Cosmos, 1998. 67–77.

———. "Maneirismo e barroco na literatura de viagens. O relato de naufrágios e a noção de modelo, a *Peregrinação* e a noção de aventura." In *Poéticas da viagem na literatura.* Lisbon: Cosmos, 1998. 53–65.

———. "Les récits de naufrages de l'Histoire Tragico-Maritime': combinatoires et sens tragique de la représentation." In *A viagem na literatura,* ed. Maria Alzira Seixo. Cursos da Arrábida 1. Mem Martins: Europa-América, 1997. 103–25.

Seixo, Maria Alzira, and Alberto Carvalho, eds. *A História Trágico-Marítima: análises e perspectivas.* Viagem 1. Lisbon: Cosmos, 1996.

Silva, Innocencio Francisco da. *Diccionario bibliographico portuguez: estudos . . . applicaveis a Portugal e ao Brasil.* Vol. 1. Lisbon: Imprensa Nacional, 1858. 22 vols.

Silva, Vítor Manuel Pires de Aguiar e. *Maneirismo e barroco na poesia lírica portuguesa.* Coimbra: Centro de Estudos Românicos, 1971.

Simões, João Gaspar. *História do romance português.* Vol. 1. Lisbon: Estúdios Cor, 1967. 3 vols.

Snow, Joseph T. "Alfonso as Troubadour: The Fact and the Fiction." In *Emperor of Culture: Alfonso X the Learned of Castile and His Thirteenth-Century Renaissance,* ed. Robert I. Burns. Philadelphia: University of Pennsylvania Press, 1990. 124–40.

———. "'Cantando e con Dança': Alfonso X, King David, the *Cantigas de Santa Maria* and the *Psalms.*" *La corónica* 27.2 (1999): 61–73.

[Souza, Maria Reynolds de, Teresa Joaquim, Dina Canço, Pedro Pires, and Isabel de Castro, eds.] *O rosto feminino da expansão portuguesa: congresso internacional realizado em Lisboa, Portugal, 21–25 de Novembro de 1994.* Cadernos Condição Feminina 43. Vol. 1. Lisbon: Comissão para a Igualdade e para os Direitos das Mulheres, 1995. 2 vols.

Soveral, Carlos Eduardo de. "História Trágico-Marítima." In *Dicionário de literatura*, 3d ed., ed. Jacinto do Prado Coelho. 5 vols. Porto: Figueirinhas, 1985.

Stegagno Picchio, Luciana. "O canto molhado: contributo para o estudo das biografias camonianas." *Arquivos do Centro Cultural Português* 16 (1981): 243–65.

Subrahmanyam, Sanjay. *The Career and Legend of Vasco da Gama*. Cambridge, England: Cambridge University Press, 1997.

Tabucchi, Antonio. "Interpretazioni della 'História Trágico-Marítima' nelle licenze per il suo 'imprimatur'." *Quaderni portoghesi* 5 (1979): 19–43.

Tonnies, Ana. "O silêncio das personagens femininas em relatos de naufrágios dos séculos XVI e XVII." In Souza, Joaquim, Canço, Pires, and Castro. 245–51.

Warnke, Frank J. *Versions of Baroque: European Literature in the Seventeenth Century*. New Haven: Yale University Press, 1972.

Wicki, José. "As relações de viagens dos jesuítas na carreira das naus da Índia de 1541 a 1598." In *II Seminário Internacional de História Indo-Portuguesa: Actas,* ed. Luís de Albuquerque and Inácio Guerreiro. Lisbon: Instituto de Investigação Científica Tropical, 1985. 4–17.

Wright, Janice, comp. "Reference Bibliography." *La corónica* 26.2 (1998): 91–129.

Zurbach, Christine. "História e ficção nos relatos de naufrágios. O caso da 'Relação da muy notavel perda do Galeão Grande *São João*'." In Seixo and Carvalho 209–24.

PERMISSIONS

The University of Minnesota Press gratefully acknowledges permission to reprint the following in this book.

INDEX

JOSIAH BLACKMORE is associate professor of Portuguese at the University of Toronto. He is coeditor (with Gregory S. Hutcheson) of *Queer Iberia: Sexualities, Cultures, and Crossings from the Middle Ages to the Renaissance*. He has written on Portuguese poetry and historiography and on the nineteenth-century Portuguese novel. He translated "Account of the Very Remarkable Loss of the Great Galleon *S. João*" for the new edition of *The Tragic History of the Sea*, edited by C. R. Boxer and recently published by the University of Minnesota Press.